© Houghton Mifflin Harcourt Publishing Company • Cover Image Credits: (Ground Squirrel) ©Don Johnston/All Canada Photos/Getty Images; (Sawtooth Range. Idaho) ©Ron and Patty Thomas Photography/E+/Getty Images

Volume 1

Made in the United States
Text printed on 100%
recycled paper

Houghton Mifflin Harcourt

2017 Edition

Copyright © by Houghton Mifflin Harcourt Publishing Company

Printed in the U.S.A.

ISBN 978-0-544-71060-3

15   0928   23 22

4500842439   D E F G

Dear Students and Families,

Welcome to **Go Math!**, Grade 4! In this exciting mathematics program, there are hands-on activities to do and real-world problems to solve. Best of all, you will write your ideas and answers right in your book. In **Go Math!**, writing and drawing on the pages helps you think deeply about what you are learning, and you will really understand math!

By the way, all of the pages in your **Go Math!** book are made using recycled paper. We wanted you to know that you can Go Green with **Go Math!**

Sincerely,

The Authors

Made in the United States
Text printed on 100% recycled paper

GO MATH!

Authors

Juli K. Dixon, Ph.D.
Professor, Mathematics Education
University of Central Florida
Orlando, Florida

Edward B. Burger, Ph.D.
President, Southwestern University
Georgetown, Texas

Steven J. Leinwand
Principal Research Analyst
American Institutes for
    Research (AIR)
Washington, D.C.

Contributor

Rena Petrello
Professor, Mathematics
Moorpark College
Moorpark, CA

Matthew R. Larson, Ph.D.
K-12 Curriculum Specialist for
    Mathematics
Lincoln Public Schools
Lincoln, Nebraska

Martha E. Sandoval-Martinez
Math Instructor
El Camino College
Torrance, California

English Language Learners Consultant

Elizabeth Jiménez
CEO, GEMAS Consulting
Professional Expert on English
    Learner Education
Bilingual Education and
    Dual Language
Pomona, California

Place Value and Operations with Whole Numbers

Big Idea Develop a conceptual understanding of multi-digit multiplication, and division, including addition and subtraction to one million. Develop factors, multiples, and number patterns.

Big Idea

GO DIGITAL

Go online! Your math lessons are interactive. Use *i*Tools, Animated Math Models, the Multimedia eGlossary, and more.

Chapter 1 Overview

In this chapter, you will explore and discover answers to the following **Essential Questions**:

- How can you use place value to compare, add, subtract, and estimate with whole numbers?
- How do you compare and order whole numbers?
- What are some strategies you can use to round whole numbers?
- How is adding and subtracting 5- and 6-digit numbers similar to adding and subtracting 3-digit numbers?

Personal Math Trainer
Online Assessment and Intervention

4 Divide by 1-Digit Numbers 195

Chapter 4 Overview

In this chapter, you will explore and discover answers to the following **Essential Questions**:

- How can you divide by 1-digit numbers?
- How can you use remainders in division problems?
- How can you estimate quotients?
- How can you model division with a 1-digit divisor?

Chapter 5 Overview

In this chapter, you will explore and discover answers to the following **Essential Questions**:

- How can you find factors and multiples, and how can you generate and describe number patterns?

- How can you use models or lists to find factors?

- How can you create a number pattern?

5 Factors, Multiples, and Patterns 277

VOLUME 2
Fractions and Decimals

Big Idea Develop a conceptual understanding of fraction equivalence and comparison. Use this understanding to add and subtract fractions with like denominators, to multiply fractions by whole numbers, and to relate fractions and decimals.

GO DIGITAL

Go online! Your math lessons are interactive. Use *i*Tools, Animated Math Models, the Multimedia *e*Glossary, and more.

Chapter 6 Overview

Essential Questions:
- What strategies can you use to compare fractions and write equivalent fractions?
- What models can help you compare and order fractions?
- How can you find equivalent fractions?
- How can you solve problems that involve fractions?

Chapter 7 Overview

Essential Questions:
- How do you add or subtract fractions that have the same denominator?
- Why do you add or subtract the numerators and not the denominators?
- Why do you rename mixed numbers when adding or subtracting fractions?
- How do you know that your sum or difference is reasonable?

Chapter 8 Overview

In this chapter, you will explore and discover answers to the following **Essential Questions**:

• How do you multiply fractions by whole numbers?

• How can you write a product of a whole number and a fraction as a product of a whole number and a unit fraction?

Practice and Homework

Lesson Check and Spiral Review in every lesson

Chapter 9 Overview

In this chapter, you will explore and discover answers to the following **Essential Questions**:

• How can you record decimal notation for fractions and compare decimal fractions?

• Why can you record tenths and hundredths as decimals and fractions?

• What are some different models you can use to find equivalent fractions?

• How can you compare decimal fractions?

x

Geometry, Measurement, and Data

Big Idea Develop a conceptual understanding that geometric figures can be analyzed and classified based on their properties, including angle measures. Develop relative sizes of measurement units and apply area and perimeter formulas for rectangles.

GO DIGITAL

Go online! Your math lessons are interactive. Use *i*Tools, Animated Math Models, the Multimedia *e*Glossary, and more.

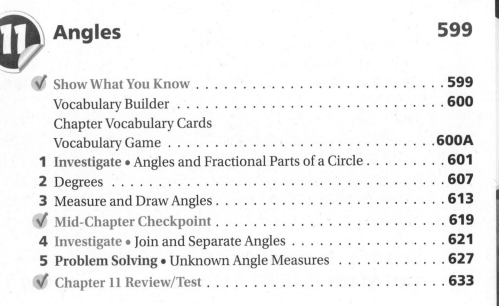

Chapter 10 Overview

Essential Questions:
- How can you draw and identify lines and angles, and how can you classify shapes?
- What are the building blocks of geometry?
- How can you classify triangles and quadrilaterals?
- How do you recognize symmetry in a polygon?

Chapter 11 Overview

Essential Questions:
- How can you measure angles and solve problems involving angle measures?
- How can you use fractions and degrees to understand angle measures?
- How can you use a protractor to measure and classify angles?
- How can equations help you find the measurement of an angle?

Chapter 12 Overview

In this chapter, you will explore and discover answers to the following **Essential Questions**:

- How can you use relative sizes of measurements to solve problems and to generate measurement tables that show a relationship?

- How can you compare metric units of length, mass, or liquid volume?

- How can you compare customary units of length, weight, or liquid volume?

Practice and Homework

Lesson Check and Spiral Review in every lesson

Chapter 13 Overview

In this chapter, you will explore and discover answers to the following **Essential Questions**:

- How can you use formulas for perimeter and area to solve problems?

- How are area and perimeter different?

- What are some methods you can use to find area and perimeter of a figure?

- How could two different rectangles have the same perimeter or the same area?

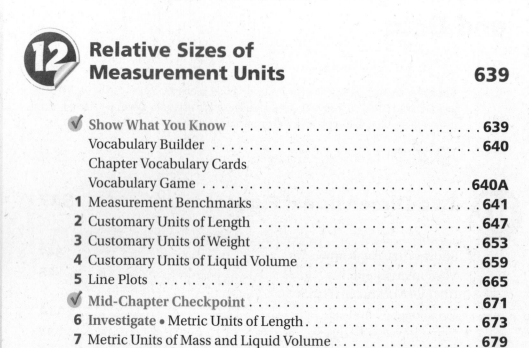

12 Relative Sizes of Measurement Units 639

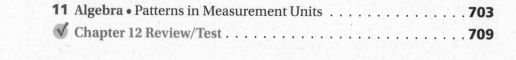

13 Algebra: Perimeter and Area 715

Science, Technology, Engineering, and Math (STEM) Activities STEM 1

Big Idea Place Value and Operations with Whole Numbers

BIG IDEA Develop a conceptual understanding of multidigit multiplication and division, including addition and subtraction to one million. Develop factors, multiples, and number patterns.

Space Shuttle launching from Kennedy Space Center ▶

Food in Space

The United States is planning a manned mission to Mars. The crew must take all of its food along on the journey, because there is no food available on Mars.

Get Started

Work with a partner. You are in charge of planning the amount of food needed for the Mars mission. Decide how much food will be needed for the entire trip. Use the Important Facts to help you plan. **Explain** your thinking.

Important Facts

- Length of trip to Mars: 6 months
- Length of stay on Mars: 6 months
- Length of return trip to Earth: 6 months
- Number of astronauts: 6
- 2 cups of water weigh 1 pound.
- 1 month = 30 days (on average).
- Each astronaut needs 10 cups of water and 4 pounds of food each day.

_____

_____

_____

_____

_____

_____

_____

_____

_____

_____

_____

Completed by _____

Place Value, Addition, and Subtraction to One Million

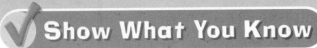
Show What You Know

Personal Math Trainer
Online Assessment and Intervention

Check your understanding of important skills.

Name _____

▶ **Tens and Ones** Write the missing numbers.

1. 27 = _____ tens _____ ones

2. 93 = _____ tens _____ ones

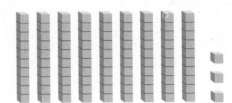

▶ **Regroup Hundreds as Tens** Regroup. Write the missing numbers.

3. 5 hundreds 4 tens = _____ tens

4. 8 hundreds 9 tens = _____ tens

▶ **Two-Digit Addition and Subtraction** Add or subtract.

5.   27
        + 34

6.   95
        + 46

7.   84
        − 27

Math in the Real World

The home stadium of the Philadelphia Phillies is a large baseball park in Philadelphia, PA. Use the following clues to find the stadium's maximum capacity.
- The 5-digit number has a 4 in the greatest place-value position and a 1 in the least place-value position.
- The digit in the thousands place has a value of 3,000.
- The digit in the hundreds place is twice the digit in the thousands place.
- There is a 5 in the tens place.

Vocabulary Builder

Write the review words with a ✓ on the Word Line, from greatest to least place value.

Place Value

greatest
_____
_____
_____
_____
least
_____

Review Words

✓ hundreds

 inverse operations

✓ ones

✓ tens

✓ ten thousands

✓ thousands

Preview Words

estimate

expanded form

period

round

standard form

word form

▶ Understand Vocabulary

Read the definition. Which word does it describe?

1. To replace a number with another number that tells about how many or how much _____

2. A way to write numbers by showing the value of each digit

   _____

3. A number close to an exact amount _____

4. Each group of three digits separated by commas in a

   multi-digit number _____

5. A way to write numbers by using the digits 0–9, with each digit

   having a place value _____

GO DIGITAL
• Interactive Student Edition
• Multimedia eGlossary

Chapter 1 Vocabulary

estimate (*noun*)

estimación

31

expanded form

forma desarrollada

32

inverse operations

operaciones inversas

43

period

período

65

round

redondear

82

standard form

forma normal

87

thousands

miles

91

word form

en palabras

97

A way to write numbers by showing the value of each digit

Example: 253 = 200 + 50 + 3

A number that is close to an exact amount. An estimate tells about how much or about how many

---

Each group of three digits in a multi-digit number; periods are usually separated by commas or spaces

Example: 85,643,900 has three periods.

Period			Period		
hundred thousands	ten thousands	thousands	hundreds	tens	ones

Operations that undo each other, such as addition and subtraction or multiplication and division

Example: $6 \times 8 = 48$ and $48 \div 6 = 8$

A way to write numbers by using the digits 0-9, with each digit having a place value

Example: 3,450 ⟵ standard form

To replace a number with another number that tells about how many or how much

---

A way to write numbers by using words

Example: Four hundred fifty-three thousand, two hundred twelve

---

The period after the ones period in the base-ten number system

Period			Period		
hundred thousands	ten thousands	thousands	hundreds	tens	ones

Game

Going to Space

Word Box

estimate

expanded form

inverse operations

period

round

standard form

thousands

word form

For 2 players

Materials

- 1 red playing piece
- 1 blue playing piece
- Clue Cards
- 1 number cube

How to Play

1. Put your playing piece on START.

2. Toss the number cube, and move that many spaces.

3. If you land on one of these spaces:

   Blue Space Follow the directions.

   Red Space Take a Clue Card from the pile. Read the question. If you answer correctly, keep the card. If you do not, return the card to the bottom of the pile.

4. Collect at least 5 Clue Cards. Move around the track as many times as you need to.

5. When you have 5 Clue Cards, follow the closest center path to reach FINISH. You must reach FINISH by exact count.

6. The first player to reach FINISH wins.

TAKE A
CLUE CARD

Rockets have
turbo-boost!
Move ahead 1.

TAKE A
CLUE CARD

FINISH

Bad weather
delays launch.
Go back 1.

Engines need repair.
Go back 1.

TAKE A
CLUE CARD

FINISH

Launch is
a go!
Move ahead 1.

START ▶

TAKE A
CLUE CARD

The Write Way

Reflect

Choose one idea. Write about it in the space below.

- Describe how to write a three-digit number in three different ways.

- Is 44,000 a good estimate of 43,986? Explain how you know.

- Explain and illustrate two ways to round numbers.

Name _____

Model Place Value Relationships

Essential Question How can you describe the value of a digit?

Learning Objective You will model and describe the value of a digit using place value relationships.

🔑 Unlock the Problem

🔒 Activity Build numbers through 10,000.

Materials ■ base-ten blocks

1	10	100	1,000	10,000

    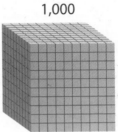 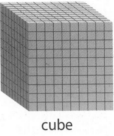

?

cube	long	flat	cube	_____
1	10 ones	_____ tens	_____ hundreds	_____ thousands

A small cube represents 1.

_____ small cubes make a long. The long represents _____.

_____ longs make a flat. The flat represents _____.

_____ flats make a large cube. The large cube represents _____.

---

1. Describe a pattern in the shapes of the models. What will be the shape of the model for 10,000?

_____

_____

_____

 Math Talk

Math Processes and Practices ⑤

Model What other type of base-ten block could you use to model 100,000?

2. Describe a pattern you see in the sizes of the models. How will the size of the model for 100,000 compare to the size of the model for 10,000?

_____

_____

_____

Value of a Digit The value of a digit depends on its place-value position in the number. A place-value chart can help you understand the value of each digit in a number. The value of each place is 10 times the value of the place to the right.

 Write 894,613 in the chart. Find the value of the digit 9.

MILLIONS			THOUSANDS			ONES		
Hundreds	Tens	Ones	Hundreds	Tens	Ones	Hundreds	Tens	Ones
			8 hundred thousands	9 ten thousands	4 thousands	6 hundreds	1 ten	3 ones
			800,000	90,000	4,000	600	10	3

The value of the digit 9 is 9 ten thousands, or _____.

 Compare the values of the underlined digits.

2,3<u>0</u>4   16,1<u>3</u>5

Math Talk

Math Processes and Practices ⑥

Describe how you can compare the values of the digits without drawing a model.

STEP 1 Find the value of 3 in 2,304.

Show 2,304 in a place-value chart.

THOUSANDS			ONES		
Hundreds	Tens	Ones	Hundreds	Tens	Ones

Think: The value of the digit 3 is _____.

Model the value of the digit 3.

STEP 2 Find the value of 3 in 16,135.

Show 16,135 in a place-value chart.

THOUSANDS			ONES		
Hundreds	Tens	Ones	Hundreds	Tens	Ones

Think: The value of the digit 3 is _____.

Model the value of the digit 3.

Each hundred is 10 times as many as 10, so 3 hundreds is ten times as many as 3 tens.

So, the value of 3 in 2,304 is _____ times the value of 3 in 16,135.

6

Name _____

1. Complete the table below.

Number	1,000,000	100,000	10,000	1,000	100	10	1
Model	?	?	?				
Shape				cube	flat	long	cube
Group				10 hundreds	10 tens	10 ones	1 one

Find the value of the underlined digit.

2. 7̲03,890

_____

3. 63,5̲40

_____

4. 1̲8̲2,034

_____

✅ **5.** 345,̲890

_____

Compare the values of the underlined digits.

6. 2̲,000 and 2̲00

The value of 2 in _____ is _____

times the value of 2 in _____ .

✅ **7.** 4̲0 and 4̲00

The value of 4 in _____ is _____

times the value of 4 in _____ .

On Your Own

Find the value of the underlined digit.

8. 23̲0,001

_____

9. 803̲,040

_____

10. 46,84̲2

_____

11. 9̲80,650

_____

12. Greg has collected 4,385 pennies and Hannah has collected 3,899 pennies. How many times as great as the value of 3 in 4,385 is the value of 3 in 3,899?

_____

13. GO DEEPER Shawn wants to model the number 13,450 using base-ten blocks. How many large cubes, flats, and longs does he need to model the number?

_____

Problem Solving • Applications

Use the table for 14.

14. **GO DEEPER** What is the value of the digit 7 in the population of Memphis? What is the value of the digit 1 in the population of Denver? How many times as great as the value of the digit 1 in the population of Cleveland is this value?

_____

15. **THINK SMARTER** How many models of 100 do you need to model 3,200? Explain.

_____

_____

_____

City Populations	
City	**Population***
Cleveland	431,369
Denver	610,345
Memphis	676,640
*2009 U. S. Census Bureau Estimation	

16. **Math Processes and Practices 6** Sid wrote 541,309 on his paper. Using numbers and words, **explain** how the number would change if he exchanged the digits in the hundred thousands and tens places.

_____

_____

_____

_____

WRITE *Math* • **Show Your Work**

17. **THINK SMARTER** For numbers 17a–17e, select True or False for each statement.

17a. The value of 7 in 375,081 is 7,000. ○ True ○ False

17b. The value of 6 in 269,480 is 600,000. ○ True ○ False

17c. The value of 5 in 427,593 is 500. ○ True ○ False

17d. The value of 1 in 375,081 is 10. ○ True ○ False

17e. The value of 4 in 943,268 is 40,000. ○ True ○ False

Model Place Value Relationships

Learning Objective You will model and describe the value of a digit using place value relationships.

Find the value of the underlined digit.

1. 6,0<u>3</u>5

2. 43,<u>7</u>82

3. 506,08<u>7</u>

4. 4<u>9</u>,254

_____ _____ _____ _____

5. 1<u>3</u>6,422

6. 673,<u>5</u>12

7. <u>8</u>14,295

8. 73<u>6</u>,144

_____ _____ _____ _____

Compare the values of the underlined digits.

9. 6,<u>3</u>00 and 5<u>3</u>0

The value of 3 in _____ is _____ times

the value of 3 in _____ .

10. <u>2</u>,783 and 7,<u>2</u>83

The value of 2 in _____ is _____ times

the value of 2 in _____ .

Problem Solving Real World

Use the table for 11–12.

11. What is the value of the digit 9 in the attendance at the Redskins vs. Titans game?

_____

12. The attendance at which game has a 7 in the ten thousands place?

_____

Football Game Attendance	
Game	**Attendance**
Redskins vs. Titans	69,143
Ravens vs. Panthers	73,021
Patriots vs. Colts	68,756

13. **WRITE** ▸ *Math* How does a digit in the ten thousands place compare to a digit in the thousands place?

_____

_____

_____

Lesson Check

1. During one season, a total of 453,193 people attended a baseball team's games. What is the value of the digit 5 in the number of people?

_____

_____

2. Hal forgot the number of people at the basketball game. He does remember that the number had four digits and a 3 in the tens place. Write a number that Hal could be thinking of.

_____

_____

Spiral Review

3. Hot dog buns come in packages of 8. For the school picnic, Mr. Spencer bought 30 packages of hot dog buns. How many hot dog buns did he buy?

_____

4. There are 8 students on the minibus. Five of the students are boys. What fraction of the students are boys?

_____

5. The clock below shows the time when Amber leaves home for school. At what time does Amber leave home?

6. Jeremy drew a polygon with four right angles and four sides with the same length.

_____

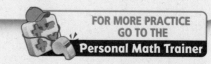
FOR MORE PRACTICE
GO TO THE
Personal Math Trainer

Read and Write Numbers

Essential Question How can you read and write numbers through hundred thousands?

Learning Objective You will read and write whole numbers through hundred thousands.

Unlock the Problem

The International Space Station uses 262,400 solar cells to change sunlight to electricity.

Write 262,400 in standard form, word form, and expanded form.

 Use a place-value chart.

Each group of three digits separated by a comma is called a **period**. Each period has hundreds, tens, and ones. The greatest place-value position in the thousands period is hundred thousands.

Write 262,400 in the place-value chart below.

PERIOD →   PERIOD →

THOUSANDS			ONES		
Hundreds	Tens	Ones	Hundreds	Tens	Ones

The number 262,400 has two periods, thousands and ones.

Standard Form: 262,400

Word Form: two hundred sixty-two thousand, four hundred

Expanded Form: 200,000 + 60,000 + 2,000 + 400

Math Talk

Math Processes and Practices ⑦

Look for Structure How can you use a place value chart to find which digit in a number has the greatest value?

Try This! Use place value to read and write numbers.

A Standard Form: _____

Word Form: ninety-two thousand, one hundred seventy

Expanded Form:

90,000 + 2,000 + _____ + 70

B Standard Form: 200,007

Word Form:
two hundred _____ , _____

Expanded Form:

_____ + 7

1. How can you use place value and period names to read and write 324,904 in word form?

_____

_____

_____

Read and write the number in two other forms.

2. four hundred eight thousand, seventeen

_____

_____

3. 65,058

_____

_____

Math Talk

Math Processes and Practices ②

Symbols and Words
Explain how you can use the expanded form of a number to write the number in standard form.

On Your Own

Read and write the number in two other forms.

4. five hundred eight thousand

_____

5. forty thousand, six hundred nineteen

_____

6. 570,020

_____

_____

7. $400,000 + 60,000 + 5,000 + 100$

_____

_____

8. THINK SMARTER During the week of the county fair, fifteen thousand, six hundred nine entry tickets were sold. Is it correct to write the number as 15,069? Explain.

_____

_____

9. GO DEEPER There were 94,172 people at a football game on Saturday. On Monday, 1,000 fewer people were at a football game. In word form, how many people were at the football game on Monday?

_____

_____

10. Richard got 263,148 hits when he did an Internet search. What is the value of the digit 6 in this number? Explain.

_____

Name _____

11. **THINK SMARTER** Yvonne wrote the numbers sixteen thousand, nine hundred eighteen and 64,704 on the board. Which of the numbers has a greater value in the thousands place?

_____

12. **GO DEEPER** Matthew found the sum of 3 thousands 4 hundreds 3 tens 1 one + 4 thousands 8 hundreds 3 tens 5 ones. Victoria found the sum of 5 thousands 7 hundreds 4 ones + 3 thousands 2 hundreds 3 tens 1 one. Who had the greater sum? What was the greater sum?

_____

Problem Solving • Applications

Use the table for 13–15.

13. **Math Processes and Practices ④ Use Graphs** Which city has a population of two hundred fifty-five thousand, one hundred twenty-four?

_____

14. Write the population of Raleigh in expanded form and word form.

Major Cities in North Carolina	
City	**Population***
Durham	229,171
Greensboro	255,124
Raleigh	405,612

*U.S. Census Bureau 2008 Estimated Population

_____

_____

15. **THINK SMARTER** **What's the Error?** Sophia said that the expanded form for 605,970 is 600,000 + 50,000 + 900 + 70. Describe Sophia's error and give the correct answer.

_____

_____

_____

_____

Unlock the Problem

16. **GO DEEPER** Mark tossed six balls while playing a number game. Three balls landed in one section, and three balls landed in another section. His score is greater than one hundred thousand. What could his score be?

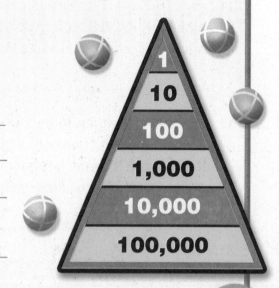

a. What do you know? _____

_____

_____

b. How can you use what you know about place value

to find what Mark's score could be? _____

_____

_____

_____

_____

_____

c. Draw a diagram to show one way to solve the problem.

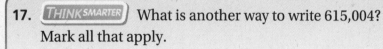

d. Complete the sentences.

Three balls could have landed in the

_____ section.

Three balls could have landed in the

_____ section.

Mark's score could be _____

_____ .

17. **THINK SMARTER** What is another way to write 615,004? Mark all that apply.

Ⓐ six hundred fifteen thousand, four

Ⓑ six hundred five thousand, fourteen

Ⓒ 60,000 + 10,000 + 5,000 + 4

Ⓓ 600,000 + 10,000 + 5,000 + 4

Name _____

Read and Write Numbers

Learning Objective You will read and write whole numbers through hundred thousands.

Read and write the number in two other forms.

1. six hundred ninety-two thousand, four

standard form: 692,004; _____

expanded form: 600,000 + _____

90,000 + 2,000 + 4 _____

_____

2. 314,207

_____

_____

_____

_____

3. 600,000 + 80,000 + 10

_____

_____

_____

_____

Use the number 913,256.

4. Write the name of the period that has the digits 913.

_____

5. Write the digit in the ten thousands place.

_____

6. Write the value of the digit 9.

_____

Problem Solving

Use the table for 7 and 8.

Population in 2008

State	Population
Alaska	686,293
South Dakota	804,194
Wyoming	532,668

7. Which state had a population of eight hundred four thousand, one hundred ninety-four?

_____

8. What is the value of the digit 8 in Alaska's population?

_____

9. **WRITE** ▸*Math* Is *70 thousand* written in standard form or word form? Explain.

_____

_____

_____

Lesson Check

1. Based on a 2008 study, children 6–11 years old spend sixty-nine thousand, one hundred eight minutes a year watching television. What is this number written in standard form?

   _____

2. What is the value of the digit 4 in the number 84,230?

   _____

Spiral Review

3. An ant has 6 legs. How many legs do 8 ants have?

   _____

4. Latricia's vacation is in 4 weeks. There are 7 days in a week. How many days is it until Latricia's vacation?

   _____

5. Marta collected 363 cans. Diego collected 295 cans. How many cans did Marta and Diego collect?

   _____

6. The city Tim lives in has 106,534 people. What is the value of the 6 in 106,534?

   _____

FOR MORE PRACTICE
GO TO THE
Personal Math Trainer

Name _____

Compare and Order Numbers

Essential Question How can you compare and order numbers?

Learning Objective You will compare and order whole numbers based on the values of the digits in each number using >, =, and < symbols.

Unlock the Problem

Grand Canyon National Park in Arizona had 651,028 visitors in July 2008 and 665,188 visitors in July 2009. In which year did the park have more visitors during the month of July?

- How many visitors were there in July 2008?

  _____

- How many visitors were there in July 2009?

  _____

🔑 Example 1 Use a place-value chart.

You can use a place-value chart to line up the digits by place value. Line up the ones with the ones, the tens with the tens, and so on. Compare 651,028 and 665,188.

Write 651,028 and 665,188 in the place-value chart below.

THOUSANDS			ONES		
Hundreds	Tens	Ones	Hundreds	Tens	Ones

Start at the left. Compare the digits in each place-value position until the digits differ.

STEP 1 Compare the hundred thousands.

651,028

665,188

6 hundred thousands ◯ 6 hundred thousands
        └ Write <, >, or =.

The digits in the hundred thousands place are the same.

STEP 2 Compare the ten thousands.

651,028

665,188

5 ten thousands ◯ 6 ten thousands
        └ Write <, >, or =.

5 ten thousands is less than 6 ten thousands so, 651,028 < 665,188.

Since 651,028 < 665,188, there were more visitors in July 2009 than in July 2008.

Chapter 1   17

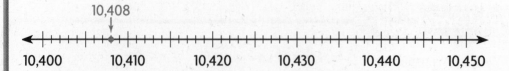 **Example 2** Use a number line to order 10,408; 10,433; and 10,416 from least to greatest.

Locate and label each point on the number line. The first one is done for you.

10,408
↓

◀─┼┼┼┼┼┼┼┼┼◆┼┼┼┼┼┼┼┼┼┼┼┼┼┼┼┼┼┼┼┼┼┼┼┼┼┼┼┼┼┼┼┼─▶
10,400   10,410   10,420   10,430   10,440   10,450

Think: Numbers to the left are closer to 0.

So, the numbers from least to greatest are 10,408; 10,416; and 10,433.

$10,408 < 10,416 < 10,433$

 **Share and Show**

1. Compare 15,327 and 15,341.
   Write <, >, or =. Use the number line to help.

◀─┼┼┼─▶
15,300   15,310   15,320   15,330   15,340   15,350   15,360

15,327 ◯ 15,341

Compare. Write <, >, or =.

2. $631,328 ◯ $640,009

✓3. 56,991 ◯ 52,880

4. 708,561 ◯ 629,672

5. 143,062 ◯ 98,643

Order from greatest to least.

✓6. 20,650; 21,150; 20,890

_____

 **Math Talk** Math Processes and Practices ②

Use Reasoning Why do you not start with the ones digits when comparing three multi-digit numbers?

Name _____

Compare. Write <, >, or =.

7. $2,212 ◯ $2,600

8. 88,304 ◯ 88,304

9. $524,116 ◯ $61,090

10. 751,272 ◯ 851,001

Order from least to greatest.

11. 41,090; 41,190; 40,009

12. 910,763; 912,005; 95,408

_____

_____

Math Processes and Practices 7 Identify Relationships **Algebra** Write all of the digits that can replace each ■.

13. 567 < 5■5 < 582

14. 464,545 > 4■3,535 > 443,550

_____

_____

15. **GO DEEPER** Leah's car has 156,261 miles on the odometer. Casey's car has 165,002 miles on the odometer. Mike's car has 145,834 miles on the odometer. Whose car has the most miles? Order the number of miles from least to greatest.

_____

16. **GO DEEPER** At Monica's Used Cars, the sales staff set a goal of $25,500 in sales each week. The sales for three weeks were $28,288; $25,369; and $25,876. Which total did not meet the goal?

_____

17. **THINK SMARTER** **What's the Error?** Max said that 36,594 is less than 5,980 because 3 is less than 5. **Describe** Max's error and give the correct answer.

_____

_____

Problem Solving • Applications

Use the picture graph for 18–20.

18. **Math Processes and Practices ④ Use Graphs** In which month shown did Grand Canyon National Park have about 7,500 tent campers?

_____

19. **GO DEEPER** How many more campers were there in July and August than in June and September?

_____

20. What if during the month of October, the park had 22,500 tent campers? How many symbols would be placed on the picture graph for October?

_____

Grand Canyon National Park Tent Campers

Month (2008)	Estimated Number of Campers
June	🏕️ 🏕️
July	🏕️ 🏕️ 🏕️
August	🏕️ 🏕️ 🏕️
September	🏕️ 🏕️

Key: Each 🏕️ = 5,000.

21. **THINK SMARTER** **What's the Question?** Compare: 643,251; 633,512; and 633,893. The answer is 633,512.

_____

_____

Personal Math Trainer

22. **THINK SMARTER +** Zachary's school set a goal of collecting 12,155 cans of food each day. In the first 3 days the school collected 12,250 cans; 10,505 cans; and 12,434 cans. Write each number in the box that tells whether or not the school met its goal.

| 12,250 | 10,505 | 12,434 |

Met the daily goal	Did not meet the daily goal

Compare and Order Numbers

Learning Objective You will compare and order whole numbers based on the values of the digits in each number using >, =, and < symbols.

Compare. Write <, >, or =.

1. 3,273 (<) 3,279

2. $1,323 ( ) $1,400

3. 52,692 ( ) 52,692

4. $413,005 ( ) $62,910

5. 382,144 ( ) 382,144

6. 157,932 ( ) 200,013

7. 401,322 ( ) 410,322

8. 989,063 ( ) 980,639

9. 258,766 ( ) 258,596

Order from least to greatest.

10. 23,710; 23,751; 23,715

11. 52,701; 54,025; 5,206

_____

_____

12. 465,321; 456,321; 456,231

13. $330,820; $329,854; $303,962

_____

_____

Problem Solving Real World

14. An online newspaper had 350,080 visitors in October, 350,489 visitors in November, and 305,939 visitors in December. What is the order of the months from greatest to least number of visitors?

_____

15. The total land area in square miles of each of three states is shown below.
    Colorado: 103,718
    New Mexico: 121,356
    Arizona: 113,635
What is the order of the states from least to greatest total land area?

_____

16. **WRITE** ▸*Math* Suppose the leftmost digits of two numbers are 8 and 3. Can you tell which number is greater? Explain.

_____

_____

_____

Lesson Check

1. At the yearly fund-raising drive, the nonprofit company's goal was to raise $55,500 each day. After three days, it had raised $55,053; $56,482; and $55,593. Which amount was less than the daily goal?

_____

2. List these numbers in order from greatest to least: 90,048; 93,405; 90,543

_____

Spiral Review

3. Write a fraction that is less than $\frac{5}{6}$ and has a denominator of 8.

_____

4. What is the perimeter of the rectangle below?

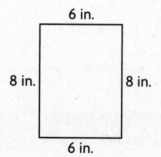

6 in.

8 in.   8 in.

6 in.

_____

5. A website had 826,140 hits last month. What is the value of the 8 in 826,140?

_____

6. Write 680,705 in expanded form.

_____

FOR MORE PRACTICE
GO TO THE
Personal Math Trainer

Name _____

Round Numbers

Essential Question How can you round numbers?

Learning Objective You will round whole numbers using place value understanding.

Unlock the Problem

During May 2008, the Mount Rushmore National Monument in South Dakota welcomed 138,202 visitors. A website reported that about 1 hundred thousand people visited the park during that month. Was the estimate reasonable?

- Underline what you are asked to find.
- Circle the information you will use.

An **estimate** tells you about how many or about how much. It is close to an exact amount. You can **round** a number to find an estimate.

One Way Use a number line.

To round a number to the nearest hundred thousand, find the hundred thousands it is between.

_____ < 138,202 < _____

Use a number line to see which hundred thousand 138,202 is closer to.

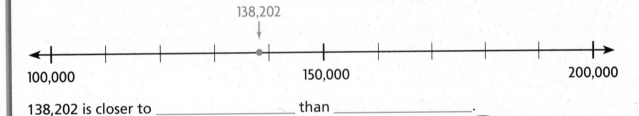

138,202 is closer to _____ than _____.

So, 1 hundred thousand is a reasonable estimate for 138,202.

Math Talk

Math Processes and Practices ④

Use Models How can you use a model to round numbers?

1. What number is halfway between 100,000 and 200,000?

_____

2. How does knowing where the halfway point is help you find which hundred thousand 138,202 is closer to? Explain.

_____

_____

_____

🔑 Another Way Use place value.

Mount Rushmore is located 5,725 feet above sea level. About how high is Mount Rushmore above sea level, to the nearest thousand feet?

To round a number to the nearest thousand, find the thousands it is between.

_____ < 5,725 < _____

Look at the digit in the place-value position to the right.

5,725

Think: The digit in the hundreds place is 7. So, 5,725 is closer to 6,000 than 5,000.

So, Mount Rushmore is about _____ feet above sea level.

Math Talk

Math Processes and Practices ⑥

Explain the difference in using a model and using place value when rounding numbers.

---

3. What number is halfway between 70,000 and 80,000?

_____

4. What is 75,000 rounded to the nearest ten thousand? Explain.

_____

_____

_____

Math Idea
When a number is exactly half way between two rounding numbers, round to the greater number.

Try This! Round to the place value of the underlined digit.

Ⓐ 6̲4,999

_____

Ⓑ 8̲50,000

_____

Ⓒ 30̲1,587

_____

Ⓓ 10̲,832

_____

Share and Show MATH BOARD

1. Suppose 255,113 people live in a city. Is it reasonable to say that about 300,000 people live in the city? Use the number line to help you solve the problem. Explain.

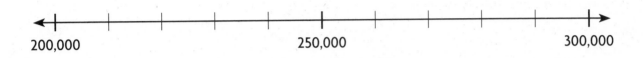

200,000   250,000   300,000

_____

_____

Round to the place value of the underlined digit.

2. 934,567   ✓ 3. 641,267   4. 234,890   ✓ 5. 347,456

_____   _____   _____   _____

On Your Own

6. **GO DEEPER** To the nearest hundred, a factory produced 3,600 jars of applesauce on Thursday and 4,200 jars of applesauce on Friday. To the nearest thousand, how many jars of applesauce did they produce during the two days?

_____

Problem Solving • Applications Real World

7. **THINK SMARTER** The number 2, 00 is missing a digit. The number rounded to the nearest thousand is 3,000. List all of the possibilities for the missing digit. Explain your answer.

_____

_____

_____

_____

8. **GO DEEPER** A male elephant weighs 6,728 pounds. A female elephant weighs 5,843 pounds. To the nearest hundred, what is the total weight of the two elephants?

_____

9. **THINK SMARTER +** About 300,000 people attended a festival. For numbers 9a–9e choose Yes or No to show whether each number could be the exact number of people that attended the festival.

9a. 351,213   ○ Yes   ○ No

9b. 249,899   ○ Yes   ○ No

9c. 252,348   ○ Yes   ○ No

9d. 389,001   ○ Yes   ○ No

9e. 305,992   ○ Yes   ○ No

Connect to Science

Data Gathering

Some scientists count and measure groups of things. Benchmarks can be used to estimate the size of a group or a population. A *benchmark* is a known number of things that helps you understand the size or amount of a different number of things.

Use the benchmark to find a reasonable estimate for the number of coquina shells it would take to fill a jar.

It would take about 5 times the benchmark to fill the jar.
$100 + 100 + 100 + 100 + 100 = 500$

The most reasonable estimate for the number of coquina shells it would take to fill the jar is 500 shells.

Benchmark   200; 500;
100 shells   or 5,000

Math Processes and Practices ① Evaluate Reasonableness Use the benchmark to find a reasonable estimate. Circle the reasonable estimate.

10.

500 beads   1,500; 2,500;
                 or 3,500

11.

10,000 blades   1,000; 10,000;
of grass   or 100,000

Name _____

Round Numbers

Learning Objective You will round whole numbers using place value understanding.

Round to the place value of the underlined digit.

1. 8<u>6</u>2,840

   862,840   **860,000**

     ↑

  less than 5

2. 123,<u>4</u>99

_____

3. <u>5</u>52,945

_____

- Look at the digit to the right.

- If the digit to the right is *less than* 5, the digit in the rounding place stays the same.

- If the digit to the right is *5 or greater,* the digit in the rounding place increases by one.

- Write zeros for the digits to the right of the rounding place.

4. 3<u>8</u>9,422

_____

5. <u>2</u>09,767

_____

6. 19<u>1</u>,306

_____

7. <u>6</u>6,098

_____

Problem Solving Real World

Use the table for 8–9.

8. Find the height of Mt. Whitney in the table. Round the height to the nearest thousand feet.

_____ feet

9. What is the height of Mt. Bona rounded to the nearest ten thousand feet?

_____ feet

Mountain Heights		
Name	State	Height (feet)
Mt. Bona	Alaska	16,500
Mt. Whitney	California	14,494

10. **WRITE** ▸*Math* Jessie says to round 763,400 to the nearest ten thousand, he will round to 770,000. Is he right? Explain.

_____

_____

Lesson Check

1. What is 247,039 rounded to the nearest thousand?

_____

_____

2. To the nearest ten thousand, the population of Vermont was estimated to be about 620,000 in 2008. What might have been the exact population of Vermont in 2008?

_____

_____

Spiral Review

3. Write the symbol that makes the following number sentence true.

$546,322 \bigcirc $540,997

4. Pittsburgh International Airport had approximately 714,587 passengers in August 2009. Write a number that is greater than 714,587.

_____

_____

5. June made a design with 6 equal tiles. One tile is yellow, 2 tiles are blue, and 3 tiles are purple. What fraction of the tiles are yellow or purple?

_____

6. The fourth grade collected 40,583 cans and plastic bottles. Write this number in word form.

_____

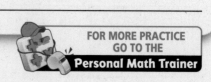

FOR MORE PRACTICE
GO TO THE
Personal Math Trainer

Name _____

 **Mid-Chapter Checkpoint**

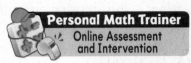
Vocabulary

Choose the best term from the box.

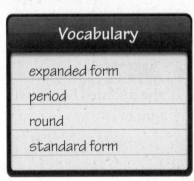

Vocabulary
expanded form
period
round
standard form

1. The _____ of 23,850 is 20,000 + 3,000 + 800 + 50. (p. 11)

2. You can _____ to find *about* how much or how many. (p. 23)

3. In 192,860 the digits 1, 9, and 2 are in the same

   _____. (p. 11)

Concepts and Skills

Find the value of the underlined digit.

4. 3<u>8</u>0,671 _____

5. 10,6<u>9</u>8 _____

6. <u>6</u>50,234 _____

Write the number in two other forms.

7. 293,805

   _____

   _____

8. 300,000 + 5,000 + 20 + 6

   _____

   _____

Compare. Write <, >, or =.

9. 457,380 ◯ 458,590

10. 390,040 ◯ 39,040

11. 11,809 ◯ 11,980

Round to the place of the underlined digit.

12. <u>1</u>40,250 _____

13. 10,<u>4</u>50 _____

14. 12<u>6</u>,234 _____

15. Last year, three hundred twenty-three thousand people visited the museum. What is this number written in standard form?

_____

16. **GO DEEPER** Rachael rounded 16,473 to the nearest hundred. Then she rounded her answer to the nearest thousand. What is the final number?

_____

17. What is the highest volcano in the Cascade Range?

Cascade Range Volcanoes		
Name	**State**	**Height (ft)**
Lassen Peak	CA	10,457
Mt. Rainier	WA	14,410
Mt. Shasta	CA	14,161
Mt. St. Helens	WA	8,364

_____

18. Richard got 263,148 hits when he did an Internet search. What is the value of the digit 6 in this number?

_____

Name _____

Rename Numbers

Essential Question How can you rename a whole number?

Learning Objective You will represent an equivalent form of a whole number by using models and regrouping.

Investigate

Materials ▪ base-ten blocks

You can regroup numbers to rename them.

A. Use large cubes and flats to model 1,200. Draw a quick picture to record your model.

The model shows _____ large cube and _____ flats.

Another name for 1,200 is _____ thousand _____ hundreds.

B. Use only flats to model 1,200.
Draw a quick picture to record your model.

The model shows _____ flats.

Another name for 1,200 is _____ hundreds.

Draw Conclusions

1. How is the number of large cubes and flats in the first model related to the number of flats in the second model?

_____

_____

2. Can you model 1,200 using only longs? Explain.

_____

_____

3. You renamed 1,200 as hundreds. How can you rename
1,200 as tens? Explain.

_____

_____

4. THINK SMARTER What would the models in Step A and Step B
look like for 5,200? How can you rename 5,200 as hundreds?

_____

_____

Make Connections

You can also use a place-value chart to help rename numbers.

THOUSANDS			ONES		
Hundreds	Tens	Ones	Hundreds	Tens	Ones
5	0	0,	0	0	0

└──────┘ 5 hundred thousands
└────────────┘ 50 ten thousands
└──────────────────┘ 500 thousands
└────────────────────────┘ 5,000 hundreds
└──────────────────────────────┘ 50,000 tens
└────────────────────────────────────┘ 500,000 ones

Write 32 hundreds on the place-value chart below. What is 32
hundreds written in standard form?

THOUSANDS			ONES		
Hundreds	Tens	Ones	Hundreds	Tens	Ones

└────────────────┘ 32 hundreds

32 hundreds written in standard form is _____ .

Math Processes and Practices ⑦

Look for Structure How can
a place-value chart help you
rename numbers?

Name _____

Rename the number. Draw a quick picture to help.

1. 150

_____ tens

2. 1,400

_____ hundreds

3. 2 thousands 3 hundreds

_____ hundreds

4. 13 hundreds

_____ thousand _____ hundreds

Rename the number. Use the place-value chart to help.

5. 18 thousands = _____

THOUSANDS			ONES		
Hundreds	Tens	Ones	Hundreds	Tens	Ones

6. 570,000 = 57 _____

THOUSANDS			ONES		
Hundreds	Tens	Ones	Hundreds	Tens	Ones

Rename the number.

7. 580 = _____ tens

8. 740,000 = _____ ten thousands

9. 8 hundreds 4 tens = 84 _____

10. 29 thousands = _____

Unlock the Problem

11. **THINK SMARTER** A toy store is ordering 3,000 remote control cars. The store can order the cars in sets of 10. How many sets of 10 does the store need to order?

a. What information do you need to use?

_____

_____

b. What do you need to find?

_____

_____

c. How can renaming numbers help you solve this problem?

_____

_____

d. Describe a strategy you can use to solve the problem.

_____

_____

e. How many sets of 10 remote control cars does the store need to buy?

_____

---

12. **GO DEEPER** Ivan sold 53 boxes of oranges on Friday and 27 boxes on Saturday during a citrus sale. There were 10 oranges in each box. How many oranges did he sell in all?

_____

13. **Math Processes and Practices 2** **Use Reasoning** A store sold a total of 15,000 boxes of buttons last month, and 12,000 boxes this month. If the store sold 270,000 buttons, how many buttons were in each box?

_____

---

14. **THINK SMARTER** For numbers 14a–14d, select True or False for each statement.

14a. 9 hundreds 3 tens can be renamed as 39 tens.   ○ True   ○ False

14b. 370,000 can be renamed as 37 ten thousands.   ○ True   ○ False

14c. 780 can be renamed as 78 tens.   ○ True   ○ False

14d. 42,000 can be renamed as 42 thousands.   ○ True   ○ False

Rename Numbers

Learning Objective You will represent an equivalent form of a whole number by using models and regrouping.

Rename the number. Use the place-value chart to help.

1. 760 hundreds = ___76,000___

THOUSANDS			ONES		
Hundreds	Tens	Ones	Hundreds	Tens	Ones
	7	6,	0	0	0

2. 24 ten thousands = _____

THOUSANDS			ONES		
Hundreds	Tens	Ones	Hundreds	Tens	Ones

Rename the number.

3. 120,000 = _____
ten thousands

4. 4 thousands 7 hundreds = 47 _____

Problem Solving Real World

5. For the fair, the organizers ordered 32 rolls of tickets. Each roll of tickets has 100 tickets. How many tickets were ordered in all?

6. An apple orchard sells apples in bags of 10. The orchard sold a total of 2,430 apples one day. How many bags of apples was this?

_____

7. ▌WRITE ▶Math Explain how you can rename 5,400 as hundreds. Include a quick picture or a place-value chart in your explanation.

_____

Lesson Check

1. A dime has the same value as 10 pennies. Marley brought 290 pennies to the bank. How many dimes did Marley get?

_____

2. A citrus grower ships grapefruit in boxes of 10. One season, the grower shipped 20,400 boxes of grapefruit. How many grapefruit were shipped?

_____

Spiral Review

3. There were 2,605 people at the basketball game. A reporter rounded this number to the nearest hundred for a newspaper article. What number did the reporter use?

_____

4. To get to Level 3 in a game, a player must score 14,175 points. Ann scores 14,205 points, Ben scores 14,089 points, and Chuck scores 10,463 points. Which score is greater than the Level 3 score?

_____

5. Henry counted 350 lockers in his school. Hayley counted 403 lockers in her school. How does the 3 in 350 compare to the 3 in 403?

_____

6. There are 4 muffins on each plate. There are 0 plates of lemon muffins. How many lemon muffins are there?

_____

FOR MORE PRACTICE
GO TO THE
Personal Math Trainer

Add Whole Numbers

Essential Question How can you add whole numbers?

Learning Objective You will add multi-digit whole numbers and determine whether solutions are reasonable.

Unlock the Problem Real World

Alaska is the largest state in the United States by area. Its land area is 570,374 square miles and its water surface area is 86,051 square miles. Find the total area of Alaska.

 Find the sum.

Add. 570,374 + 86,051

Think: It is important to line up the addends by place value when adding two numbers.

- Underline what you are asked to find.
- Circle the information you will use.

▲ The area of Alaska is outlined in the photo above.

STEP 1 Add the ones.

Add the tens. Regroup.

12 tens = 1 hundred _____ tens

$$\begin{array}{r} 5\overset{1}{70,374} \\ +\ 86,051 \\ \hline \end{array}$$

STEP 2 Add the hundreds.

Add the thousands.

$$\begin{array}{r} 5\overset{1}{70,374} \\ +\ 86,051 \\ \hline 25 \end{array}$$

STEP 3 Add the ten thousands.

Regroup.

15 ten thousands =

1 hundred thousand _____ ten thousands

$$\begin{array}{r} \overset{1}{5}7\overset{1}{0,374} \\ +\ 86,051 \\ \hline 6,425 \end{array}$$

Math Talk Math Processes and Practices ⑧

Draw Conclusions How do you know when to regroup when adding?

STEP 4 Add the hundred thousands.

$$\begin{array}{r} \overset{1}{5}7\overset{1}{0,374} \\ +\ 86,051 \\ \hline 56,425 \end{array}$$

So, the total area of Alaska is _____ square miles.

Estimate You can estimate to tell whether an answer is reasonable. To estimate a sum, round each addend before you add.

🔑 Example Estimate. Then find the sum.

Juneau has an area of 2,717 square miles. Valdez has an area of 222 square miles. What is their combined area?

A Estimate. Use the grid to help you align the addends by place value.

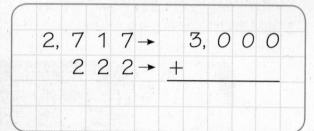

2, 7 1 7 → 3, 0 0 0   Round to the nearest thousand.

2 2 2 → +_____   Round to the nearest hundred.

So, the combined area of Juneau and Valdez is about _____ square miles.

B Find the sum.

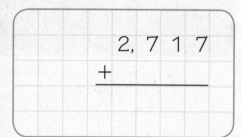

2, 7 1 7

+_____

Think: Begin by adding the ones.

> ⚠️ **ERROR Alert**
> Remember to align the addends by place value.

So, the combined area of Juneau and Valdez is _____ square miles.

• Is the sum reasonable? Explain.

_____

Share and Show

1. Use the grid to find 738,901 + 162,389.

Use the grid to align the addends by place value.

Name _____

Estimate. Then find the sum.

2. Estimate: _____

$$72{,}931$$
$$+18{,}563$$

3. Estimate: _____

$$432{,}068$$
$$+239{,}576$$

4. Estimate: _____

$$64{,}505$$
$$+38{,}972$$

Math Talk Math Processes and Practices 6

Explain how estimating helps you know if your answer is reasonable.

On Your Own

Estimate. Then find the sum.

5. Estimate: _____

$$839{,}136$$
$$+120{,}193$$

6. Estimate: _____

$$186{,}231$$
$$+\ 88{,}941$$

7. Estimate: _____

$$744{,}201$$
$$+168{,}900$$

8. **GO DEEPER** For the first football game of the season, 62,732 fans attended. The number of fans at the second game was 469 more than at the first game. What is the total number of fans that attended the first two games?

9. **GO DEEPER** Daisy's Flower Shop sold 135,649 flowers during its first year. The second year, the shop sold 9,754 more flowers than it did its first year. The third year, it sold 1,343 more flowers than it did in the second year. How many flowers did the shop sell during the three years?

_____

Math Processes and Practices 2 **Reason Abstractly Algebra** Find the missing number and name the property you used to find it. Write *Commutative* or *Associative.*

10. $(4{,}580 + 5{,}008) + 2{,}351 = 4{,}580 + (\boxed{} + 2{,}351)$

_____

Remember

Commutative Property

$4 + 5 = 5 + 4$

Associative Property

$4 + (7 + 3) = (4 + 7) + 3$

11. $7{,}801 + \boxed{} = 4{,}890 + 7{,}801$ _____

12. $2{,}592 + 3{,}385 = 3{,}385 + \boxed{}$ _____

Problem Solving • Applications

Use the table for 13–14.

13. **THINK SMARTER** What is the combined population of the three major Alaskan cities? Estimate to verify your answer.

_____

14. **Math Processes and Practices 6** The digit 5 occurs two times in the population of Fairbanks. What is the value of each 5? **Explain** your answer.

_____

_____

_____

Major Cities of Alaska

City	Population*
Anchorage	286,174
Fairbanks	35,252
Juneau	30,796

*2009 U.S. Census Bureau estimates

15. **GO DEEPER** Kaylie has 164 stamps in her collection. Her friend Nellie has 229 more stamps than Kaylie. How many stamps do Kaylie and Nellie have?

_____

| **WRITE** ▸ *Math* • **Show Your Work**

16. **THINK SMARTER** Alaska's Glacier Bay National Park had 431,986 visitors one year. The next year, the park had 22,351 more visitors than the year before. How many people visited during the two years? Show your work and explain how you found your answer.

_____

_____

_____

_____

_____

Name _____

Add Whole Numbers

Learning Objective You will add multi-digit whole numbers and determine whether solutions are reasonable.

Estimate. Then find the sum.

1. Estimate: __90,000__

```
  11
63,824 →  60,000
+ 29,452 → + 30,000
93,276    90,000
```

2. Estimate: _____

```
 73,404
+ 27,865
```

3. Estimate: _____

```
403,446
+ 396,755
```

4. Estimate: _____

```
137,638
+ 52,091
```

5. Estimate: _____

```
200,629
+ 28,542
```

6. Estimate: _____

```
212,514
+ 396,705
```

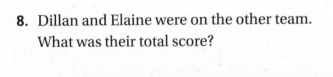

Problem Solving

Use the table for 7–9.

7. Beth and Cade were on one team. What was their total score?

   _____

8. Dillan and Elaine were on the other team. What was their total score?

   _____

9. Which team scored the most points?

   _____

Individual Game Scores	
Student	Score
Beth	251,567
Cade	155,935
Dillan	188,983
Elaine	220,945

10. **WRITE** *Math* Write a story problem that can be solved by finding the sum of 506,211 and 424,809. Then solve the problem.

_____

_____

Lesson Check

1. The coastline of the United States is 12,383 miles long. Canada's coastline is 113,211 miles longer than the coastline of the United States. How long is the coastline of Canada?

2. Germany is the seventh largest European country and is slightly smaller by area than Montana. Germany has a land area of 134,835 square miles and a water area of 3,011 square miles. What is the total area of Germany?

Spiral Review

3. In an election, about 500,000 people voted in all. What could be the exact number of people who voted in the election?

4. In 2007, Pennsylvania had approximately 121,580 miles of public roads. What is 121,580 rounded to the nearest thousand?

5. Order these numbers from least to greatest: 749,340; 740,999; 740,256

6. Which symbol makes the following statement true?

   $413,115 \bigcirc $431,511

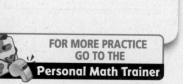
FOR MORE PRACTICE
GO TO THE
Personal Math Trainer

Name _____

Subtract Whole Numbers

Essential Question How can you subtract whole numbers?

Learning Objective You will subtract multi-digit whole numbers and determine whether solutions are reasonable.

Unlock the Problem

Mt. Bear and Mt. Bona are two mountains in Alaska. Mt. Bear is 14,831 feet tall and Mt. Bona is 16,421 feet tall. How much taller is Mt. Bona than Mt. Bear?

Estimate. 16,000 − 15,000 = _____

Subtract. 16,421 − 14,831

▲ Mt. Bear and Mt. Bona are in the St. Elias Mountain Range located in the Wrangell-St. Elias National Park and Preserve in Alaska.

STEP 1 Subtract the ones.

Regroup to subtract the tens.

4 hundreds 2 tens =

3 hundreds _____ tens

$$\begin{array}{r} \overset{\scriptstyle 3\,12}{16,\!4\!\!\!/21} \\ -14,\!831 \\ \hline \end{array}$$

STEP 2 Regroup to subtract the hundreds.

6 thousands 3 hundreds =

5 thousands _____ hundreds

$$\begin{array}{r} \overset{\scriptstyle 13}{\underset{}{5\ \overset{\scriptstyle 3\,12}{16,\!4\!\!\!/21}}} \\ -14,\!831 \\ \hline 90 \end{array}$$

STEP 3 Subtract the thousands.

Subtract the ten thousands.

$$\begin{array}{r} \overset{\scriptstyle 13}{\underset{}{5\ \overset{\scriptstyle 3\,12}{16,\!4\!\!\!/21}}} \\ -14,\!831 \\ \hline ,\!590 \end{array}$$

So, Mt. Bona is _____ feet taller than Mt. Bear. Since _____ is

close to the estimate of _____, the answer is reasonable.

Try This! Use addition to check your answer.

$$\begin{array}{r} \overset{\scriptstyle 13}{\cancel{6}} \\ 5\ \cancel{6}12 \\ 1\cancel{6},421 \\ -14,831 \\ \hline 1,590 \end{array}$$

$$\begin{array}{r} 1\ \ 1 \\ 1,590 \\ +14,831 \\ \hline \end{array}$$

So, the answer checks.

Share and Show MATH BOARD

1. Subtract. Use the grid to record the problem.

$637,350 - 43,832$

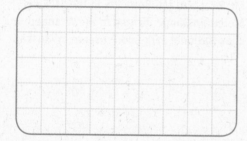

Math Talk Math Processes and Practices 8

Draw Conclusions How do you know which places to regroup to subtract?

Estimate. Then find the difference.

2. Estimate: _____

$$\begin{array}{r} 14,659 \\ -11,584 \\ \hline \end{array}$$

 3. Estimate: _____

$$\begin{array}{r} 456,912 \\ -\ 37,800 \\ \hline \end{array}$$

4. Estimate: _____

$$\begin{array}{r} 407,001 \\ -184,652 \\ \hline \end{array}$$

On Your Own

Estimate. Then find the difference.

5. Estimate: _____

$$\begin{array}{r} 942,385 \\ -461,803 \\ \hline \end{array}$$

6. Estimate: _____

$$\begin{array}{r} 798,300 \\ -348,659 \\ \hline \end{array}$$

7. Estimate: _____

$$\begin{array}{r} 300,980 \\ -159,000 \\ \hline \end{array}$$

Name _____

Practice: Copy and Solve Subtract. Add to check.

8. 653,809 − 256,034

9. 258,197 − 64,500

10. 496,004 − 398,450

11. 500,000 − 145,609

 Reason Abstractly Algebra Find the missing digit.

12.
$$\begin{array}{r} 6{,}532 \\ -4{,}1\ 5 \\ \hline 2{,}407 \end{array}$$

13.
$$\begin{array}{r} \ 08{,}665 \\ -659{,}420 \\ \hline 149{,}245 \end{array}$$

14.
$$\begin{array}{r} 697{,}320 \\ -432{,}\ 08 \\ \hline 264{,}712 \end{array}$$

Problem Solving • Applications

Use the table for 15–16.

15. **Math Processes and Practices ①** **Estimate Reasonableness** How many more acres were grown in 1996 than in 1986? Estimate to check the reasonableness of your answer.

_____

_____

16. What is the difference between the greatest number of acres and the least number of acres used for growing oranges?

_____

Orange Groves in Florida

Year	Acres
1966	673,086
1976	628,657
1986	466,256
1996	656,598

17. **GO DEEPER** Workers at a paper company count the number of boxes of paper in the warehouse each month. In January, there were 106,341 boxes of paper. In February, there were 32,798 fewer boxes than there were in January. In March, there were 25,762 fewer boxes than there were in February. How many boxes were in the warehouse in March?

18. **THINK SMARTER** There are 135,663 kilometers of U.S. coastline that border the Pacific Ocean. There are 111,866 kilometers of U.S. coastline that border the Atlantic Ocean. How many more kilometers of U.S. coastline border the Pacific Ocean than the Atlantic Ocean? Solve the problem and show how to check your answer.

_____

19. **THINKSMARTER** **What's the Error?** Maryland has an area of 12,407 square miles. Texas has an area of 268,601 square miles. How much larger is Texas than Maryland?

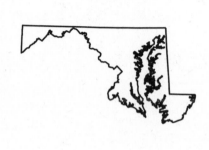

Read how Janice solved the problem. Find her error.

Solve the problem and correct her error.

Texas: 268,601 square miles
Maryland: 12,407 square miles
I can subtract to find the difference.

$$\begin{array}{r} 268{,}601 \\ -\ 12{,}407 \\ \hline 144{,}531 \end{array}$$

So, Texas is _____ square miles larger than Maryland.

- **Math Processes and Practices ❸** **Verify Reasoning of Others** Describe Janice's error.

_____

_____

Subtract Whole Numbers

Learning Objective You will subtract multi-digit whole numbers and determine whether solutions are reasonable.

Estimate. Then find the difference.

1. Estimate: __600,000__

   $$\begin{array}{r} 7\ \overset{9}{10}\ 15\ 6\ 13 \\ 7\cancel{8}\cancel{0},\cancel{5}\cancel{7}\cancel{3} \\ -\ 229{,}615 \\ \hline 550{,}958 \end{array}$$

   Think: 780,573 rounds to 800,000.
   229,615 rounds to 200,000.
   So an estimate is 800,000 − 200,000 = 600,000.

2. Estimate: _____

   $$\begin{array}{r} 428{,}731 \\ -\ 175{,}842 \\ \hline \end{array}$$

3. Estimate: _____

   $$\begin{array}{r} 920{,}026 \\ -\ 535{,}722 \\ \hline \end{array}$$

4. Estimate: _____

   $$\begin{array}{r} 253{,}495 \\ -\ 48{,}617 \\ \hline \end{array}$$

Problem Solving · Real World

Use the table for 5 and 6.

5. How many more people attended the Magic's games than attended the Pacers' games?

   _____

6. How many fewer people attended the Pacers' games than attended the Clippers' games?

   _____

Season Attendance for Three NBA Teams	
Team	**Attendance**
Indiana Pacers	582,295
Orlando Magic	715,901
Los Angeles Clippers	670,063

7. **WRITE** ▸*Math* Write a story problem that can be solved by finding the difference of 432,906 and 61,827. Then solve the problem.

   _____

   _____

   _____

Lesson Check

1. This year, a farm planted 400,000 corn stalks. Last year, the farm planted 275,650 corn stalks. How many more corn stalks did the farm plant this year than last year?

_____

2. One machine can make 138,800 small paper clips in one day. Another machine can make 84,250 large paper clips in one day. How many more small paper clips than large paper clips are made by the two machines in one day?

_____

Spiral Review

3. In three baseball games over a weekend, 125,429 people came to watch. The next weekend, 86,353 people came to watch the games. How many people total watched the six baseball games?

_____

4. Kevin read the number "two hundred seven thousand, forty-eight" in a book. What is this number in standard form?

_____

5. A museum had 275,608 visitors last year. What is this number rounded to the nearest thousand?

_____

6. At the Millville Theater, a play ran for several weeks. In all, 28,175 people saw the play. What is the value of the digit 8 in 28,175?

_____

© Houghton Mifflin Harcourt Publishing Company

FOR MORE PRACTICE
GO TO THE
Personal Math Trainer

Name _____

Problem Solving • Comparison Problems with Addition and Subtraction

Essential Question How can you use the strategy *draw a diagram* to solve comparison problems with addition and subtraction?

Learning Objective You will use the strategy *draw a diagram* to solve comparison problems with addition and subtraction.

Unlock the Problem

Hot air balloon festivals draw large crowds of people. The attendance on the first day of one festival was 17,350. On the second day the attendance was 18,925. How many more people attended the hot air balloon festival on the second day?

Use the graphic organizer to help you solve the problem.

Read the Problem

What do I need to find?	**What information do I need to use?**	**How will I use the information?**
Write what you need to find.	_____ people attended on the first day, _____ people attended on the second day.	What strategy can you use?
_____		_____
_____		_____
_____		_____

Solve the Problem

I can draw a bar model and write an equation to represent the problem.

18,925

17,350	

$18,925 - 17,350 =$ _____

So, _____ more people attended the festival on the second day.

🔑 Try Another Problem

During an event, a hot air balloon traveled a distance of 5,110 feet during the first trip and 850 feet more during the second trip. How far did it travel during the second trip?

Read the Problem

What do I need to find?	What information do I need to use?	How will I use the information?

Solve the Problem

- Is your answer reasonable? Explain how you know.

_____

_____

Math Talk

Math Processes and Practices ⑧

Generalize How can inverse operations be used to check your answer?

Name _____

Unlock the Problem

√ Use the Problem Solving MathBoard

√ Underline important facts.

√ Choose a strategy you know.

1. Hot air balloons are able to fly at very high altitudes. A world record height of 64,997 feet was set in 1988. In 2005, a new record of 68,986 feet was set. How many feet higher was the 2005 record than the 1988 record?

First, draw a diagram to show the parts of the problem.

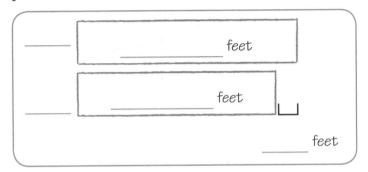

Next, write the problem you need to solve.

_____

Last, solve the problem to find how many feet higher the 2005 record was than the 1988 record.

So, the 2005 record was _____ feet higher.

▲ Dr. Vijaypat Singhania flew the world's largest hot-air balloon when he made his record-breaking flight. The balloon he flew was over 20 stories tall.

2. What if a new world altitude record of 70,000 feet was set? How many feet higher would the new record be than the 2005 record?

_____

3. Last year, the ticket sales for a commercial hot air balloon ride were $109,076. This year, the ticket sales were $125,805. How much more were the ticket sales this year?

_____

4. A musician's first album sells 234,499 copies the first week it was released. During the second week, another 432,112 albums were sold. How many more albums were sold during the second week than the first week?

_____

On Your Own

Use the information in the table for 5–6.

5. **Math Processes and Practices ④** **Use Models** Steve Fossett attempted to fly around the world in a balloon several times before he succeeded in 2002. How many more miles did he fly during the 2002 flight than during the August 1998 flight?

Steve Fossett's Balloon Flights	
Year	**Distance in Miles**
1996	2,200
1997	10,360
1998 (January)	5,803
1998 (August)	14,235
2001	3,187
2002	20,482

_____

6. **GO DEEPER** Is the combined distance for the 1998 flights more or less than the distance for the 2002 flight? By how much? Explain.

_____

_____

_____

7. **THINK SMARTER** There were 665 hot air balloon pilots at a hot air balloon race. There were 1,550 more ground crew members than there were pilots. How many pilots and ground crew members were there all together?

_____

Personal Math Trainer

8. **THINK SMARTER +** The first year Becky owned her car she drove it 14,378 miles. The second year she drove it 422 fewer miles than the first year. She bought the car with 16 miles on it. How many miles were on the car at the end of the second year? Show your work.

_____

_____

_____

Problem Solving • Comparison Problems with Addition and Subtraction

Learning Objective You will use the strategy *draw a diagram* to solve comparison problems with addition and subtraction.

Use the information in the table for 1–3.

Surface Area of the Great Lakes	
Lake	**Surface Area (in square miles)**
Lake Superior	31,700
Lake Michigan	22,278
Lake Huron	22,973
Lake Erie	9,906
Lake Ontario	7,340

1. How many square miles larger is the surface area of Lake Huron than the surface area of Lake Erie?

   Think: How can a bar model help represent the problem? What equation can be written?

   Lake Huron | 22,973

   Lake Erie | 9,906 | ?

   $22,973 - 9,906 = \underline{13,067}$ square miles

   _____
   13,067 square miles

2. Which lake has a surface area that is 14,938 square miles greater than the surface area of Lake Ontario? Draw a model and write a number sentence to solve the problem.

   _____

3. Lake Victoria has the largest surface area of all lakes in Africa. Its surface area is 26,828 square miles. How much larger is the surface area of Lake Superior than that of Lake Victoria?

   _____

4. **WRITE** ▸*Math* Write a comparison problem you can solve using addition or subtraction. Draw a bar model to represent the situation. Describe how the information in the bar model is related to the problem.

   _____

Lesson Check

1. The Mariana Trench in the Pacific Ocean is about 36,201 feet deep. The Puerto Rico Trench in the Atlantic Ocean is about 27,493 feet deep. Draw a bar model to find how many feet deeper the Mariana Trench is than the Puerto Rico Trench.

2. At 1,932 feet, Crater Lake in Oregon, is the deepest lake in the United States. The world's deepest lake, Lake Baykal in Russia, is 3,383 feet deeper. Draw a bar model to find how deep Lake Baykal is.

Spiral Review

3. Write a number that is greater than 832,458, but less than 832,500.

4. A stadium in Pennsylvania seats 107,282 people. A stadium in Arizona seats 71,706 people. Based on these facts, how many more people does the stadium in Pennsylvania seat than the stadium in Arizona?

5. What is 399,713 rounded to the place value of the underlined digit?

6. About 400,000 people visited an art museum in December. What could be the exact number of people who visited the art museum?

FOR MORE PRACTICE
GO TO THE
Personal Math Trainer

Name _____

✓ Chapter 1 Review/Test

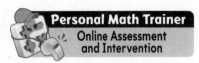

1. Select a number for ■ that will make a true comparison. Mark all that apply.

$$703,209 > \blacksquare$$

- (A) 702,309
- (C) 703,209
- (E) 730,029
- (B) 703,029
- (D) 703,290
- (F) 730,209

2. **GO DEEPER** Nancy wrote the greatest number that can be made using each of these digits exactly once.

| 5 | 3 | 4 | 9 | 8 | 1 |

Part A

What was Nancy's number? How do you know this is the greatest possible number for these digits?

Part B

What is the least number that can be made using each digit exactly once? Explain why the value of the 4 is greater than the value of the 5.

GO DIGITAL Assessment Options
Chapter Test

For 3–4, use the table.

U.S. Mountain Peaks					
Name	State	Height (ft)	Name	State	Height (ft)
Blanca Peak	CO	14,345	Mount Whitney	CA	14,494
Crestone Peak	CO	14,294	University Peak	AK	14,470
Humboldt Peak	CO	14,064	White Mountain	CA	14,246

3. Write the name of each mountain peak in the box that describes its height, in feet.

Between 14,000 feet and 14,300 feet	Between 14,301 feet and 14,500 feet

4. Circle the name of the tallest peak. Explain how you know which of the mountain peaks is the tallest.

5. Mr. Rodriguez bought 420 pencils for the school. If there are 10 pencils in a box, how many boxes did he buy?

(A) 42

(B) 420

(C) 430

(D) 4,200

6. Bobby and Cheryl each rounded 745,829 to the nearest ten thousand. Bobby wrote 750,000 and Cheryl wrote 740,000. Who is correct? Explain the error that was made.

Name _____

7. The total season attendance for a college team's home games, rounded to the nearest ten thousand, was 270,000. For numbers 7a–7d, select Yes or No to tell whether the number could be the exact attendance.

7a. 265,888   ○ Yes   ○ No

7b. 260,987   ○ Yes   ○ No

7c. 274,499   ○ Yes   ○ No

7d. 206,636   ○ Yes   ○ No

For 8–10, use the table.

The table shows recent population data for Sacramento, California.

Population of Sacramento, CA			
Age in years	Population	Age in years	Population
Under 5	35,010	20 to 34	115,279
5 to 9	31,406	35 to 49	92,630
10 to 14	30,253	50 to 64	79,271
15 to 19	34,219	65 and over	49,420

8. How many children are under 10 years old? Show your work.

9. How many people are between the ages of 20 and 49? Show your work.

10. How many more children are under the age of 5 than between the ages of 10 and 14? Show your work.

11. For numbers 11a–11d, select True or False for each sentence.

11a.   The value of 7 in 375,092
       is 7,000.   ○ True   ○ False

11b.   The value of 5 in 427,593
       is 500.   ○ True   ○ False

11c.   The value of 2 in 749,021
       is 200.   ○ True   ○ False

11d.   The value of 4 in 842,063
       is 40,000.   ○ True   ○ False

12. Select another way to show 403,871. Mark all that apply.

   Ⓐ   four hundred three thousand, eight hundred one

   Ⓑ   four hundred three thousand, seventy-one

   Ⓒ   four hundred three thousand, eight hundred seventy-one

   Ⓓ   400,000 + 38,000 + 800 + 70 + 1

   Ⓔ   400,000 + 3,000 + 800 + 70 + 1

   Ⓕ   4 hundred thousands + 3 thousands + 8 hundreds +
       7 tens + 1 one

Personal Math Trainer

13. THINK SMARTER ➕   Lexi, Susie, and Rial are playing an online word
    game. Rial scores 100,034 points. Lexi scores 9,348 fewer points
    than Rial and Susie scores 9,749 more points than Lexi. What is
    Susie's score? Show your work.

14. There were 13,501 visitors to a museum in June. What is this
    number rounded to the nearest ten thousand? Explain how
    you rounded.

    _____

    _____

15. New Mexico has an area of 121,298 square miles. California has an area of 155,779 square miles. How much greater is the area, in square miles, of California than the area of New Mexico? Show your work and explain how you know the answer is reasonable.

16. Circle the choice that completes the statement.

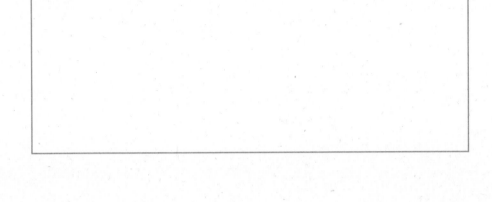

10,000 less than 24,576 is | equal to / greater than / less than | 1,000 less than 14,576

17. Match the number to the value of its 5.

45,678 •   • 500

757,234•   • 50

13,564 •   • 50,000

3,450 •   • 5,000

18. During September and October, a total of 825,150 visitors went to Grand Canyon National Park. If 448,925 visitors went to the park in September, how many visitors went to the park in October?
Show your work.

19. A college baseball team had 3 games in April. Game one had an attendance of 14,753 people. Game two had an attendance of 20,320 people. Game three had an attendance of 14,505 people. Write the games in order from the least attendance to the greatest attendance. Use pictures, words, or numbers to show how you know.

20. Caden made a four-digit number with a 5 in the thousands place, a 5 in the ones place, a 6 in the tens place, and a 4 in the hundreds place. What was the number?

_____

Multiply by 1-Digit Numbers

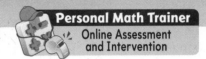

Personal Math Trainer
Online Assessment and Intervention

✓ Show What You Know

Check your understanding of important skills.

Name _____

▶ **Arrays** Write a multiplication sentence for the array.

1.

2.

_____   _____   _____   _____

▶ **Multiplication Facts** Find the product.

3. _____ = 9 × 6

4. _____ = 7 × 8

5. 8 × 4 = _____

▶ **Regroup Through Thousands**
Regroup. Write the missing numbers.

6. 9 tens 10 ones = _____ hundred

7. 60 hundreds = _____ thousands

8. 25 tens = _____ hundreds 5 tens

9. 14 ones = _____ ten _____ ones

10. 3 tens 12 ones = _____ tens 2 ones

Math in the Real World

The Arctic Lion's Mane Jellyfish is one of the largest known animals. Its tentacles can be as long as 120 feet. Find how this length compares to your height. Round your height to the nearest foot. 120 feet is _____ times as long as _____ feet.

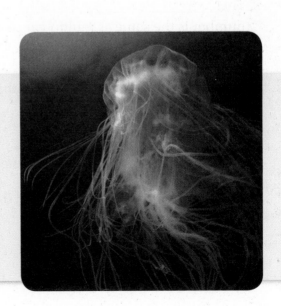

Vocabulary Builder

▶ **Visualize It** •

Complete the flow map, using the words with a ✓.

Multiplying

What can you do?	What can you use?	What are some examples?
_____ products.	→	Use _____ and mental math.	→	$3 \times 48 = $ ■ ↓ ↓ $3 \times 50 = 150$
_____ ones as tens.	→	Use _____ .	→	12 ones = 1 ten 2 ones

▶ **Understand Vocabulary** •

Complete the sentences.

1. The _____ states that multiplying a sum by a
   number is the same as multiplying each addend by the number and then
   adding the products.

2. A number that is multiplied by another number to find a product

   is called a _____ .

3. A method of multiplying in which the ones, tens, hundreds, and

   so on are multiplied separately and then the products are added together is

   called the _____ method.

GO DIGITAL
• Interactive Student Edition
• Multimedia eGlossary

Distributive Property

propiedad distributiva

23

estimate (*verb*)

estimar

30

factor

factor

33

partial product

producto parcial

61

place value

valor posicional

68

product

producto

72

regroup

reagrupar

78

round

redondear

82

To find an answer that is close to the exact amount

The property that states that multiplying a sum by a number is the same as multiplying each addend by the number and then adding the products

Example: $5 \times (10 + 6) = (5 \times 10) + (5 \times 6)$

A method of multiplying in which the ones, tens, hundreds, and so on are multiplied separately and then the products are added together

$$
\begin{array}{r}
182 \\
\times \quad 6 \\
\hline
600 \\
480 \leftarrow \text{Partial products} \\
+ \quad 12 \\
\hline
1{,}092
\end{array}
$$

A number that is multiplied by another number to find a product

Example: $4 \times 5 = 20$

factor   factor

The answer to a multiplication problem

Example: $4 \times 5 = 20$

product

The value of a digit in a number, based on the location of the digit

To replace a number with another number that tells about how many or how much

To exchange amounts of equal value to rename a number

Example: $5 + 8 = 13$ ones or 1 ten 3 ones

Picture It

For 3 to 4 players

Materials

- timer
- sketch pad

How to Play

1. Take turns to play.

2. To take a turn, choose a word from the Word Box, but do not tell the word to the other players.

3. Set the timer for 1 minute.

4. Draw pictures and numbers to give clues about the word.

5. The first player to guess the word before time runs out gets 1 point. If that player can use the word in a sentence, he or she gets 1 more point. Then that player gets a turn choosing a word.

6. The first player to score 10 points wins.

Word Box

Distributive Property
estimate
factor
partial product
place value
product
regroup
round

The Write Way

Reflect

Choose one idea. Write about it.

- Explain the Distributive Property so that a younger child could understand it.
- Write two questions you have about regrouping.
- Describe the steps you would take find the product of 354 and 6.

Name _____

Multiplication Comparisons

Essential Question How can you model multiplication comparisons?

Learning Objective You will use models to interpret a multiplication equation as a comparison and write a comparison sentence.

You can use multiplication to compare amounts. For example, you can think of $15 = 3 \times 5$ as a comparison in two ways:

Remember
The Commutative Property states that you can multiply two factors in any order and get the same product.

15 is 3 times as many as 5.

15		
5	5	5

5

15 is 5 times as many as 3.

15				
3	3	3	3	3

3

Unlock the Problem

Carly has 9 pennies. Jack has 4 times as many pennies as Carly. How many pennies does Jack have?

 Draw a model and write an equation to solve.

• What do you need to compare?

_____

_____

MODEL

Carly

Jack

RECORD

Use the model to write an equation and solve.

$n = $ _____ $\times$ _____

$n = $ _____

The value of n is 36.

Think: n is how many pennies Jack has.

So, Jack has _____ pennies.

Math Talk Math Processes and Practices ①

Describe what is being compared and explain how the comparison model relates to the equation.

• **THINK SMARTER** Explain how the equation for *4 is 2 more than 2* is different from the equation for *4 is 2 times as many as 2*.

_____

_____

_____

Chapter 2 63

Example Draw a model and write an equation to solve.

Miguel has 3 times as many rabbits as Sara. Miguel has 6 rabbits. How many rabbits does Sara have?

- How many rabbits does Miguel have? _____
- How many rabbits does Sara have?

_____

_____

MODEL

Think: You don't know how many rabbits Sara has. Use n for Sara's rabbits.

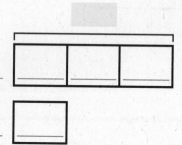

_____

_____

So, Sara has 2 rabbits.

RECORD

Use the model to write an equation and solve.

$6 = $ _____ $\times$ _____

$6 = 3 \times$ _____   Think: 3 times what number equals 6?

The value of n is 2.

Think: n is how many rabbits Sara has.

Try This! Write an equation or a comparison sentence.

A Write an equation.

21 is 7 times as many as 3.

_____ = _____ $\times$ _____

B Write a comparison sentence.

$8 \times 5 = 40$

_____ times as many as _____ is _____.

Share and Show MATH BOARD

1. There are 8 students in the art club. There are 3 times as many students in chorus. How many students are in chorus?

_____

_____

So, there are _____ students in chorus.

Write an equation and solve.

$n = $ _____ $\times$ _____

$n = $ _____

The value of n is _____.

Math Talk

Math Processes and Practices ⑥

Explain how you could write the equation a different way.

Name _____

Draw a model and write an equation.

2. 6 times as many as 2 is 12.

☑ **3.** 20 is 4 times as many as 5.

_____

_____

Write a comparison sentence.

4. $18 = 9 \times 2$

_____ is _____ times as many as _____.

☑ **5.** $8 \times 4 = 32$

_____ times as many as _____ is _____.

On Your Own

Write a comparison sentence.

6. $5 \times 7 = 35$

_____ times as many as _____ is _____.

7. $54 = 6 \times 9$

_____ is _____ times as many as _____.

8. **GO DEEPER** One week, Jake and Sally collected canned goods for a food drive. On Monday, Jake collected 4 boxes and Sally collected 2 boxes. At the end of the week, Jake had 3 times as many boxes as he had on Monday. Sally had 4 times as many boxes as she had on Monday. Together, how many boxes of canned goods did they have at the end of the week?

_____

9. **GO DEEPER** Nando has 4 goldfish. Jill has 3 goldfish. Cooper has 2 times as many goldfish as Nando and Jill combined. Write an equation that compares the number of goldfish Cooper has with the number of goldfish that Nando and Jill have.

_____

10. **Math Processes and Practices ②** **Represent a Problem** Write a comparison sentence about pet food that could be represented using the equation $12 = 4 \times 3$.

_____

_____

_____

© Houghton Mifflin Harcourt Publishing Company

Unlock the Problem Real World

11. **THINK SMARTER** Luca has 72 baseball cards. This is 8 times as many cards as Han has. How many baseball cards does Han have?

a. What do you need to find? _____

_____

b. How can you use a model to find the number of cards Han has?

_____

c. Draw the model.

d. Write an equation and solve.

_____ = _____ × _____

_____ = _____

So, Han has _____ baseball cards.

12. **THINK SMARTER** Complete the statements to describe each model.

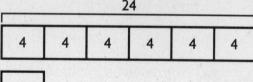

24
4	4	4	4	4	4

4

24
6	6	6	6

6

24 is [   ] times as many as [   ].   24 is [   ] times as many as [   ].

Name _____

Multiplication Comparisons

Learning Objective You will use models to interpret a multiplication equation as a comparison and write a comparison sentence.

Write a comparison sentence.

1. $6 \times 3 = 18$

___6___ times as many as ___3___ is ___18___.

2. $63 = 7 \times 9$

_____ is _____ times as many as _____.

3. $5 \times 4 = 20$

_____ times as many as _____ is _____.

4. $48 = 8 \times 6$

_____ is _____ times as many as _____.

Write an equation.

5. 2 times as many as 8 is 16.

_____

6. 42 is 6 times as many as 7.

_____

7. 3 times as many as 5 is 15.

_____

8. 36 is 9 times as many as 4.

_____

Problem Solving · Real World

9. Alan is 14 years old. This is twice as old as his brother James is. How old is James?

_____

10. There are 27 campers. This is nine times as many as the number of counselors. How many counselors are there?

_____

11. **WRITE** ▸ *Math* Draw a model, and write an equation to represent "4 times as many as 3 is 12." Explain your work.

_____

_____

Lesson Check

1. Write an equation that represents this comparison sentence.

   24 is 4 times as many as 6.

   _____

   _____

2. Write a comparison sentence that represents this equation.

   $5 \times 9 = 45$

   _____

   _____

Spiral Review

3. Which symbol makes the following statement true?

   547,098 ◯ 574,908

4. What is the standard form for $200,000 + 80,000 + 700 + 6$?

   _____

5. Sean and Leah are playing a computer game. Sean scored 72,491 points. Leah scored 19,326 points more than Sean. How many points did Leah score?

   _____

6. A baseball stadium has 38,496 seats. Rounded to the nearest thousand, how many seats is this?

   _____

© Houghton Mifflin Harcourt Publishing Company

FOR MORE PRACTICE
GO TO THE
Personal Math Trainer

Name _____

Comparison Problems

Essential Question How does a model help you solve a comparison problem?

Learning Objective You will solve real-world problems with whole numbers involving multiplicative comparison using drawings and equations.

Unlock the Problem

Evan's dog weighs 7 times as much as Oxana's dog. Together, the dogs weigh 72 pounds. How much does Evan's dog weigh?

Example 1 Use a multiplication model.

STEP 1 Draw a model. Let *n* represent the unknown.

Think: Let *n* represent how much Oxana's dog weighs. Together, the dogs weigh 72 pounds.

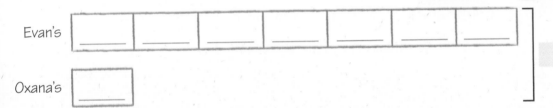

Evan's

Oxana's

STEP 2 Use the model to write an equation. Find the value of *n*.

_____ × *n* = _____   **Think:** There are 8 parts. The parts together equal 72.

8 × _____ = 72   **Think:** What times 8 equals 72?

The value of *n* is 9.

n is how much _____ weighs.

STEP 3 Find how much Evan's dog weighs.

Think: Evan's dog weighs 7 times as much as Oxana's dog.

Evan's dog = _____ × _____   Multiply.

= _____

So, Evan's dog weighs 63 pounds.

Math Talk

Math Processes and Practices 6

Attend to Precision How can you tell if you found the correct weight of Evan's dog?

To find how many times as much, use a multiplication model. To find how many more or fewer, model the addition or subtraction.

Evan's dog weighs 63 pounds. Oxana's dog weighs 9 pounds. How much more does Evan's dog weigh than Oxana's dog?

🔓 Example 2 Use an addition or subtraction model.

STEP 1 Draw a model. Let n represent the unknown.

Think: Let n represent the difference.

_____ | _____ |

_____ | |

_____

STEP 2 Use the model to write an equation. Find the value of n.

_____ − _____ = n **Think:** The model shows a difference.

  63 − 9 = _____   Subtract.

The value of n is _____.

n is _____.

So, Evan's dog weighs 54 pounds more than Oxana's dog.

Share and Show MATH BOARD

Math Talk

Math Processes and Practices ④

Use Models How do you know which model to use to solve a comparison problem?

1. Maria's dog weighs 6 times as much as her rabbit. Together the pets weigh 56 pounds. What does Maria's dog weigh?

   Draw a model. Let n represent the unknown.

   Write an equation to find the value of n. $7 \times n =$ _____. n is _____ pounds.

   Multiply to find how much Maria's dog weighs. $8 \times 6 =$ _____

   So, Maria's dog weighs _____ pounds.

Name _____

Draw a model. Write an equation and solve.

✓ **2.** Last month Kim trained 3 times as many dogs as cats. If the total number of cats and dogs she trained last month is 28, how many cats did Kim train?

Draw a model.   Write an equation and solve.

_____

_____

_____

✓ **3.** How many more dogs than cats did Kim train?

Draw a model.   Write an equation and solve.

_____

_____

_____

On Your Own

Practice: Copy and Solve Draw a model.

Write an equation and solve.

4. At the dog show, there are 4 times as many boxers as spaniels. If there are a total of 30 dogs, how many dogs are spaniels?

_____

5. There are 5 times as many yellow labs as terriers in the dog park. If there are a total of 18 dogs, how many dogs are terriers?

_____

6. Ben has 3 times as many guppies as goldfish. If he has a total of 20 fish, how many guppies does he have?

_____

7. GO DEEPER Carlita saw 5 times as many robins as cardinals while bird watching. She saw a total of 24 birds. How many more robins did she see than cardinals?

_____

Problem Solving • Applications

8. **GO DEEPER** To get to a dog show, Mr. Luna first drives
7 miles west from his home and then 3 miles north. Next,
he turns east and drives 11 miles. Finally, he turns north
and drives 4 miles to the dog show. How far north of
Mr. Luna's home is the dog show?

To solve the problem, Dara and Cliff drew diagrams.
Which diagram is correct? Explain.

_____

_____

_____

_____

9. **Math Processes and Practices 2** **Use Reasoning** Valerie and Bret have a total
of 24 dog show ribbons. Bret has twice as many ribbons as
Valerie. How many ribbons does each have?

_____

_____

WRITE ► *Math*
Show Your Work

10. **THINK SMARTER** Noah built a fenced dog
run that is 8 yards long and 6 yards wide.
He placed posts at every corner and every
yard along the length and width of the run.
How many posts did he use?

_____

11. **THINK SMARTER** Last weekend, Mandy collected 4 times as many shells as
Cameron. Together, they collected 40 shells. How many shells did Mandy
collect? Complete the bar model. Then, write an equation and solve.

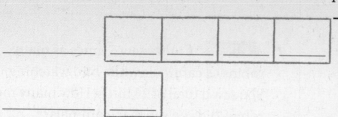

Comparison Problems

Learning Objective You will solve real-world problems with whole numbers involving multiplicative comparison using drawings and equations.

Draw a model. Write an equation and solve.

1. Stacey made a necklace using 4 times as many blue beads as red beads. She used a total of 40 beads. How many blue beads did Stacey use?

Think: Stacey used a total of 40 beads. Let n represent the number of red beads.

blue: n n n n ⎤ 40
red: n ⎦

$5 \times n = 40; 5 \times 8 = 40;$ _____

$4 \times 8 = 32$ blue beads _____

2. At the zoo, there were 3 times as many monkeys as lions. Tom counted a total of 24 monkeys and lions. How many monkeys were there?

_____

_____

Problem Solving · Real World

3. Rafael counted a total of 40 white cars and yellow cars. There were 9 times as many white cars as yellow cars. How many white cars did Rafael count?

_____

4. Sue scored a total of 35 points in two games. She scored 6 times as many points in the second game as in the first. How many more points did she score in the second game?

_____

5. **WRITE** ▸*Math* Write a problem involving *how much more than* and solve it. Explain how drawing a diagram helped you solve the problem.

_____

_____

Lesson Check

1. Sari has 3 times as many pencil erasers as Sam. Together, they have 28 erasers. How many erasers does Sari have?

_____

2. In Sean's fish tank, there are 6 times as many goldfish as guppies. There are a total of 21 fish in the tank. How many more goldfish are there than guppies?

_____

Spiral Review

3. Barbara has 9 stuffed animals. Trish has 3 times as many stuffed animals as Barbara. How many stuffed animals does Trish have?

_____

4. There are 104 students in the fourth grade at Allison's school. One day, 15 fourth-graders were absent. How many fourth-graders were at school that day?

_____

5. Joshua has 112 rocks. Jose has 98 rocks. Albert has 107 rocks. Write the boy's names in order from the least to the greatest number of rocks owned.

_____

6. Alicia has 32 stickers. This is 4 times as many stickers as Benita has. How many stickers does Benita have?

_____

FOR MORE PRACTICE GO TO THE Personal Math Trainer

Name _____

Multiply Tens, Hundreds, and Thousands

Essential Question How does understanding place value help you multiply tens, hundreds, and thousands?

Learning Objective You will use place value to multiply tens, hundreds, and thousands.

Unlock the Problem

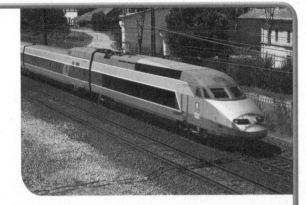

Each car on a train has 200 seats. How many seats are on a train with 8 cars?

Find 8×200.

One Way Draw a quick picture.

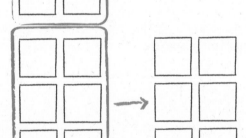

T

Think: 10 hundreds = 1,000

Think: 6 hundreds = 600

$1,000 + 600 =$ _____

Another Way Use place value.

$8 \times 200 = 8 \times$ _____ hundreds

$=$ _____ hundreds

$=$ _____ **Think:** 16 hundreds is 1 thousand, 6 hundreds.

So, there are _____ seats on a train with 8 cars.

Math Talk

Math Processes and Practices ⑦

Look for a Pattern How can finding 8×2 help you find 8×200?

❶ Other Ways

Ⓐ Use a number line.

Bob's Sled Shop rents 4,000 sleds each month.
How many sleds does the store rent in 6 months?

Find 6 × 4,000.

Multiplication can be thought of as repeated addition.
Draw jumps to show the product.

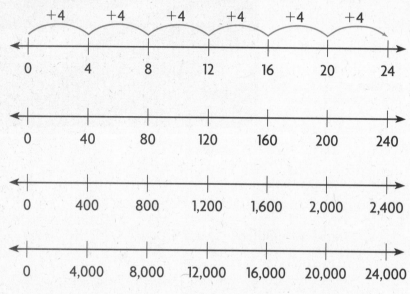

$6 \times 4 = 24$ ← basic fact

$6 \times 40 = 240$

$6 \times 400 = 2,400$

$6 \times 4,000 = 24,000$

So, Bob's Sled Shop rents _____ sleds in 6 months.

Ⓑ Use patterns.

Basic fact:

$3 \times 7 = 21$ ← basic fact

$3 \times 70 = 210$

$3 \times 700 =$ _____

$3 \times 7,000 =$ _____

Basic fact with a zero:

$8 \times 5 = 40$ ← basic fact

$8 \times 50 = 400$

$8 \times 500 =$ _____

$8 \times 5,000 =$ _____

- How does the number of zeros in the product of 8 and 5,000
  compare to the number of zeros in the factors? Explain.

_____

_____

Math Talk

Math Processes and Practices ⑤

Use Patterns to tell how the
number of zeros in the factors
and products changes in
Example B.

Name _____

1. Use the drawing to find 2×500.

$2 \times 500 =$ _____

Complete the pattern.

2. $3 \times 8 = 24$

$3 \times 80 =$ _____

$3 \times 800 =$ _____

$3 \times 8,000 =$ _____

3. $6 \times 2 = 12$

$6 \times 20 =$ _____

$6 \times 200 =$ _____

$6 \times 2,000 =$ _____

4. $4 \times 5 =$ _____

$4 \times 50 =$ _____

$4 \times 500 =$ _____

$4 \times 5,000 =$ _____

Find the product.

5. $6 \times 500 = 6 \times$ _____ hundreds

$=$ _____ hundreds

$=$ _____

6. $9 \times 5,000 = 9 \times$ _____ thousands

$=$ _____ thousands

$=$ _____

On Your Own

Find the product.

7. $7 \times 6,000 =$ _____

8. $4 \times 80 =$ _____

9. $3 \times 500 =$ _____

Math Processes and Practices ② **Use Reasoning Algebra Find the missing factor.**

10. _____ $\times 9,000 = 63,000$

11. $7 \times$ _____ $= 56,000$

12. $8 \times$ _____ $= 3,200$

13. Math Processes and Practices ⑤ **Communicate** How does the number of zeros in the product of 8 and 5,000 compare to the number of zeros in the factors? Explain.

_____

_____

🔑 Unlock the Problem

14. **THINK SMARTER** Joe's Fun and Sun rents beach chairs. The store rented 300 beach chairs each month in April and in May. The store rented 600 beach chairs each month from June through September. How many beach chairs did the store rent during the 6 months?

a. What do you need to know? _____

_____

b. How will you find the number of beach chairs? _____

_____

c. Show the steps you use to solve the problem.

d. Complete the sentences.

For April and May, a total of _____ beach chairs were rented.

For June through September, a total of

_____ beach chairs were rented.

Joe's Fun and Sun rented _____ beach chairs during the 6 months.

---

15. **GO DEEPER** Mariah makes bead necklaces. Beads are packaged in bags of 50 and bags of 200. Mariah bought 4 bags of 50 beads and 3 bags of 200 beads. How many

beads did Mariah buy? _____

---

16. **THINK SMARTER** Carmen has three books of 20 stamps and five books of 10 stamps. How many stamps does Carmen have? Complete the equation using the numbers on the tiles.

_____ × 20 + _____ × 10 = _____

3	5
110	50
60	100

Multiply Tens, Hundreds, and Thousands

Learning Objective You will use place value to multiply tens, hundreds, and thousands.

Find the product.

1. $4 \times 7{,}000 =$ ___28,000___

Think: $4 \times 7 = 28$
So, $4 \times 7{,}000 = 28{,}000$

2. $9 \times 60 =$ _____

3. $8 \times 200 =$ _____

4. $5 \times 6{,}000 =$ _____

5. $7 \times 800 =$ _____

6. $8 \times 90 =$ _____

7. $6 \times 3{,}000 =$ _____

8. $3 \times 8{,}000 =$ _____

9. $5 \times 500 =$ _____

10. $9 \times 4{,}000 =$ _____

Problem Solving · Real World

11. A bank teller has 7 rolls of coins. Each roll has 40 coins. How many coins does the bank teller have?

_____

12. Theo buys 5 packages of paper. There are 500 sheets of paper in each package. How many sheets of paper does Theo buy?

_____

13. **WRITE** ▸*Math* Explain how finding 7×20 is similar to finding $7 \times 2{,}000$. Then find each product.

_____

_____

© Houghton Mifflin Harcourt Publishing Company

Lesson Check

1. A plane is traveling at a speed of 400 miles per hour. How far will the plane travel in 5 hours?

2. One week, a clothing factory made 2,000 shirts in each of 6 different colors. How many shirts did the factory make in all?

Spiral Review

3. Write a comparison sentence to represent this equation.

$$6 \times 7 = 42$$

4. The population of Middleton is six thousand, fifty-four people. Write this number in standard form.

5. In an election for mayor, 85,034 people voted for Carl Green and 67,952 people voted for Maria Lewis. By how many votes did Carl Green win the election?

6. Meredith picked 4 times as many green peppers as red peppers. If she picked a total of 20 peppers, how many green peppers did she pick?

FOR MORE PRACTICE
GO TO THE
Personal Math Trainer

Name _____

Estimate Products

Essential Question How can you estimate products by rounding and determine if exact answers are reasonable?

Learning Objective You will estimate products using place value understanding to round multi-digit whole numbers to given place values and determine if exact answers are reasonable.

Unlock the Problem

An elephant can reach as high as 23 feet with its trunk. It uses its trunk to pick up objects that weigh up to 3 times as much as a 165-pound person. About how much weight can an African elephant pick up with its trunk?

- Cross out the information you will not use.
- Circle the numbers you will use.
- How will you use the numbers to solve the problem?

_____

One Way Estimate by rounding.

STEP 1 Round the greater factor to the nearest hundred.

3×165

↓

3×200

STEP 2 Use mental math.

Think: $3 \times 200 = 3 \times 2$ hundreds

$= 6$ hundreds

$= \underline{\hspace{1cm}}$

So, an African elephant can pick up about 600 pounds with its trunk.

Another Way Estimate by finding two numbers the exact answer is between.

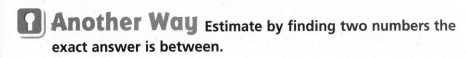

3×165 3×165

↓   ↓

$3 \times 100 = \underline{\hspace{1cm}}$ $3 \times 200 = \underline{\hspace{1cm}}$

Think: 165 is between 100 and 200. Use those numbers to estimate.

An African elephant is the largest living land mammal.

So, the African elephant can pick up between 300 and 600 pounds.

1. Is 200 less than or greater than 165? _____

2. So, would the product of 3 and 165 be less than or

   greater than 600? _____

Math Talk | Math Processes and Practices ⑥

Compare Is the exact answer closer to 300 or 600? Why?

Describe Reasonableness You can estimate a product to find whether an exact answer is reasonable.

 Tell whether an exact answer is reasonable.

Eva's horse eats 86 pounds each week. Eva solved the equation below to find how much feed she needs for 4 weeks.

$4 \times 86 = \blacksquare$

Eva says she needs 344 pounds of feed.
Is her answer reasonable?

 One Way Estimate.

4×86

↓ Think: Round to the nearest ten.

_____ × _____ = _____

344 is close to 360.

 Another Way Find two numbers the exact answer is between.

4×86 4×86

↓   ↓

_____ × _____ = _____   _____ × _____ = _____

_____ is between _____ and _____.

So, 344 pounds of feed is reasonable.

Share and Show

1. Estimate the product by rounding.

    $5 \times 2,213$

    ↓

    _____ × _____ = _____

2. Estimate the product by finding two numbers the exact answer is between.

    $5 \times 2,213$ $5 \times 2,213$

    _____ × _____ = _____   _____ × _____ = _____

Math Talk   Math Processes and Practices ⑥

How do you know that an exact answer of 11,065 is reasonable? **Explain.**

Name _____

Tell whether the exact answer is reasonable.

3. Kira needs to make color copies of a horse show flyer. The printer can make 24 copies in 1 minute. Kira says the printer makes 114 copies in 6 minutes.

_____

_____

_____

4. Jones Elementary is having a car wash to raise money for a community horse trail. Each car wash ticket costs $8. Tiara says the school will receive $1,000 if 125 tickets are sold.

_____

_____

_____

On Your Own

Tell whether the exact answer is reasonable.

5. (Math Processes and Practices ①) **Evaluate Reasonableness** Mrs. Hense sells a roll of coastal Bermuda horse hay for $58. She says she will make $174 if she sells 3 rolls.

_____

_____

_____

6. Mr. Brown sells horse supplies. A pair of riding gloves sells for $16. He says he will make $144 if he sells 9 pairs.

_____

_____

_____

7. GO DEEPER Path A and Path B are walking paths used for horses. Path A is 118 feet long. Path B is 180 feet long. Carlos walks his horse down each path 3 times. Which path did Carlos use to walk his horse about 500 feet? Explain.

_____

_____

_____

_____

8. THINK SMARTER Students in the third grade sell 265 tickets to the school play. Students in the fourth grade sell 3 times as many tickets as the third grade students. Estimate the number of tickets the fourth grade students sold by finding the two numbers the exact answer is between.

The students sold between

0		300	
300	and	600	tickets.
600		900	
800		1,200	

Connect to Reading

Make Predictions

As you read a story, you make predictions about what might happen next or about how the story will end.

When you solve a math problem, you make predictions about what your answer might be.

An *estimate* is a prediction because it helps you to determine whether your answer is correct. For some problems, it is helpful to make two estimates—one that is less than the exact answer and one that is greater.

Predict whether the exact answer will be *less than* or *greater than* the estimate. Explain your answer.

9. **THINK SMARTER** The food stand at the zoo sold 2,514 pounds of hamburger last month. The average cost of a pound of hamburger is $2. Jeremy estimates that about $6,000 worth of hamburger was sold last month.

_____

_____

_____

_____

10. **GO DEEPER** A zoo bought 2,240 pounds of fresh food for the bears this month. The average cost of a pound of food is $4. Jeremy estimates that about $8,000 was spent on fresh food for the bears this month.

_____

_____

_____

_____

Name _____

Estimate Products

Learning Objective You will estimate products using place value understanding to round multi-digit whole numbers to given place values and determine if exact answers are reasonable.

Estimate the product by rounding.

1. 4 × 472

    4 × 472

      ↓

    4 × **500**

      2,000
_____

2. 2 × 6,254

_____

3. 9 × 54

_____

4. 5 × 5,503

_____

Find two numbers the exact answer is between.

5. 3 × 567

_____

6. 6 × 7,381

_____

7. 4 × 94

_____

8. 8 × 684

_____

Problem Solving Real World

9. Isaac drinks 8 glasses of water each day. He says he will drink 2,920 glasses of water in a year that has 365 days. Is the exact answer reasonable? **Explain.**

_____

_____

_____

10. Most Americans throw away about 1,365 pounds of trash each year. Is it reasonable to estimate that Americans throw away over 10,000 pounds of trash in 5 years? **Explain.**

_____

_____

_____

11. **WRITE** ▸*Math* Describe a real-life multiplication situation for which an estimate makes sense.

_____

_____

Lesson Check

1. A theater has 4,650 seats. If the theater sells all the tickets for each of its 5 shows, about how many tickets will the theater sell?

_____

2. Washington Elementary has 4,358 students. Jefferson High School has 3 times as many students as Washington Elementary. About how many students does Jefferson High School have?

_____

Spiral Review

3. Diego has 4 times as many autographed baseballs as Melanie has. Diego has 24 autographed baseballs. How many autographed baseballs does Melanie have?

_____

4. Mr. Turkowski bought 4 boxes of envelopes at the office supply store. Each box has 500 envelopes. How many envelopes did Mr. Turkowski buy?

_____

5. Pennsylvania has a land area of 44,816 square miles. What is the land area of Pennsylvania rounded to the nearest hundred?

_____

6. The table shows the types of DVDs customers rented from Sunshine Movie Rentals last year.

Movie Rentals	
Type	Number Rented
Comedy	6,720
Drama	4,032
Action	5,540

How many comedy and action movies were rented last year?

_____

FOR MORE PRACTICE GO TO THE Personal Math Trainer

Name _____

Multiply Using the Distributive Property

Essential Question How can you use the Distributive Property to multiply a 2-digit number by a 1-digit number?

Learning Objective You will use the Distributive Property to multiply a 2-digit number by a 1-digit number.

Investigate

Materials ■ color pencils, grid paper

You can use the Distributive Property to break apart numbers to make them easier to multiply.

The **Distributive Property** states that multiplying a sum by a number is the same as multiplying each addend by the number and then adding the products.

A. Outline a rectangle on the grid to model 6 × 13.

B. Think of 13 as 5 + 8. Break apart the model to show 6 × (5 + 8). Label and shade the smaller rectangles. Use two different colors.

Use the Distributive Property. Find the product each smaller rectangle represents. Then find the sum of the products. Record your answers.

_____ × _____ = _____

_____ × _____ = _____

_____ + _____ = _____

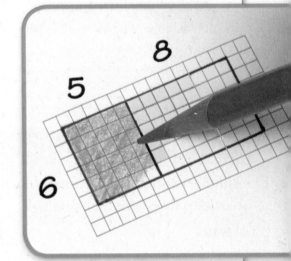

C. Model 6 × 13 again. Think of 13 as a different sum. Break apart the model to show 6 × (_____ + _____). Find the product each smaller rectangle represents. Then find the sum of the products. Record your answers.

_____ × _____ = _____

_____ × _____ = _____

_____ + _____ = _____

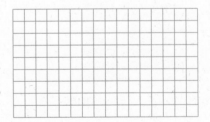

Draw Conclusions

1. Explain how you found the total number of squares in each model in Steps B and C.

_____

_____

_____

2. Compare the sums of the products in Steps B and C with those of your classmates. What can you conclude?

_____

_____

3. [THINK SMARTER] To find 7×23, is it easier to break apart the factor, 23, as $20 + 3$ or $15 + 8$? Explain.

_____

_____

Make Connections

Another way to model the problem is to use base-ten blocks to show tens and ones.

STEP 1

Use base-ten blocks to model 6×13.

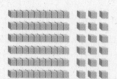

6 rows of 1 ten 3 ones

STEP 2

Break the model into tens and ones.

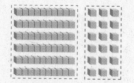

(6×1 ten)   (6×3 ones)

(6×10)   (6×3)

_____   _____

STEP 3

Add the tens and the ones to find the product.

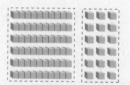

(6×10) + (6×3)

60   +   18

_____

So, $6 \times 13 = 78$.

In Step 2, the model is broken into two parts. Each part shows a **partial product**. The partial products are 60 and 18.

Math Talk   Math Processes and Practices ④

Model Mathematics Why is this a good model for the problem?

Name _____

Model the product on the grid. Record the product.

1. $3 \times 13 =$ _____

2. $5 \times 14 =$ _____

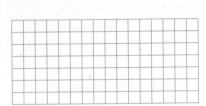

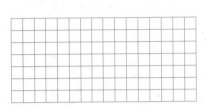

Find the product.

3. $6 \times 14 =$ _____

4. $5 \times 18 =$ _____

5. $4 \times 16 =$ _____

Use grid paper or base-ten blocks to model the product. Then record the product.

6. $7 \times 12 =$ _____

7. $5 \times 16 =$ _____

8. $9 \times 13 =$ _____

Problem Solving • Applications Real World

9. Math Processes and Practices 6 Explain how modeling partial products can be used to find the products of greater numbers.

_____

_____

_____

10. *THINK SMARTER* Use the Distributive Property to model the product on the grid. Record the product.

$4 \times 14 =$ _____

11. **THINK SMARTER** Kyle went to a fruit market. The market sells a wide variety of fruits and vegetables. The picture at the right shows a display of oranges.

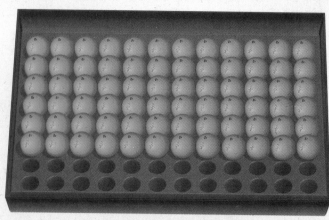

Write a problem that can be solved using the picture.

Pose a problem.

_____
_____
_____
_____
_____
_____
_____

Solve your problem.

_____
_____
_____
_____
_____
_____
_____

• **GO DEEPER** Describe how you could change the problem by changing the number of rows of oranges and the number of empty spaces in the picture. Then solve the problem.

_____
_____
_____
_____

Multiply Using the Distributive Property

Learning Objective You will use the Distributive Property to multiply a 2-digit number by a 1-digit number.

Model the product on the grid. Record the product.

1. $4 \times 19 =$ ___76___

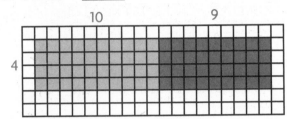

$4 \times 10 = 40$ and $4 \times 9 = 36$

$40 + 36 = 76$

2. $5 \times 13 =$ _____

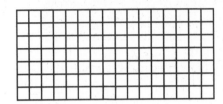

Find the product.

3. $4 \times 14 =$ _____

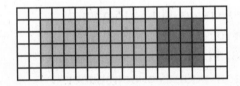

4. $3 \times 17 =$ _____

5. $6 \times 15 =$ _____

Problem Solving Real World

6. Michael arranged his pennies in the following display.

How many pennies does Michael have in all?

_____

7. **WRITE** ▸ *Math* Explain how you can use a model to find 6×17.

_____

_____

_____

_____

Lesson Check

1. The model shows how Maya planted flowers in her garden.

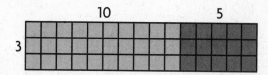

How many flowers did Maya plant?

2. The model below represents the expression 5 × 18.

How many tens will there be in the final product?

Spiral Review

3. Center City has a population of twenty-one thousand, seventy people. Write the population in standard form.

4. Central School collected 12,516 pounds of newspaper to recycle. Eastland School collected 12,615 pounds of newspapers. How many more pounds of newspaper did Eastland School collect than Central School?

5. Allison has 5 times as many baseball cards as football cards. In all, she has 120 baseball and football cards. How many baseball cards does Allison have?

6. A ruby-throated hummingbird beats its wings about 53 times each second. About how many times does a ruby-throated hummingbird beat its wings in 5 seconds?

FOR MORE PRACTICE
GO TO THE
Personal Math Trainer

Name _____

Multiply Using Expanded Form

Essential Question How can you use expanded form to multiply a multidigit number by a 1-digit number?

Learning Objective You will use expanded form to multiply by a 1-digit number.

 Unlock the Problem Real World

🔑 Example 1 Use expanded form.

Multiply. 5 × 143

5 × 143 = 5 × (_____ + _____ + _____)   Write 143 in expanded form.

= (5 × 100) + (_____ × _____) + (_____ × _____)   Use the Distributive Property.

SHADE THE MODEL	THINK AND RECORD

STEP 1
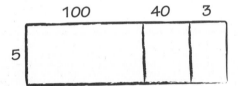

Multiply the hundreds.

(5 × 100) + (5 × 40) + (5 × 3)

_____ + (5 × 40) + (5 × 3)

STEP 2
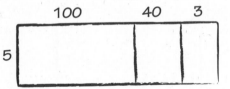

Multiply the tens.

(5 × 100) + (5 × 40) + (5 × 3)

500 + _____ + (5 × 3)

STEP 3
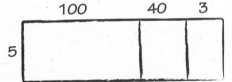

Multiply the ones.

(5 × 100) + (5 × 40) + (5 × 3)

500 + 200 + _____

STEP 4
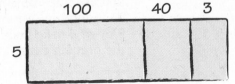

Add the partial products.

500
200
+ 15

So, 5 × 143 = _____ .

 Math Talk

Math Processes and Practices ①

Evaluate Reasonableness How do you know your answer is reasonable?

🔑 Example 2 Use expanded form.

The gift shop at the animal park orders 3 boxes of toy animals. Each box has 1,250 toy animals. How many toy animals does the shop order?

Multiply. $3 \times 1,250$

STEP 1

Write 1,250 in expanded form. Use the Distributive Property.

$3 \times 1,250 = 3 \times ($ _____ $+$ _____ $+$ _____ $)$

$= (3 \times 1,000) + ($ _____ $\times$ _____ $) + ($ _____ $\times$ _____ $)$

STEP 2

Add the partial products.

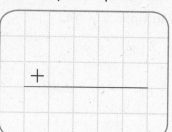

So, the shop ordered _____ animals.

Share and Show

1. Find 4×213. Use expanded form.

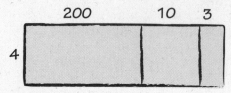

$4 \times 213 =$ _____ $\times ($ _____ $+$ _____ $+$ _____ $)$

$= ($ _____ $\times$ _____ $) + ($ _____ $\times$ _____ $) + ($ _____ $\times$ _____ $)$

Use the Distributive Property.

$=$ _____ $+$ _____ $+$ _____

$=$ _____

Record the product. Use expanded form to help.

☑ **2.** $4 \times 59 =$ _____

☑ **3.** $3 \times 288 =$ _____

Math Talk Math Processes and Practices ②

Represent a Problem How did using the Distributive Property make finding the product easier?

Name _____

On Your Own

Record the product. Use expanded form to help.

4. $4 \times 21 =$ _____

5. $6 \times 35 =$ _____

6. **GO DEEPER** A hotel has 128 rooms on each floor. There are 4 floors in all. If 334 of the rooms in the hotel have been cleaned, how many rooms still need to be cleaned?

_____

7. **GO DEEPER** Ben wants to buy 2 blue sweaters for $119 each and 3 brown sweaters for $44 each. How much will Ben spend on the five sweaters?

_____

WRITE ▸ *Math*
Show Your Work

8. **GO DEEPER** A jeweler has 36 inches of silver chain. She needs 5 times that much to make some necklaces and 3 times that amount to make some bracelets. How much silver chain does the jeweler need to make her necklaces and bracelets?

_____

9. **GO DEEPER** Gretchen walks her dog 3 times a day. Each time she walks the dog, she walks 1,760 yards. How many yards does she walk her dog in 3 days?

_____

10. **Math Processes and Practices 4** **Write an Expression** Which expression could you write to show how to multiply 9×856 using place value and expanded form?

_____

11. **GO DEEPER** Jennifer bought 4 packages of tacks. There are 48 tacks in a package. She used 160 of the tacks to put up posters. How many tacks does she have left? Explain.

_____

_____

_____

_____

Problem Solving • Applications

Use the table for 12–13.

Sacco Nursery Plant Sale Prices per Tree		
Tree	Regular Price	Discounted Price (4 or more)
Flowering Cherry	$59	$51
Italian Cypress	$79	$67
Muskogee Crape Myrtle	$39	$34
Royal Empress	$29	$25

12. What is the total cost of 3 Italian cypress trees?

_____

13. **THINK SMARTER** **What's the Error?**
Tanya says that the difference in the
cost of 4 flowering cherry trees and
4 Muskogee crape myrtles is $80.
Is she correct? Explain.

_____

_____

_____

WRITE *Math* • **Show Your Work**

14. **WRITE** *Math* What is the greatest possible product
of a 2-digit number and a 1-digit number? Explain
how you know.

_____

_____

_____

15. **THINK SMARTER** Multiply 5 × 381 using place value and expanded form.
Select a number from each box to complete the expression.

$$(5 \times \boxed{\begin{matrix} 30 \\ 300 \end{matrix}}) + (5 \times \boxed{\begin{matrix} 8 \\ 80 \end{matrix}}) + (5 \times \boxed{\begin{matrix} 1 \\ 10 \end{matrix}})$$

Multiply Using Expanded Form

Learning Objective You will use expanded form to multiply by a 1-digit number.

Record the product. Use expanded form to help.

1. $7 \times 14 =$ _____98_____

  $7 \times 14 = 7 \times (10 + 4)$

    $= (7 \times 10) + (7 \times 4)$

    $= 70 + 28$

    $= 98$

2. $8 \times 43 =$ _____

3. $6 \times 532 =$ _____

4. $5 \times 923 =$ _____

5. The fourth-grade students at Riverside School are going on a field trip. There are 68 students on each of the 4 buses. How many students are going on the field trip?

6. There are 5,280 feet in one mile. Hannah likes to walk 5 miles each week for exercise. How many feet does Hannah walk each week?

_____ _____

7. **WRITE** ▸*Math* Explain how you can find 3×584 using expanded form.

_____

_____

_____

Lesson Check

1. Write an expression that shows how to multiply 7 × 256 using expanded form and the Distributive Property.

_____

_____

2. Sue uses the expression (8 × 3,000) + (8 × 200) + (8 × 9) to help solve a multiplication problem. What is Sue's multiplication problem?

_____

_____

Spiral Review

3. What is another way to write 9 × 200?

_____

_____

4. What is the value of the digit 4 in 46,000?

_____

_____

5. Chris bought 6 packages of napkins for his restaurant. There were 200 napkins in each package. How many napkins did Chris buy?

_____

6. List these numbers in order from **least** to **greatest**.

8,251; 8,125; 8,512

_____

FOR MORE PRACTICE
GO TO THE
Personal Math Trainer

Name _____

Multiply Using Partial Products

Essential Question How can you use place value and partial products to multiply by a 1-digit number?

Learning Objective You will use place value understanding and partial products to multiple a whole number of up to 4-digits by a 1-digit whole number.

 Unlock the Problem

CONNECT How can you use what you know about the Distributive Property to break apart numbers to find products of 3-digit and 1-digit numbers?

• How can you write 182 as a sum of hundreds, tens, and ones?

_____

 Use place value and partial products.

Multiply. 6 × 182   **Estimate.** 6 × 200 = _____

SHADE THE MODEL	THINK AND RECORD
STEP 1 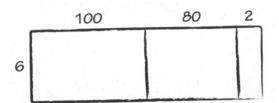	182 × 6 ← Multiply the hundreds. 6 × 1 hundred = 6 hundreds
STEP 2 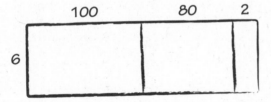	182 × 6 600 ← Multiply the tens. 6 × 8 tens = 48 tens
STEP 3 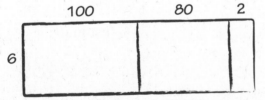	182 × 6 600 480 ← Multiply the ones. 6 × 2 ones = 12 ones
STEP 4 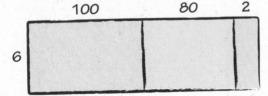	182 × 6 600 480 + 12 ← Add the partial products.

So, 6 × 182 = 1,092. Since 1,092 is close to the estimate of 1,200, it is reasonable.

Math Talk   Math Processes and Practices ②

Use Reasoning How can you use the Distributive Property to find 4 × 257?

🔑 Example

Use place value and partial products.

Multiply. 2 × 4,572   **Estimate.** 2 × 5,000 = _____

$$\begin{array}{r} 4,572 \\ \times \quad 2 \\ \hline \end{array}$$

← 2 × 4 thousands = 8 thousands

← 2 × 5 hundreds = 1 thousand

← 2 × 7 tens = 1 hundred, 4 tens

← 2 × 2 ones = 4 ones

← Add the partial products.

Share and Show MATH BOARD

1. Use the model to find 2 × 137.

	100	30	7
2			

$$\begin{array}{r} 137 \\ \times \quad 2 \\ \hline \\ + \\ \hline \end{array}$$

Estimate. Then record the product.

2. Estimate: _____

$$\begin{array}{r} 190 \\ \times \quad 3 \\ \hline \\ + \\ \hline \end{array}$$

✓3. Estimate: _____

$$\begin{array}{r} 471 \\ \times \quad 4 \\ \hline \\ + \\ \hline \end{array}$$

✓4. Estimate: _____

$$\begin{array}{r} \$3,439 \\ \times \quad 7 \\ \hline \\ + \\ \hline \end{array}$$

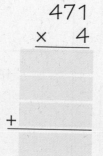

Math Talk

Math Processes and Practices ⑥

Explain how using place value and expanded form makes it easier to find products.

Name _____

On Your Own

Estimate. Then record the product.

5. Estimate: _____

$$\begin{array}{r} \$53 \\ \times\ \ 4 \\ \hline \\ + \ \ \\ \hline \\ \end{array}$$

6. Estimate: _____

$$\begin{array}{r} \$473 \\ \times\ \ \ 9 \\ \hline \\ \\ + \ \ \\ \hline \\ \end{array}$$

7. Estimate: _____

$$\begin{array}{r} 608 \\ \times\ \ \ 6 \\ \hline \\ \\ + \ \ \\ \hline \\ \end{array}$$

Practice: Copy and Solve Estimate. Then record the product.

8. 2×78

9. $2 \times \$210$

10. $9 \times \$682$

11. $8 \times 8{,}145$

Math Processes and Practices ② Use Reasoning Algebra Find the missing digit.

12.
$$\begin{array}{r} \boxed{}5 \\ \times\ \ 7 \\ \hline 455 \end{array}$$

13.
$$\begin{array}{r} 248 \\ \times\ \ 3 \\ \hline \boxed{}44 \end{array}$$

14.
$$\begin{array}{r} \$395 \\ \times\ \ \boxed{} \\ \hline \$2{,}370 \end{array}$$

15.
$$\begin{array}{r} 3{,}748 \\ \times\ \ \ \ 4 \\ \hline 1\ \boxed{}{,}992 \end{array}$$

16. **GO DEEPER** A store bought 9 cases of light bulbs in May and 8 cases in June. There are 48 light bulbs in a case. How many light bulbs did the store buy in May and June?

17. **GO DEEPER** Mr. Wilson saved $2,500 to buy airline tickets for his family. He bought 6 airline tickets for $372 each. How much of his savings does Mr. Wilson have after he buys the tickets?

18. **GO DEEPER** Coach Ramirez bought 8 cases of bottled water for a road race. There are 24 bottles in each case. After the race, 34 bottles of water were left. How many bottles were used at the race? Explain.

_____

_____

_____

© Houghton Mifflin Harcourt Publishing Company

Problem Solving • Applications

19. **Math Processes and Practices ④ Use Diagrams** Look at the picture. Kylie has 832 songs on her portable media player. Lance has 3 times as many songs. How many fewer songs can Lance add to his player than Kylie can add to hers?

_____

20. **GO DEEPER** James wants to buy the new portable media player shown. He has 5 times as many songs as Susan. Susan has 1,146 songs. Will all of his songs fit on the portable media player? How many songs does James have?

_____

Up To 9,000 Songs

Battery Life For Audio: 22 Hours

• • • • • **WRITE** ❭ _Math_ • **Show Your Work** • • • • • •

21. **THINK SMARTER** The sum of a 3-digit number and a 1-digit number is 217. The product of the numbers is 642. If one number is between 200 and 225, what are the numbers?

_____

22. **THINK SMARTER** Mrs. Jackson bought 6 gallons of juice for a party. Each gallon has 16 cups. After the party, 3 cups of juice were left over. At the party, how many cups did people drink? Show your work and explain how you found your answer.

_____

_____

_____

Multiply Using Partial Products

Learning Objective You will use place value understanding and partial products to multiple a whole number of up to 4-digits by a 1-digit whole number.

Estimate. Then record the product.

1. Estimate: 1,200

$$
\begin{array}{r}
243 \\
\times\ \ 6 \\
\hline
1,200 \\
240 \\
+\ \ \ 18 \\
\hline
1,458
\end{array}
$$

2. Estimate: _____

$$
\begin{array}{r}
640 \\
\times\ \ 3 \\
\hline
\end{array}
$$

3. Estimate: _____

$$
\begin{array}{r}
\$149 \\
\times\ \ 5 \\
\hline
\end{array}
$$

4. Estimate: _____

$$
\begin{array}{r}
721 \\
\times\ \ 8 \\
\hline
\end{array}
$$

5. Estimate: _____

$$
\begin{array}{r}
293 \\
\times\ \ 4 \\
\hline
\end{array}
$$

6. Estimate: _____

$$
\begin{array}{r}
\$416 \\
\times\ \ 6 \\
\hline
\end{array}
$$

7. Estimate: _____

$$
\begin{array}{r}
961 \\
\times\ \ 2 \\
\hline
\end{array}
$$

8. Estimate: _____

$$
\begin{array}{r}
837 \\
\times\ \ 9 \\
\hline
\end{array}
$$

Problem Solving Real World

9. A maze at a county fair is made from 275 bales of hay. The maze at the state fair is made from 4 times as many bales of hay. How many bales of hay are used for the maze at the state fair?

_____

10. Pedro gets 8 hours of sleep each night. How many hours does Pedro sleep in a year with 365 days?

_____

11. **WRITE** ▸Math Explain how you can find 4 × 754 using two different methods.

_____

_____

Lesson Check

1. A passenger jet flies at an average speed of 548 miles per hour. At that speed, how many miles does the plane travel in 4 hours?

2. Use the model to find 3×157.

	100	50	7
3			

_____

_____

Spiral Review

3. The school fun fair made $1,768 on games and $978 on food sales. How much money did the fun fair make on games and food sales?

4. Use the table below.

State	Population
North Dakota	646,844
Alaska	698,473
Vermont	621,760

List the states from least to greatest population.

_____

_____

_____

_____

5. A National Park covers 218,375 acres. What is this number written in expanded form?

6. Last year a business had profits of $8,000. This year its profits are 5 times as great. What are this year's profits?

_____

_____

_____

_____

© Houghton Mifflin Harcourt Publishing Company

FOR MORE PRACTICE
GO TO THE
Personal Math Trainer

Name _____

 Mid-Chapter Checkpoint

Vocabulary

Choose the best term from the box to complete the sentence.

Vocabulary

Distributive Property
factor
partial product

1. To find the product of a two-digit number and a 1-digit number, you can multiply the tens, multiply the ones, and find the sum of each _____. (p. 88)

2. The _____ states that multiplying a sum by a number is the same as multiplying each addend by the number and then adding the products. (p. 87)

Concepts and Skills

Write a comparison sentence.

3. $5 \times 9 = 45$

   _____ times as many as _____ is _____.

4. $24 = 6 \times 4$

   _____ is _____ times as many as _____.

5. $54 = 6 \times 9$

   _____ is _____ times as many as _____.

6. $8 \times 6 = 48$

   _____ times as many as _____ is _____.

Estimate. Then record the product.

7. Estimate: _____

   $\begin{array}{r} 75 \\ \times\ 5 \\ \hline \end{array}$

8. Estimate: _____

   $\begin{array}{r} 12 \\ \times\ 6 \\ \hline \end{array}$

9. Estimate: _____

   $\begin{array}{r} 28 \\ \times\ 3 \\ \hline \end{array}$

10. Estimate: _____

   $\begin{array}{r} \$43 \\ \times\ 6 \\ \hline \end{array}$

Record the product. Use expanded form to help.

11. $5 \times 64 =$ _____

12. $3 \times 272 =$ _____

13. There are 6 times as many dogs as cats. If the total number of dogs and cats is 21, how many dogs are there?

_____

14. The table below shows the number of calories in 1 cup of different kinds of berries. How many calories are in 4 cups of blackberries?

Berry Nutrition	
Berry	Number of Calories in 1 Cup
Blackberries	62
Blueberries	83
Raspberries	64
Strawberries	46

_____

15. **GO DEEPER** The skating rink rented 218 pairs of skates during the month of April and 3 times that many in May. How many pairs of skates did the skating rink rent during April and May?

_____

Name _____

Multiply Using Mental Math

Essential Question How can you use mental math and properties to help you multiply numbers?

Learning Objective You will use mental math and properties of operations to multiply a whole number of up to 4-digits by a 1-digit whole number.

Unlock the Problem

Properties of Multiplication can make multiplication easier.

There are 4 sections of seats in the Playhouse Theater. Each section has 7 groups of seats. Each group has 25 seats. How many seats are there in the theater?

Find 4 × 7 × 25.

4 × 7 × 25 = 4 × 25 × 7   Commutative Property

= _____ × 7   Think: 4 × 25 = 100

= _____   Think: 100 × 7 = 700

So, there are 700 seats in the theater.

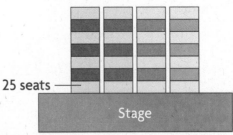

25 seats —

Stage

Math Talk   Math Processes and Practices ⑧

Draw Conclusions What do you know about 4 × 25 that will help you find 6 × 25?

Try This! Use mental math and properties.

Ⓐ Find (6 × 10) × 10.

(6 × 10) × 10 = 6 × (10 × 10)   Associative Property

= 6 × _____

= _____

Ⓑ Find (4 × 9) × 250.

(4 × 9) × 250 = 250 × (4 × 9)   Commutative Property

= (250 × 4) × 9   Associative Property

= _____ × 9

= _____

Remember

The Associative Property states that you can group factors in different ways and get the same product. Use parentheses to group the factors you multiply first.

Chapter 2   **107**

More Strategies Choose the strategy that works best with the
numbers in the problems.

🔑 Examples

A **Use friendly numbers.**

Multiply. 24×250

Think: $24 = 6 \times 4$ and $4 \times 250 = 1,000$

$24 \times 250 = 6 \times 4 \times 250$

$\qquad\qquad = 6 \times \underline{\hspace{2cm}}$

$\qquad\qquad = \underline{\hspace{2cm}}$

B **Use halving and doubling.**

Multiply. 16×50

Think: 16 can be divided evenly by 2.

$16 \div 2 = 8 \qquad$ Find half of 16.

$8 \times 50 = \underline{\hspace{2cm}} \qquad$ Multiply.

$2 \times 400 = \underline{\hspace{2cm}} \qquad$ Double 400.

C **Use addition.**

Multiply. 4×625

Think: 625 is 600 plus 25.

$4 \times 625 = 4 \times (600 + 25)$

$\qquad\qquad = (4 \times 600) + (4 \times 25)$

$\qquad\qquad = \underline{\hspace{1.5cm}} + \underline{\hspace{1.5cm}}$

$\qquad\qquad = \underline{\hspace{1.5cm}}$

D **Use subtraction.**

Multiply. 5×398

Think: 398 is 2 less than 400.

$5 \times 398 = 5 \times (400 - 2)$

$\qquad\qquad = (5 \times \underline{\hspace{1.5cm}}) - (5 \times 2)$

$\qquad\qquad = 2,000 - \underline{\hspace{1.5cm}}$

$\qquad\qquad = \underline{\hspace{1.5cm}}$

• What property is being used in Examples C and D?_____

Share and Show

1. Break apart the factor 112 to find 7×112
by using mental math and addition.

$7 \times 112 = 7 \times (\underline{\hspace{2cm}} + 12)$

$\qquad = \underline{\hspace{4cm}}$

$\qquad = \underline{\hspace{4cm}}$

$\qquad = \underline{\hspace{4cm}}$

Find the product. Tell which strategy you used.

2. $4 \times 6 \times 50$

☑**3.** 5×420

☑**4.** 6×298

_____   _____   _____

_____   _____   _____

On Your Own

> **Math Talk** Math Processes and Practices ⑦
>
> **Identify Relationships**
> How is using an addition strategy related to using a subtraction strategy?

Find the product. Tell which strategy you used.

5. 14×50

6. 32×25

7. $8 \times 25 \times 23$

_____   _____   _____

_____   _____   _____

Practice: Copy and Solve Use a strategy to find the product.

8. 16×400

9. $3 \times 31 \times 10$

10. 3×199

11. $3 \times 1,021$

Math Processes and Practices ⑦ Identify Relationships Algebra Use mental math to find the unknown number.

12. $21 \times 40 = 840$, so $21 \times 42 =$ _____.

13. $9 \times 60 = 540$, so $18 \times 30 =$ _____.

14. **GO DEEPER** The science museum sells dinosaur models to schools and libraries for $107 each. The town library buys 3 models. The town elementary school buys 5 models. What is the total cost of the models the town buys?

_____

15. **GO DEEPER** Kyle and Karen each bought 6 books of ride tickets at the fair. Each book has 15 tickets. How many tickets did they buy altogether?

_____

Problem Solving • Applications

Use the table for 16–18.

16. **GO DEEPER** Three thousand, forty-three people buy tickets at the gate for Section N and one hundred people buy tickets at the gate for Section L. How much money is collected for Section N and Section L at the gate?

_____

Arena Ticket Prices Per Game			
Section	Full Season	15-Game Plan	Gate Price
K	$44	$46	$48
L	$30	$32	$35
M	$25	$27	$30
N	$20	$22	$25

17. **Math Processes and Practices ❶** **Use Diagrams** Tina and 3 of her friends buy the full season plan for Section M. If there are 45 games in the full season, how much money do they spend?

_____

WRITE ▸ *Math* · **Show Your Work**

18. **THINK SMARTER** When the full season tickets first went on sale, 2,000 Full Season tickets sold for Section N. Two weeks after the tickets first went on sale, another 1,500 full season tickets were sold for Section N. How much money was spent on full season tickets for Section N in total? How much more money was spent when the tickets first went on sale than after the first two weeks?

_____

Personal Math Trainer

19. **THINK SMARTER +** Find 6 × 407. Show your work and explain why the strategy you chose works best with the factors.

_____

_____

_____

_____

Multiply Using Mental Math

Learning Objective You will use mental math and properties of operations to multiply a whole number of up to 4-digits by a 1-digit whole number.

Find the product. Tell which strategy you used.

1. 6×297 **Think:** $297 = 300 - 3$
   $6 \times 297 = 6 \times (300 - 3)$
   $= (6 \times 300) - (6 \times 3)$
   $= 1,800 - 18$
   $= 1,782$

   1,782;

   use subtraction

2. $14 \times 25 \times 4$

3. 8×604

4. 50×28

_____   _____   _____

_____   _____   _____

Problem Solving · Real World

5. Section J in an arena has 20 rows. Each row has 15 seats. All tickets cost $18 each. If all the seats are sold, how much money will the arena collect for Section J?

6. At a high-school gym, the bleachers are divided into 6 equal sections. Each section can seat 395 people. How many people can be seated in the gym?

_____   _____

7. **WRITE** ▸*Math* Show how to multiply 6×298 using friendly numbers and then using properties and mental math. Write about which method you like better and why.

_____

_____

_____

_____

Lesson Check

1. Pencils come in cartons of 24 boxes. A school bought 50 cartons of pencils for the start of school. Each box of pencils cost $2. How much did the school spend on pencils?

_____

2. The school also bought 195 packages of markers. There are 6 markers in a package. How many markers did the school buy?

Spiral Review

3. Alex has 175 baseball cards. Rodney has 3 times as many baseball cards as Alex. How many fewer cards does Alex have than Rodney?

_____

4. A theater seats 1,860 people. The last 6 shows have been sold out. Estimate the total number of people attending the last 6 shows.

_____

5. At one basketball game, there were 1,207 people. At the next game, there were 958 people. How many people were at the two games?

_____

6. Bill bought 4 jigsaw puzzles. Each puzzle has 500 pieces. How many pieces are in all the puzzles?

FOR MORE PRACTICE GO TO THE Personal Math Trainer

Name _____

Problem Solving • Multistep Multiplication Problems

Essential Question When can you use the *draw a diagram* strategy to solve a multistep multiplication problem?

Learning Objective You will use the strategy *draw a diagram* to solve multistep multiplication problems.

🔑 Unlock the Problem

At the sea park, one section in the stadium has 9 rows with 18 seats in each row. In the center of each of the first 6 rows, 8 seats are in the splash zone. How many seats are not in the splash zone?

Use the graphic organizer to help you solve the problem.

Read the Problem	Solve the Problem
What do I need to find? I need to find the number of seats that _____ in the splash zone.	I drew a diagram of the section to show 9 rows of 18 seats. In the center, I outlined a section to show the 6 rows of 8 seats in the splash zone.

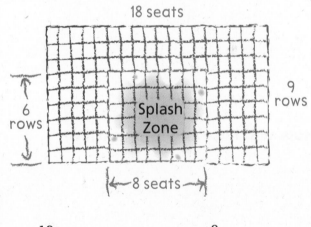

What information do I need to use?

There are 9 rows with _____ seats in each row of the section.

There are 6 rows with _____ seats in each row of the splash zone.

How will I use the information?

I can _____ to find both the number of seats in the section and the number of seats in the splash zone.

$$\begin{array}{r} 18 \\ \times\ 9 \\ \hline \end{array}$$ ← total number of seats in the section

$$\begin{array}{r} 8 \\ \times 6 \\ \hline \end{array}$$ ← seats in the splash zone

1. What else do you need to do to solve the problem?

_____

_____

Try Another Problem

At the sea park, one section of the shark theater has 8 rows with 14 seats in each row. In the middle of the section, 4 rows of 6 seats are reserved. How many seats are not reserved?

Read the Problem	Solve the Problem
What do I need to find?	
What information do I need to use?	
How will I use the information?	

2. How did your diagram help you solve the problem?

_____

_____

Math Talk

Math Processes and Practices ②

Reason Abstractly How do you know your answer is correct?

© Houghton Mifflin Harcourt Publishing Company • Image Credits: (t) ©Ingram Publishing/Alamy

Name _____

Share and Show

Unlock the Problem

√ Use the Problem Solving MathBoard
√ Underline important facts.
√ Choose a strategy you know.

1. The seats in Sections A and B of the stadium are all taken for the last show. Section A has 8 rows of 14 seats each. Section B has 6 rows of 16 seats each. How many people are seated in Sections A and B for the last show?

   First, draw and label a diagram. **Next**, find the number of seats in each section.

	Section A	Section B

   Last, find the total number of seats. _____ + _____ = _____

   There are _____ people seated in Sections A and B for the last show.

WRITE *Math*
Show Your Work

2. What if Sections A and B each had 7 rows? How many people would have been seated in Sections A and B?

   _____

3. Brenda's vegetable garden has 13 rows with 8 plants in each row. Brenda plans to plant peppers in the first 2 rows and the last 2 rows of the garden. The rest of the rows will be tomatoes. How many tomato plants will Brenda plant?

   _____

4. **GO DEEPER** There are 8 rows of 22 chairs set up for an awards ceremony at the school. In each row, the 2 chairs on each end are reserved for students receiving awards. The rest of the chairs are for guests. How many chairs are there for guests?

   _____

On Your Own

Use the graph for 5–6.

5. **GO DEEPER** Mr. Torres took his students to the dolphin show. Each row in the stadium had 11 seats. One adult sat at each end of a row, and each group of 4 students was seated between 2 adults. Mr. Torres sat by himself. How many adults were there?

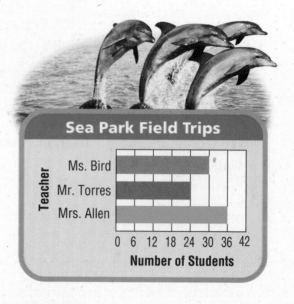

Sea Park Field Trips

6. **WRITE** ▸*Math* Another stadium section has 24 rows of 10 seats each. Describe at least two ways Mrs. Allen's class can sit if an equal number of students sits in each row.

WRITE ▸*Math* · **Show Your Work** · · · · · ·

7. **THINK SMARTER** Carol, Ann, and Liz each bought a toy fish. Carol's fish is 10 inches longer than Ann's fish. Liz's fish is 2 inches longer than twice the length of Ann's fish. Ann's fish is 12 inches long. Find the length of each toy fish.

8. **Math Processes and Practices 1** **Evaluate Relationships** Nell made a secret code. Each code word has 2 letters. Each word begins with a consonant and ends with a vowel. How many code words can Nell make with 3 consonants and 2 vowels?

9. **THINK SMARTER** Allie is building a patio. The patio will have 8 tiles in each of 13 rows. She has already built the center section with 4 tiles in each of 7 rows. How many more tiles are needed to complete the patio? Show your work.

Problem Solving • Multistep Multiplication Problems

Learning Objective You will use the strategy *draw a diagram* to solve multistep multiplication problems.

Solve each problem.

1. A community park has 6 tables with a chessboard painted on top. Each board has 8 rows of 8 squares. When a game is set up, 4 rows of 8 squares on each board are covered with chess pieces. If a game is set up on each table, how many total squares are NOT covered by chess pieces?

   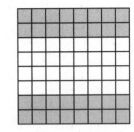

   $4 \times 8 = 32$

   $32 \times 6 = \blacksquare$

   _____ **192 squares**

2. Jonah and his friends go apple picking. Jonah fills 5 baskets. Each basket holds 15 apples. If 4 of Jonah's friends pick the same amount as Jonah, how many apples do Jonah and his friends pick in all? Draw a diagram to solve the problem.

   _____

3. **WRITE** ►*Math* Write a word problem that can be solved using multiplication of two-digit numbers. Solve your word problem and explain the solution.

   _____

   _____

   _____

   _____

Lesson Check

1. At a tree farm, there are 9 rows of 36 spruce trees. In each row, 14 of the spruce trees are blue spruce. How many spruce trees are NOT blue spruce?

2. Ron is tiling a countertop. He needs to place 54 square tiles in each of 8 rows to cover the counter. He wants to randomly place 8 groups of 4 blue tiles each and have the rest of the tiles be white. How many white tiles will Ron need?

Spiral Review

3. Juan reads a book with 368 pages. Savannah reads a book with 172 fewer pages than Juan's book. How many pages are in the book Savannah reads?

4. Hailey has bottles that hold 678 pennies each. About how many pennies does she have if she has 6 bottles filled with pennies?

5. Terrence plants a garden that has 8 rows of flowers, with 28 flowers in each row. How many flowers did Terrence plant?

6. Kevin has 5 fish in his fish tank. Jasmine has 4 times as many fish as Kevin has. How many fish does Jasmine have?

© Houghton Mifflin Harcourt Publishing Company

Name _____

Multiply 2-Digit Numbers with Regrouping

Learning Objective You will use regrouping to multiply a 2-digit number by a 1-digit number.

Essential Question How can you use regrouping to multiply a 2-digit number by a 1-digit number?

Unlock the Problem

A Thoroughbred racehorse can run at speeds of up to 60 feet per second. During practice, Celia's horse runs at a speed of 36 feet per second. How far does her horse run in 3 seconds?

- Underline important information.
- Is there information you will not use? If so, cross out the information.

Example 1

Multiply. 3 × 36   **Estimate.** 3 × 40 = _____

MODEL	THINK	RECORD

STEP 1

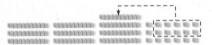

Multiply the ones.
3 × 6 ones = 18 ones
Regroup the 18 ones.

$\begin{array}{r} \overset{1}{3}6 \\ \times\ 3 \\ \hline 8 \end{array}$

Regroup 18 ones as 1 ten 8 ones.

STEP 2

Multiply the tens.
3 × 3 tens = 9 tens
Add the regrouped ten.
9 tens + 1 ten = 10 tens

$\begin{array}{r} \overset{1}{3}6 \\ \times\ 3 \\ \hline 108 \end{array}$

10 tens is the same as 1 hundred 0 tens.

So, Celia's racehorse runs _____ feet in 3 seconds.

Since _____ is close to the estimate of _____, the answer is reasonable.

Math Talk

Math Processes and Practices ③

Apply Look at Step 1. How does the model support your work?

🔓 Example 2

Multiply. 8 × 22 **Estimate.** 8 × 20 = _____

MODEL	THINK	RECORD

STEP 1

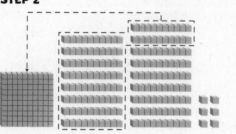

Multiply the ones.
8 × 2 ones = 16 ones

Regroup the 16 ones.

$$\begin{array}{r} \overset{1}{2}2 \\ \times\ 8 \\ \hline 6 \end{array}$$

Regroup
16 ones as
1 ten 6 ones.

STEP 2

Multiply the tens.
8 × 2 tens = 16 tens

Add the regrouped ten.
16 tens + 1 ten = 17 tens

$$\begin{array}{r} 1 \\ 22 \\ \times\ 8 \\ \hline 176 \end{array}$$

17 tens is
the same as 1
hundred 7 tens.

So, 8 × 22 = _____. Since _____ is close to the estimate

of _____, it is reasonable.

Try This! Multiply. 7 × $68

Estimate. 7 × $68	Use partial products.	Use regrouping.
	$$\begin{array}{r}\$\ 6\ 8 \\ \times\ \quad 7 \\ \hline \end{array}$$	$$\begin{array}{r}\$\ 6\ 8 \\ \times\ \quad 7 \\ \hline \end{array}$$

• **Math Processes and Practices 7** **Identify Relationships** Look at the partial products and regrouping

methods above. How are the partial products 420 and 56 related to 476?

Name _____

1. Use the model to find the product.

$$2 \times 36 = \underline{\hspace{1cm}}$$

Estimate. Then record the product.

2. Estimate: _____	3. Estimate: _____	✓ 4. Estimate: _____	✓ 5. Estimate: _____
42 × 4	32 × 2	81 × 5	$63 × 7

Math Talk

Math Processes and Practices ⑦

Look for Structure What are the steps for using place value and regrouping to find 3 × 78?

On Your Own

Estimate. Then record the product.

6. Estimate: _____	7. Estimate: _____	8. Estimate: _____	9. Estimate: _____
33 × 2	$25 × 3	36 × 8	$94 × 5

Practice: Copy and Solve **Estimate. Then record the product.**

10. 3×82 11. 9×41 12. 6×75 13. $7 \times \$23$ 14. $8 \times \$54$

Math Processes and Practices ⑦ **Identify Relationships** **Algebra** **Write a rule. Find the unknown numbers.**

15.

Carton ___	1	2	3	4	5
Eggs ___	12	24		48	

16.

Row ___		2	3	4	5	6
Seats ___		32	48	64		

17. **GO DEEPER** It will cost $73 per hour to rent a sailboat and $88 per hour to rent a ski boat. How much more will it cost to rent a ski boat than a sailboat for 4 hours?

Problem Solving • Applications

Use the table for 18–19.

18. **GO DEEPER** At the speeds shown, how much farther could a black-tailed jackrabbit run than a desert cottontail in 7 seconds?

    _____

19. A black-tailed jackrabbit hops about 7 feet in a single hop. How far can it hop in 5 seconds?

    _____

Running Speeds	
Animal	**Speed (feet per second)**
Black-tailed Jackrabbit	51
Desert Cottontail	22

▲ Desert Cottontail

20. **GO DEEPER** Mr. Wright bought a 3-pound bag of cat food and a 5-pound bag of dog food. There are 16 ounces in each pound. How many ounces of pet food did Mr. Wright buy?

    _____

21. **THINK SMARTER** The sum of two numbers is 31. The product of the two numbers is 150. What are the numbers?

    _____

22. **Math Processes and Practices ②** **Use Reasoning** 6 × 87 is greater than 5 × 87. How much greater? Explain how you know without multiplying.

    _____

    _____

WRITE ▸ Math
Show Your Work

23. **THINK SMARTER** Multiply 6 × 73. For 23a–23d, select True or False for each statement.

    23a. A reasonable estimate of the product is $420.   ○ True   ○ False

    23b. Using partial products, the products are 42 and 180.   ○ True   ○ False

    23c. Using regrouping, 18 ones are regrouped as 8 tens and 1 one.   ○ True   ○ False

    23d. The product is 438.   ○ True   ○ False

Multiply 2-Digit Numbers with Regrouping

Learning Objective You will use regrouping to multiply a 2-digit number by a 1-digit number.

Estimate. Then record the product.

1. Estimate: __150__

$$\begin{array}{r} \overset{1}{46} \\ \times\ \ 3 \\ \hline 138 \end{array}$$

2. Estimate: _____

$$\begin{array}{r} 32 \\ \times\ \ 8 \\ \hline \end{array}$$

3. Estimate: _____

$$\begin{array}{r} \$55 \\ \times\ \ 2 \\ \hline \end{array}$$

4. Estimate: _____

$$\begin{array}{r} 61 \\ \times\ \ 8 \\ \hline \end{array}$$

5. Estimate: _____

$$\begin{array}{r} 37 \\ \times\ \ 9 \\ \hline \end{array}$$

6. Estimate: _____

$$\begin{array}{r} \$18 \\ \times\ \ 7 \\ \hline \end{array}$$

7. Estimate: _____

$$\begin{array}{r} 83 \\ \times\ \ 5 \\ \hline \end{array}$$

8. Estimate: _____

$$\begin{array}{r} 95 \\ \times\ \ 8 \\ \hline \end{array}$$

 Problem Solving Real World

9. Sharon is 54 inches tall. A tree in her backyard is 5 times as tall as she is. The floor of her treehouse is at a height that is twice as tall as she is. What is the difference, in inches, between the top of the tree and the floor of the treehouse?

_____

10. Mr. Diaz's class is taking a field trip to the science museum. There are 23 students in the class, and a student admission ticket is $8. How much will the student tickets cost?

_____

11. **WRITE** ▸*Math* Compare partial products and regrouping. Describe how the methods are alike and different.

_____

_____

_____

_____

Lesson Check

1. A ferryboat makes four trips to an island each day. The ferry can hold 88 people. If the ferry is full on each trip, how many passengers are carried by the ferry each day?

2. Julian counted the number of times he drove across the Seven Mile Bridge while vacationing in the Florida Keys. He crossed the bridge 34 times. How many miles in all did Julian drive crossing the bridge?

Spiral Review

3. Sebastian wrote the population of his city as 300,000 + 40,000 + 60 + 7. Write the population of Sebastian's city in standard form.

4. A plane flew 2,190 kilometers from Chicago to Flagstaff. Another plane flew 2,910 kilometers from Chicago to Oakland. How much farther did the plane that flew to Oakland fly than the plane that flew to Flagstaff?

5. Tori buys 27 packages of miniature racing cars. Each package contains 5 cars. About how many miniature racing cars does Tori buy?

6. Use the Distributive Property to write an expression equivalent to $5 \times (3 + 4)$.

FOR MORE PRACTICE
GO TO THE
Personal Math Trainer

Multiply 3-Digit and 4-Digit Numbers with Regrouping

Learning Objective You will use regrouping to multiply a 3- and 4-digit number by a 1-digit number.

Essential Question How can you use regrouping to multiply?

Unlock the Problem

Alley Spring, in Missouri, produces an average of 567 million gallons of water per week. How many million gallons of water do the springs produce in 3 weeks?

Multiply. 3 × 567

Estimate. 3 × _____ = _____

THINK	RECORD

STEP 1

Multiply the ones.

3 × 7 ones = _____ ones
Regroup the 21 ones.

$$\begin{array}{r} 2 \\ 56\!7 \\ \times\ \ 3 \\ \hline 1 \end{array}$$

Regroup the 21 ones as 2 tens and 1 one.

STEP 2

Multiply the tens.

3 × 6 tens = _____ tens
Add the regrouped tens.
18 tens + 2 tens = 20 tens
Regroup the 20 tens.

$$\begin{array}{r} 2\,2 \\ 567 \\ \times\ \ 3 \\ \hline 01 \end{array}$$

Regroup 20 tens as 2 hundreds 0 tens.

STEP 3

Multiply the hundreds.

3 × 5 hundreds = _____ hundreds
Add the regrouped hundreds.
15 hundreds + 2 hundreds = 17 hundreds

$$\begin{array}{r} 2\,2 \\ 567 \\ \times\ \ 3 \\ \hline 1{,}701 \end{array}$$

17 hundreds is the same as 1 thousand 7 hundreds.

So, Alley Spring produces _____ million gallons of water in 3 weeks.

🔑 Example

Use an estimate or an exact answer.

The table shows the prices of three vacation packages. Jake, his parents, and his sister want to choose a package.

Lakefront Vacations

	Adult	Child
Package A	$1,299	$619
Package B	$849	$699
Package C	$699	$484

Ⓐ About how much would Package C cost Jake's family?

STEP 1

Estimate the cost for 2 adults.

$2 \times \$699$

↓

$2 \times \$700 = $ _____

STEP 2

Estimate the cost for 2 children.

$2 \times \$484$

↓

$2 \times \$500 = $ _____

STEP 3

Add to estimate the total cost.

```
      _____
  +   _____
  _____
      _____
```

So, Package C would cost Jake's family about $2,400.

Ⓑ Jake's family wants to compare the total costs of Packages A and C. Which plan costs more? How much more does it cost?

Math Talk | Math Processes and Practices ①

Analyze How did you use the information to know that you needed an estimate?

Package A

Adults	Children	Total Cost
$1,299	$619	
× 2	× 2	+

Package C

Adults	Children	Total Cost
$699	$484	
× 2	× 2	+

Subtract to compare the total costs of the packages.

```
  $3,836
- $2,366
  _____
```

Math Talk | Math Processes and Practices ①

Make Sense of Problems How did you use the information to know that you needed an exact answer?

So, Package _____ would cost _____ more

than Package _____ .

Name _____

1. Tell what is happening in Step 1 of the problem.

_____

_____

STEP 1	STEP 2	STEP 3	STEP 4
2	4 2	1 4 2	1 4 2
1,27<u>4</u>	1,27<u>4</u>	1,274	1,274
× 6	× 6	× 6	× 6
4	44	644	7,644

Estimate. Then find the product.

2. Estimate: _____

603
× 4

3. Estimate: _____

1,935
× 7

4. Estimate: _____

$8,326
× 5

Explain how you can use estimation to find how many digits the product 4 × 1,861 will have.

Math Processes and Practices ⑥

On Your Own

Estimate. Then find the product.

5. Estimate: _____

$3,316
× 8

6. Estimate: _____

$2,900
× 7

7. Estimate: _____

$4,123
× 6

8. **GO DEEPER** Mr. Jackson has $5,400 to buy supplies for the school computer lab. He buys 8 boxes of printer ink that cost $149 each and 3 printers that cost $1,017 each. How much money will Mr. Jackson have left after he buys the printer ink and printers?

_____

Practice: Copy and Solve Compare. Write <, >, or =.

9. 5 × 352 ◯ 4 × 440

10. 6 × 8,167 ◯ 9,834 × 5

11. 3,956 × 4 ◯ 5 × 7,692

12. 740 × 7 ◯ 8 × 658

13. 4 × 3,645 ◯ 5 × 2,834

14. 6,573 × 2 ◯ 4,365 × 3

Problem Solving • Applications

15. **GO DEEPER** Airplane tickets to Fairbanks, Alaska, will cost $958 each. Airplane tickets to Vancouver, Canada, will cost $734. How much can the four members of the Harrison family save on airfare by vacationing in Vancouver?

_____

16. **THINK SMARTER** Philadelphia, Pennsylvania, is 2,147 miles from Salt Lake City, Utah, and 2,868 miles from Portland, Oregon. What is the difference in the round-trip distances between Philadelphia and each of the other two cities? Explain whether you need an estimate or an exact answer.

_____

_____

WRITE *Math* • **Show Your Work**

17. **Math Processes and Practices 3** **Verify the Reasoning of Others** Joe says that the product of a 4-digit number and a 1-digit number is always a 4-digit number. Does Joe's statement make sense? Explain.

_____

_____

_____

18. **THINK SMARTER** What number is 150 more than the product of 5 and 4,892? Explain how you found the answer.

_____

_____

_____

Name _____

Multiply 3-Digit and 4-Digit Numbers with Regrouping

Learning Objective You will use regrouping to multiply a 3- and 4-digit number by a 1-digit number.

Estimate. Then find the product.

1. Estimate: __4,000__

$$\begin{array}{r} \scriptstyle 1\ 2\ 2 \\ 1{,}467 \\ \times\qquad 4 \\ \hline 5{,}868 \end{array}$$

2. Estimate: _____

$$\begin{array}{r} 5{,}339 \\ \times\qquad 6 \\ \hline \end{array}$$

3. Estimate: _____

$$\begin{array}{r} \$879 \\ \times\qquad 8 \\ \hline \end{array}$$

4. Estimate: _____

$$\begin{array}{r} 3{,}182 \\ \times\qquad 5 \\ \hline \end{array}$$

5. Estimate: _____

$$\begin{array}{r} 4{,}616 \\ \times\qquad 3 \\ \hline \end{array}$$

6. Estimate: _____

$$\begin{array}{r} \$2{,}854 \\ \times\qquad 9 \\ \hline \end{array}$$

7. Estimate: _____

$$\begin{array}{r} 7{,}500 \\ \times\qquad 2 \\ \hline \end{array}$$

8. Estimate: _____

$$\begin{array}{r} 948 \\ \times\qquad 7 \\ \hline \end{array}$$

Problem Solving · Real World

9. Lafayette County has a population of 7,022 people. Columbia County's population is 8 times as great as Lafayette County's population. What is the population of Columbia County?

10. A seafood company sold 9,125 pounds of fish last month. If 6 seafood companies sold the same amount of fish, how much fish did the 6 companies sell last month in all?

_____

_____

11. **WRITE** ▸*Math* Explain how finding 4 × 384 can help you find 4 × 5,384. Then find both products.

_____

_____

Lesson Check

1. By recycling 1 ton of paper, 6,953 gallons of water are saved. How many gallons of water are saved by recycling 4 tons of paper?

   _____

2. Esteban counted the number of steps it took him to walk to school. He counted 1,138 steps. How many steps does he take walking to and from school each day?

   _____

Spiral Review

3. A website has 13,406 people registered. What is the word form of this number?

   _____

   _____

4. In one year, the McAlister family drove their car 15,680 miles. To the nearest thousand, how many miles did they drive their car that year?

   _____

   _____

5. Connor scored 14,370 points in a game. Amy scored 1,089 fewer points than Connor. How many points did Amy score?

   _____

6. Lea buys 6 model cars that each cost $15. She also buys 4 bottles of paint that each cost $11. How much does Lea spend on model cars and paint?

   _____

FOR MORE PRACTICE
GO TO THE
Personal Math Trainer

Name _____

Solve Multistep Problems Using Equations

Essential Question How can you represent and solve multistep problems using equations?

Learning Objective You will model and solve multistep problems using equations.

? Unlock the Problem

Crismari's computer has 3 hard drives with 64 gigabytes of space each and 2 hard drives with 16 gigabytes of space each. The files on her computer use 78 gigabytes of space. How much hard drive space does her computer have left?

• Underline the important information.

🔑 One Way Use multiple single-step equations.

STEP 1 Find how much hard drive space is on 3 hard drives with 64 gigabytes of space each.

| 64 | 64 | 64 |

← 3 hard drives with 64 gigabytes.

n ← Total space on 3 hard drives with 64 gigabytes.

$3 \times 64 = n$

_____ $= n$

STEP 2 Find how much hard drive space is on 2 hard drives with 16 gigabytes of space.

| 16 | 16 |

← 2 hard drives with 16 gigabytes.

p ← Total space on 2 hard drives with 16 gigabytes.

$2 \times 16 = p$

_____ $= p$

STEP 3 Find the total hard drive space on the computer.

Total space on 64-gigabyte hard drives.　　Total space on 16-gigabyte hard drives.

| 192 | 32 |

A ← Total space on computer.

$192 + 32 = A$

_____ $= A$

STEP 4 The files use 78 gigabytes of space. Find how much hard drive space the computer has left.

space left　　space used

| y | 78 |

224 ← Total hard drive space on the computer.

$224 - 78 = y$

_____ $= y$

So, Crismari has _____ gigabytes of hard drive space left on her computer.

Order of Operations The Order of Operations is a special set of rules that gives the order in which calculations are done in an expression. First, multiply and divide from left to right. Then, add and subtract from left to right.

🔓 Another Way Use one multistep equation.

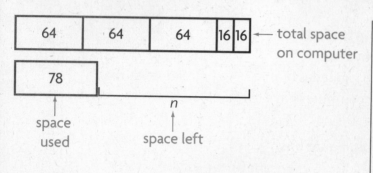

| 64 | 64 | 64 | 16 | 16 | ← total space on computer |

| 78 |
space used   space left n

$3 \times 64 + 2 \times 16 - 78 = n$

_____ + _____ × _____ − _____ = n

_____ + _____ − _____ = n

_____ − _____ = n

_____ = n

Share and Show

1. Use the order of operations to find the value of n.

$5 \times 17 + 5 \times 20 - 32 = n$

_____ + _____ × _____ − _____ = n ← First, multiply 5×17.

_____ + _____ − _____ = n ← Next, multiply 5×20.

_____ − _____ = n ← Then, add the two products.

_____ = n ← Finally, subtract to find n.

Find the value of n.

2. $3 \times 22 + 7 \times 41 - 24 = n$

_____ = n

3. $4 \times 34 + 6 \times 40 - 66 = n$

_____ = n

4. $2 \times 62 + 8 \times 22 - 53 = n$

_____ = n

5. $6 \times 13 + 9 \times 34 - 22 = n$

_____ = n

Math Talk

Math Processes and Practices ②

Use Reasoning If you solve $6 \times 3 + 2$ by adding before multiplying, will you get the same answer? Explain.

Name _____

Find the value of *n*.

6. $8 \times 42 + 3 \times 59 - 62 = n$

7. $6 \times 27 + 2 \times 47 - 83 = n$

_____ $= n$

_____ $= n$

Problem Solving • Applications

8. GO DEEPER Maggie has 3 binders with 25 stamps in each binder. She has 5 binders with 24 baseball cards in each binder. If she gives 35 stamps to a friend, how many stamps and cards does she have left?

_____

WRITE ▸ *Math*
Show Your Work

9. Math Processes and Practices ① **Evaluate** Maddox has 4 boxes with 32 marbles in each box. He has 7 boxes with 18 shells in each box. If he gets 20 marbles from a friend, how many marbles and shells does he have?

_____

Personal Math Trainer

10. THINK SMARTER ✛ The soccer team sells 54 bagels with cream cheese for $2 each and 36 muffins for $1 each during a bake sale. The coach uses the money to buy socks for the 14 players. The socks cost $6 per pair. How much money does the coach have left? Explain how you found your answer.

_____

_____

_____

_____

_____

11. **THINKSMARTER** **What's the Error?** Dominic has 5 books with 12 postcards in each book. He has 4 boxes with 20 coins in each box. If he gives 15 post cards to a friend, how many postcards and coins does he have?

Dominic drew this model.

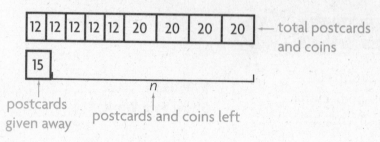

| 12 | 12 | 12 | 12 | 12 | 20 | 20 | 20 | 20 | ← total postcards and coins

| 15 |

↑ postcards given away

n

↑ postcards and coins left

Dominic used these steps to solve.

$5 \times 12 + 4 \times 20 - 15 = n$

$60 + 4 \times 20 - 15 = n$

$64 \times 20 - 15 = n$

$1{,}280 - 15 = n$

$1{,}265 = n$

Look at the steps Dominic used to solve this problem. Find and describe his error.

_____

_____

Use the correct steps to solve the problem.

_____

_____

_____

_____

So, there are _____ postcards and coins left.

Solve Multistep Problems Using Equations

Learning Objective You will model and solve multistep problems using equations.

Find the value of n.

1. $4 \times 27 + 5 \times 34 - 94 = n$

   $108 + 5 \times 34 - 94 = n$

   $108 + 170 - 94 = n$

   $278 - 94 = n$

   $184 = n$

2. $7 \times 38 + 3 \times 45 - 56 = n$

   _____ $= n$

3. $6 \times 21 + 7 \times 29 - 83 = n$

4. $9 \times 19 + 2 \times 57 - 75 = n$

   _____ $= n$

   _____ $= n$

Problem Solving · Real World

5. A bakery has 4 trays with 16 muffins on each tray. The bakery has 3 trays of cupcakes with 24 cupcakes on each tray. If 15 cupcakes are sold, how many muffins and cupcakes are left?

6. Katy bought 5 packages of stickers with 25 stickers in each package. She also bought 3 boxes of markers with 12 markers in each box. If she receives 8 stickers from a friend, how many stickers and markers does Katy have now?

_____

_____

7. **WRITE** ▸*Math* Write a word problem that could be solved by writing and solving a multistep equation. Then solve your problem.

_____

_____

_____

Lesson Check

1. What is the value of n?

   $9 \times 23 + 3 \times 39 - 28 = n$

2. What is the value of n?

   $4 \times 28 + 6 \times 17 - 15 = n$

Spiral Review

3. Write an expression that shows how you can multiply 9×475 using expanded form and the Distributive Property.

4. Write an equation that represents this comparison sentence.

   32 is 8 times as many as 4

5. Between which pair of numbers is the exact product of 379 and 8?

6. Write an expression that shows how to use the halving and doubling strategy to find 28×50.

Name _____

✓ Chapter 2 Review/Test

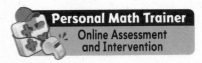

Personal Math Trainer
Online Assessment
and Intervention

For 1–3, use the table.

Prices for Trees					
Tree	Regular Price	Price for 3 or more	Tree	Regular Price	Price for 3 or more
Ivory Silk Lilac	$25	$22	Hazelnut	$9	$8
White Pine	$40	$37	Red Maple	$9	$8
Bur Oak	$35	$32	Birch	$9	$8

1. What is the cost of 3 Bur Oak trees? Show your work.

2. Mr. Tan buys 4 White Pine trees and 5 Birch trees. What is the cost of the trees? Show your work and explain how you found the answer.

3. Rudy will buy 3 Ivory Silk Lilac trees or 2 Bur Oak trees. He wants to buy the trees that cost less. What trees will he buy? How much will he save? Show your work.

4. For numbers 4a–4d, select True or False for each equation.

4a. $7 \times 194 = 1,338$ ○ True   ○ False

4b. $5 \times 5,126 = 25,630$ ○ True   ○ False

4c. $8 \times 367 = 2,926$ ○ True   ○ False

4d. $4 \times 3,952 = 15,808$ ○ True   ○ False

5. Part A

Draw a line to match each section in the model to the partial product it represents.

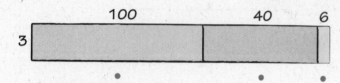

•   •   •

3×6 3×100 3×40

Part B

Then find 3×146. Show your work and explain.

Name _____

6. For numbers 6a–6c, write an equation or a comparison sentence using the numbers on the tiles.

6a.

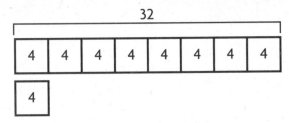

[ ] times as many as [ ] is [ ].

6b.   48

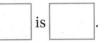

| 8 | 8 | 8 | 8 | 8 | 8 |

8

[ ] × [ ] = [ ]

6c. $9 \times 3 = 27$

[ ] times as many as [ ] is [ ].

7. Multiply 7×43. For 7a–7d, select True or False for each statement.

7a. A reasonable estimate of the product is 280.   ○ True   ○ False

7b. Using partial products, the products are 21 and 28.   ○ True   ○ False

7c. Using regrouping, 21 ones are regrouped as 1 ten and 2 ones.   ○ True   ○ False

7d. The product is 301.   ○ True   ○ False

8. It costs 9,328 points to build each apartment building in the computer game *Big City Building*. What is the cost to build 5 apartment buildings? Show your work.

9. Multiply 7×462 using place value and expanded form.
Choose the number from the box to complete the expression.

$$(7 \times \boxed{\begin{matrix} 4 \\ 40 \\ 400 \end{matrix}}) + (7 \times \boxed{\begin{matrix} 600 \\ 60 \\ 6 \end{matrix}}) + (7 \times \boxed{\begin{matrix} 2 \\ 20 \\ 200 \end{matrix}})$$

10. For numbers 10a–10b, use place value to find the product.

10a. $3 \times 600 = 3 \times \boxed{}$ hundreds

$= \boxed{}$ hundreds

$= \boxed{}$

10b. $5 \times 400 = 5 \times \boxed{}$ hundreds

$= \boxed{}$ hundreds

$= \boxed{}$

11. 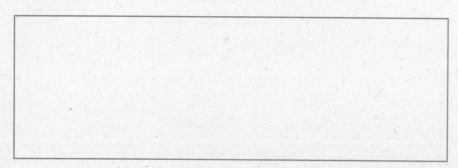 Liam has 3 boxes of baseball cards with 50 cards in each box. He also has 5 boxes with 40 basketball cards in each box. If Liam goes to the store and buys 50 more baseball cards, how many baseball and basketball cards does Liam have? Show your work.

12. There is a book sale at the library. The price for each book is $4. Which expression can be used to show how much money the library will make if it sells 289 books? Use the numbers on the tiles to complete your answer.

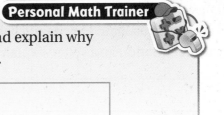

$(4 \times \text{_____}) + (4 \times \text{_____}) + (4 \times \text{_____})$

13. THINK SMARTER + Find 8×397. Show your work and explain why the strategy you chose works best with the factors.

14. A clown bought 6 bags of round balloons with 24 balloons in each bag. The clown also bought 3 bags of long balloons with 36 balloons in each bag.

Part A

How many more round balloons than long balloons did the clown buy? Show your work.

Part B

The clown also bought 5 bags of heart-shaped balloons with 14 balloons in each bag. When the clown blew up all of the round, long, and heart-shaped balloons, 23 balloons burst. How many blown-up balloons were left? Explain your answer.

15. Hector planted 185 flowers in 2 days. There were 5 volunteers, including Hector, who each planted about the same number of flowers. About how many flowers did they plant?

185
400
500
1,000

16. Jay and Blair went fishing. Together, they caught 27 fish. Jay caught 2 times as many fish as Blair. How many fish did Jay and Blair each catch? Write an equation and solve. Explain your work.

17. At the pet fair, Darlene's dog weighed 5 times as much as Leah's dog. Together, the dogs weighed 84 pounds. How much did each dog weigh? Complete the bar model. Write an equation and solve.

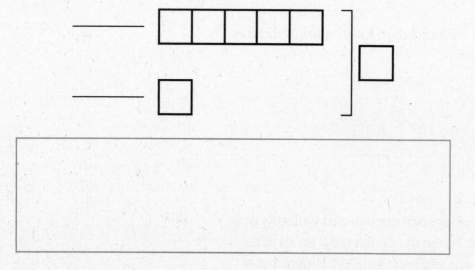

18. Use the Distributive Property to model the product on the grid. Record the product.

$4 \times 12 =$ _____

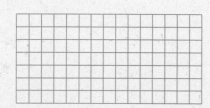

Multiply 2-Digit Numbers

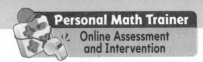

Personal Math Trainer
Online Assessment
and Intervention

✓ Show What You Know

Check your understanding of important skills.

Name _____

▶ **Practice Multiplication Facts** **Find the product.**

1. $8 \times 7 =$ _____

    $7 \times 8 =$ _____

2. $3 \times (2 \times 4) =$ _____

    $(3 \times 2) \times 4 =$ _____

▶ **2-Digit by 1-Digit Multiplication** **Find the product.**

3. 28
   $\times\ 3$

4. 56
   $\times\ 6$

5. 71
   $\times\ 5$

6. 69
   $\times\ 8$

7. 36
   $\times\ 4$

▶ **Multiply by 1-Digit Numbers** **Find the product.**

8.   72
   $\times\ 4$

9.   456
    $\times\ 5$

10. 804
    $\times\ 7$

11. 1,341
    $\times\ \ \ 9$

12. 65
    $\times\ 6$

13. 392
    $\times\ 8$

14. 1,478
    $\times\ \ \ 3$

15. $1,627
    $\times\ \ \ \ 2$

16. 584
    $\times\ 7$

17. 2,837
    $\times\ \ \ \ 4$

Math in the Real World

Yellowstone National Park, which is located in Wyoming, Montana, and Idaho, was America's first National Park. The park has over 500 geysers. Grand Geyser erupts about every 8 hours.

Based on this estimate, how many times would you see this geyser erupt if you could watch it for 1 year? There are 24 hours in a day and 365 days in a year.

Vocabulary Builder

▶ **Visualize It** ••••••••••••••••••••••••••••••••

Complete the H-diagram using the words with a ✓.

Multiplication Words	Estimation Words

▶ **Understand Vocabulary** •••••••••••••••••••••••

Draw a line to match each word or phrase with its definition.

Word

1. Commutative Property of Multiplication

2. estimate

3. compatible numbers

4. factor

5. regroup

Definition

• A number that is multiplied by another number to find a product

• To exchange amounts of equal value to rename a number

• To find an answer that is close to the exact amount

• Numbers that are easy to compute mentally

• The property that states when the order of two factors is changed, the product is the same.

• Interactive Student Edition
• Multimedia eGlossary

Chapter 3 Vocabulary

Associative Property of Multiplication

propiedad asociativa de la multiplicación

4

Commutative Property of Multiplication

Propiedad conmutativa de la multiplicación

13

compatible numbers

números compatibles

15

estimate (*verb*)

estimar

30

factor

factor

33

partial product

producto parcial

61

place value

valor posicional

68

regroup

reagrupar

78

The property that states that when the order of two factors is changed, the product is the same

Example: $3 \times 5 = 5 \times 3$

The property that states that you can group factors in different ways and still get the same product

Example: $3 \times (4 \times 2) = (3 \times 4) \times 2$

To find an answer that is close to the exact amount

Numbers that are easy to compute mentally

Example: Estimate. $176 \div 8$

160 divides easily by 8

↑

compatible number

A method of multiplying in which the ones, tens, hundreds, and so on are multiplied separately and then the products are added together

$$
\begin{array}{r}
182 \\
\times \ \ 6 \\
\hline
600 \\
480 \\
+ \ \ 12 \\
\hline
1{,}092
\end{array}
$$

480 ← Partial products

A number that is multiplied by another number to find a product

Example: $4 \times 5 = 20$

factor   factor

To exchange amounts of equal value to rename a number

Example: $5 + 8 = 13$ ones or 1 ten 3 ones

The value of a digit in a number, based on the location of the digit

Matchup

For 3 to 4 players

Materials

- 1 set of word cards

How to Play

1. Put the cards face-down in rows. Take turns to play.

2. Choose two cards and turn them face-up.

   - If the cards show a word and its meaning, it's a match. Keep the pair and take another turn.

   - If the cards do not match, turn them back over.

3. The game is over when all cards have been matched. The players count their pairs. The player with the most pairs wins.

Word Box

Associative Property of Multiplication

Commutative Property of Multiplication

compatible numbers

estimate

factor

partial product

place value

regroup

The Write Way

Reflect

Choose one idea. Write about it.

- Do 36 × 29 and 29 × 36 represent the same product? Explain why or why not.

- Explain in your words what the Associative Property of Multiplication means.

- A reader of your math advice column writes, "I can't remember what compatible numbers are or how to use them." Write a letter that helps your reader with this problem.

Name _____

Multiply by Tens

Essential Question What strategies can you use to multiply by tens?

Unlock the Problem

Animation for a computer-drawn cartoon requires about 20 frames per second. How many frames would need to be drawn for a 30-second cartoon?

- The phrase "20 frames per second" means 20 frames are needed for each second of animation. How does this help you know what operation to use?

_____

_____

One Way Use place value.

Multiply. 30 × 20

You can think of 20 as 2 tens.

30 × 20 = 30 × _____ tens

= _____ tens

= 600

Another Way Use the Associative Property.

You can think of 20 as 2 × 10.

30 × 20 = 30 × (2 × 10)

= (30 × 2) × 10

= _____ × _____

= _____

So, _____ frames would need to be drawn.

Remember

The Associative Property states that you can group factors in different ways and get the same product. Use parentheses to group the factors you multiply first.

 Math Talk

 Math Processes and Practices 7

Look for Structure How can you use place value to tell why 60 × 10 = 600?

- Compare the number of zeros in each factor to the number of zeros in the product. What do you notice?

_____

_____

🔓 Other Ways

Ⓐ **Use a number line and a pattern to multiply 15 × 20.**

Draw jumps to show the product.

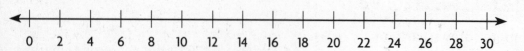

15 × 2 = _____

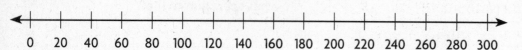

15 × 20 = _____

Ⓑ **Use mental math to find 14 × 30.**

Use the halving-and-doubling strategy.

STEP 1 Find half of 14 to make the problem simpler.	**STEP 2** Multiply.	**STEP 3** Double 210.
Think: To find half of a number, divide by 2.		Think: To double a number, multiply by 2.
14 ÷ 2 = _____	7 × 30 = _____	2 × 210 = _____

So, 14 × 30 = 420.

Try This! **Multiply.**

Use mental math to find 12 × 40.	Use place value to find 12 × 40.

Share and Show

1. Find 20 × 27. Tell which method you chose. Explain what happens in each step.

_____

_____

146

Name _____

Choose a method. Then find the product.

2. 10×12

3. 20×20

☑**4.** 40×24

☑**5.** 11×60

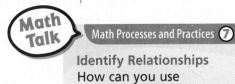

Math Talk · Math Processes and Practices ⑦

Identify Relationships
How can you use
$30 \times 10 = 300$ to
find 30×12?

On Your Own

Choose a method. Then find the product.

6. 70×55

7. 17×30

8. 30×60

9. 12×90

Math Processes and Practices ② **Reason Quantitatively** **Algebra** Find the unknown digit in the number.

10. $64 \times 40 = 2,56\blacksquare$

11. $29 \times 50 = 1,\pentagon 50$

12. $3\blacklozenge \times 47 = 1,410$

$\blacksquare =$ _____

$\pentagon =$ _____

$\blacklozenge =$ _____

13. GO DEEPER Caroline packs 12 jars of jam in a box. She has 40 boxes. She has 542 jars of jam. How many jars of jam will she have left when all the boxes are full?

14. GO DEEPER Alison is preparing for a math contest. Each day, she works on multiplication problems for 20 minutes and division problems for 10 minutes. How many minutes does Alison practice multiplication and division problems in 15 days?

Problem Solving • Applications

Use the table for 15–16.

15. **Math Processes and Practices ④ Use Graphs** How many frames did it take to produce 50 seconds of *Pinocchio*?

_____

16. **GO DEEPER** Are there fewer frames in 10 seconds of *The Flintstones* or in 14 seconds of *The Enchanted Drawing?* What is the difference in the number of frames?

_____

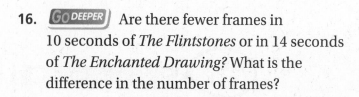

Animated Productions		
Title	Date Released	Frames per Second
The Enchanted Drawing©	1900	20
Little Nemo©	1911	16
Snow White and the Seven Dwarfs©	1937	24
Pinocchio©	1940	19
The Flintstones™	1960–1966	24

17. **THINK SMARTER** The product of my number and twice my number is 128. What is half my number? Explain how you solved the problem.

_____

_____

_____

18. **THINK SMARTER** Tanya says that the product of a multiple of ten and a multiple of ten will always have only one zero. Is she correct? Explain.

_____

_____

WRITE ▸ *Math* • **Show Your Work**

19. **THINK SMARTER** For numbers 19a–19e, select Yes or No to tell whether the answer is correct.

19a. $28 \times 10 = 280$ ○ Yes ○ No

19b. $15 \times 20 = 300$ ○ Yes ○ No

19c. $17 \times 10 = 17$ ○ Yes ○ No

19d. $80 \times 10 = 800$ ○ Yes ○ No

19e. $16 \times 30 = 1,800$ ○ Yes ○ No

Name _____

Multiply by Tens

Learning Objective You will use the Associative Property of Multiplication and place value understanding to multiply by tens.

Choose a method. Then find the product.

1. 16×60

Use the halving-and-doubling strategy.

Find half of 16: $16 \div 2 = 8$.

Multiply 60 by this number: $8 \times 60 = 480$

Double this result: $2 \times 480 = 960$

_____**960**_____

2. 80×22

3. 30×52

4. 60×20

_____   _____   _____

Problem Solving (Real World)

5. Kenny bought 20 packs of baseball cards. There are 12 cards in each pack. How many cards did Kenny buy?

6. The Hart family drove 10 hours to their vacation spot. They drove an average of 48 miles each hour. How many miles did they drive?

_____   _____

7. WRITE ►Math Write the steps for how to use a number line to multiply a 2-digit number by 20. Give an example.

_____

_____

_____

_____

Lesson Check

1. For the school play, 40 rows of chairs are set up. There are 22 chairs in each row. How many chairs are there?

2. At West School, there are 20 classrooms. Each classroom has 20 students. How many students are at West School?

Spiral Review

3. Alex has 48 stickers. This is 6 times the number of stickers Max has. How many stickers does Max have?

4. Ali's dog weighs 8 times as much as her cat. Together, the two pets weigh 54 pounds. How much does Ali's dog weigh?

5. Allison has 3 containers with 25 crayons in each. She also has 4 boxes of markers with 12 markers in each box. She gives 10 crayons to a friend. How many crayons and markers does Allison have now?

6. The state of Utah covers 82,144 square miles. The state of Montana covers 145,552 square miles. What is the total area of the two states?

FOR MORE PRACTICE
GO TO THE
Personal Math Trainer

Name _____

Estimate Products

Essential Question What strategies can you use to estimate products?

Learning Objective You will use compatible numbers and rounding to estimate products.

Unlock the Problem (Real World)

On average, the Smith family opens the door of their refrigerator 32 times each day. There are 31 days in May. About how many times is the refrigerator door opened in May?

- Underline any information you will need.

One Way Use rounding and mental math.

Estimate. 31 × 32

STEP 1 Round each factor.

31 × 32

↓   ↓

30 × 30

STEP 2 Use mental math.

3 × 3 = 9 ← basic fact

30 × 30 = _____

Math Talk

Math Processes and Practices ⑥

Compare Is the exact product greater than or less than 900? Explain.

So, the Smith family opens the refrigerator door about 900 times during the month of May.

1. On average, a refrigerator door is opened 38 times each day. About how many fewer times in May is the Smith family's refrigerator door opened than the average refrigerator door?

Show your work.

All 24 light bulbs in the Park family's home are CFL light bulbs. Each CFL light bulb uses 28 watts to produce light. About how many watts will the light bulbs use when turned on all at the same time?

🔑 Another Way Use mental math and compatible numbers.

Compatible numbers are numbers that are easy to compute mentally.

Estimate. 24 × 28

STEP 1 Use compatible numbers.

24 × 28
↓   ↓
25 × 30   Think: 25 × 3 = 75

So, about 750 watts are used.

STEP 2 Use mental math.

25 × 3 = 75

25 × 30 = _____

Try This! Estimate 26 × $79.

┌─────────────────────────────────┐   ┌──────────────────────────────────────┐
Ⓐ Round to the nearest ten   **Ⓑ Compatible numbers**

   26   × $79   26   × $79   **Think:** How can you use
   ↓   ↓   ↓   ↓   25 × 4 = 100 to
                                                                    help find 25 × 8?
_____ × _____ = _____   25   × $80 = _____

26 × $79 is about _____.   26 × $79 is about _____.

2. Explain why $2,400 and $2,000 are both reasonable estimates.

_____

_____

3. In what situation might you choose to find an estimate rather than an exact answer?

_____

_____

Share and Show

1. To estimate the product of 62 and 28 by rounding, how would you round the factors? What would the estimated product be?

_____

Name _____

Estimate the product. Choose a method.

2. 96×34

✓ **3.** $47 \times \$39$

✓ **4.** 78×72

Math Talk **Math Processes and Practices ①**

Describe how you know if an estimated product will be greater than or less than the exact answer.

On Your Own

Estimate the product. Choose a method.

5. 41×78

6. 51×73

7. 34×80

Practice: Copy and Solve Estimate the product. Choose a method.

8. 61×31

9. 52×68

10. 26×44

11. $57 \times \$69$

THINK SMARTER Find two possible factors for the estimated product.

12. 2,800

13. 8,100

14. 5,600

15. 2,400

16. **GO DEEPER** Mr. Parker jogs for 35 minutes each day. He jogs 5 days in week 1, 6 days in week 2, and 7 days in week 3. About how many minutes does he jog?

17. **GO DEEPER** There are 48 beads in a package. Candice bought 4 packages of blue, 9 packages of gold, 6 packages of red, and 2 packages of silver beads. About how many beads did Candice buy?

Problem Solving • Applications

18. **GO DEEPER** On average, a refrigerator door is opened 38 times each day. Len has two refrigerators in his house. Based on this average, about how many times in a 3-week period are the refrigerator doors opened?

    _____

19. The cost to run a refrigerator is about $57 each year. About how much will it have cost to run by the time it is 15 years old?

    _____

20. **THINK SMARTER** If Mel opens his refrigerator door 36 times every day, about how many times will it be opened in April? Will the exact answer be more than or less than the estimate? Explain.

    _____

    _____

    _____

    _____

21. **Math Processes and Practices ②** **Represent a Problem** What question could you write for this answer? The estimated product of two numbers, that are not multiples of ten, is 2,800.

    _____

    _____

• **WRITE** ▸ *Math* • **Show Your Work** • • • •

22. **THINK SMARTER** Which is a reasonable estimate for the product? Write the estimate. An estimate may be used more than once.

30×20	25×50	20×20

26×48 [_____] 28×21 [_____]

21×22 [_____] 51×26 [_____]

Estimate Products

Learning Objective You will use compatible numbers and rounding to estimate products.

Estimate the product. Choose a method.

1. 38 × 21

$$38 \times 21$$

$$40 \times 20$$

$$\underline{\quad 800 \quad}$$

2. 63 × 19

_____

3. 27 × $42

_____

4. 73 × 67

_____

5. 37 × $44

_____

6. 45 × 22

_____

Problem Solving Real World

7. A dime has a diameter of about 18 millimeters. About how many millimeters long would a row of 34 dimes be?

8. A half-dollar has a diameter of about 31 millimeters. About how many millimeters long would a row of 56 half-dollars be?

_____   _____

9. **WRITE** ▸*Math* Describe a real-life multiplication situation for which an estimate makes sense. Explain why it makes sense.

_____

_____

Lesson Check

1. What is a reasonable estimate for the product of 43×68?

_____

_____

2. Marissa burns 93 calories each time she plays fetch with her dog. She plays fetch with her dog once a day. About how many calories will Marissa burn playing fetch with her dog in 28 days?

_____

_____

Spiral Review

3. Use the model to find 3×126.

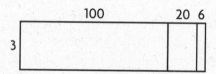

_____

4. A store sold a certain brand of jeans for $38. One day, the store sold 6 pairs of jeans of that brand. How much did the 6 pairs of jeans cost?

_____

5. The Gateway Arch in St. Louis, Missouri, weighs about 20,000 tons. Write an amount that could be the exact number of tons the Arch weighs.

_____

_____

6. What is another name for 23 ten thousands?

_____

_____

FOR MORE PRACTICE
GO TO THE
Personal Math Trainer

Name _____

Area Models and Partial Products

Essential Question How can you use area models and partial products to multiply 2-digit numbers?

Learning Objective You will use area models and partial products to multiply two 2-digit numbers.

Investigate

Materials ■ color pencils

How can you use a model to break apart factors and make them easier to multiply?

A. Outline a rectangle on the grid to model 13 × 18. Break apart the model into smaller rectangles to show factors broken into tens and ones. Label and shade the smaller rectangles. Use the colors below.

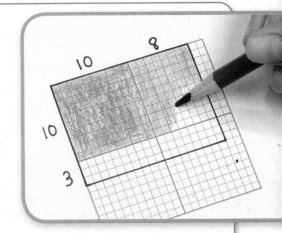

B. Find the product of each smaller rectangle. Then, find the sum of the partial products. Record your answers.

□ = 10 × 10

■ = 10 × 8

▨ = 3 × 10

▨ = 3 × 8

100 + _____ + _____ + _____ = _____

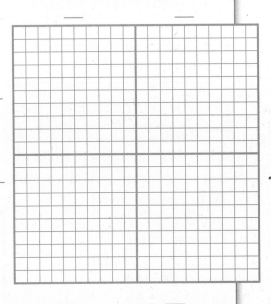

C. Draw the model again. Break apart the whole model to show factors different from those shown the first time. Label and shade the four smaller rectangles and find their products. Record the sum of the partial products to represent the product of the whole model.

_____ + _____ + _____ + _____ = _____

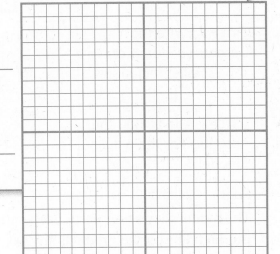

Draw Conclusions

1. Explain how you found the total number of squares in the whole model.

   _____

   _____

2. Compare the two models and their products. What can you conclude? Explain.

   _____

   _____

3. To find the product of 10 and 33, which is the easier computation, $(10 \times 11) + (10 \times 11) + (10 \times 11)$ or $(10 \times 30) + (10 \times 3)$? Explain.

   _____

   _____

Make Connections

You can draw a simple diagram to model and break apart factors to find a product. Find 15×24.

STEP 1 Draw a model to show 15×24. Break apart the factors into tens and ones to show the partial products.

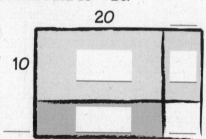

STEP 2 Write the product for each of the smaller rectangles.

(10 × 2 tens)	(10 × 4 ones)	(5 × 2 tens)	(5 × 4 ones)
(10 × 20)	(10 × 4)	(5 × 20)	(5 × 4)

STEP 3 Add to find the product for the whole model.

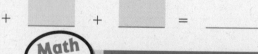

So, $15 \times 24 = 360$.

The model shows four parts. Each part represents a partial product. The partial products are 200, 40, 100, and 20.

Math Talk

Math Processes and Practices ②

Use Reasoning How does breaking apart the factors into tens and ones make finding the product easier?

Name _____

Find the product.

1. $16 \times 19 = $ _____

	10	9
10	100	90
6	60	54

2. $18 \times 26 = $ _____

	20	6
10		
8		

3. $27 \times 39 = $ _____

	30	9
20		
7		

Draw a model to represent the product.
Then record the product.

4. $14 \times 16 = $ _____

5. $23 \times 25 = $ _____

6. **Math Processes and Practices 6** **Explain** how modeling partial products can be used to find the products of greater numbers.

_____

_____

7. **GO DEEPER** Emma bought 16 packages of rolls for a party. There were 12 rolls in a package. After the party there were 8 rolls left over. How many rolls were eaten? Explain.

_____

_____

© Houghton Mifflin Harcourt Publishing Company

Sense or Nonsense?

8. **THINK SMARTER** Jamal and Kim used different ways to solve
12×15 by using partial products. Whose answer makes sense?
Whose answer is nonsense? Explain your reasoning.

Jamal's Work

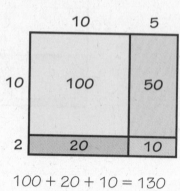

$$100 + 20 + 10 = 130$$

_____

_____

_____

Kim's Work

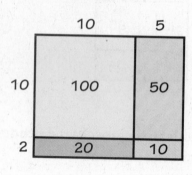

$$120 \quad + 60 = 180$$

_____

_____

_____

a. For the answer that is nonsense, write an answer that makes sense.

_____

b. Look at Kim's method. Can you think of another way Kim
could use the model to find the product? Explain.

_____

_____

_____

	10	5
10	100	50
2	20	10

9. **THINK SMARTER** Look at the model in 8b. How would the partial
products change if the product was 22×15? Explain why you think the
products changed.

_____

_____

Area Models and Partial Products

Learning Objective You will use area models and partial products to multiply two 2-digit numbers.

Draw a model to represent the product.
Then record the product.

1. 13×42

	40	2
10	400	20
3	120	6

$400 + 20 + 120 + 6 = \underline{546}$

2. 18×34

_____

3. 22×26

_____

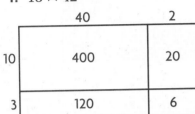 **Problem Solving** Real World

4. Sebastian made the following model to find the product 17×24.

	20	4
10	200	40
7	14	28

$200 + 40 + 14 + 28 = 282$

Is his model correct? **Explain**.

_____

_____

5. Each student in Ms. Sike's kindergarten class has a box of crayons. Each box has 36 crayons. If there are 18 students in Ms. Sike's class, how many crayons are there?

_____

6. **WRITE** ▸*Math* Describe how to model 2-digit by 2-digit multiplication using an area model.

_____

_____

Lesson Check

1. What product does the model below represent?

	20	3
10	200	30
7	140	21

_____

2. What product does the model below represent?

	13	2
10	130	20
5	65	10

_____

Spiral Review

3. Mariah builds a tabletop using square tiles. There are 12 rows of tiles and 30 tiles in each row. How many tiles does Mariah use?

_____

4. Trevor bakes 8 batches of biscuits, with 14 biscuits in each batch. He sets aside 4 biscuits from each batch for a bake sale and puts the rest in a container. How many biscuits does Trevor put in the container?

_____

5. Li feeds her dog 3 cups of food each day. About how many cups of food does her dog eat in 28 days?

_____

6. Find the product of $20 \times 9 \times 5$. Tell which property you used.

_____

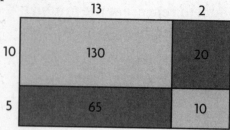

FOR MORE PRACTICE
GO TO THE
Personal Math Trainer

Name _____

Multiply Using Partial Products

Essential Question How can you use place value and partial products to multiply 2-digit numbers?

Learning Objective You will use partial products and place value understanding to multiply two 2-digit numbers.

Unlock the Problem

CONNECT You know how to break apart a model to find partial products. How can you use what you know to find and record a product?

 Multiply. 34 × 57   **Estimate.** 30 × 60 = _____

SHADE THE MODEL	THINK AND RECORD

STEP 1

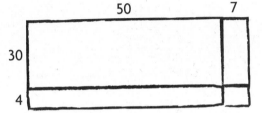

$$\begin{array}{r} 57 \\ \times\ 34 \\ \hline \end{array}$$

← Multiply the tens by the tens.
30 × 5 tens = 150 tens

STEP 2

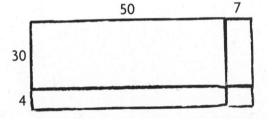

$$\begin{array}{r} 57 \\ \times\ 34 \\ \hline 1,500 \end{array}$$

← Multiply the ones by the tens.
30 × 7 ones = 210 ones

STEP 3

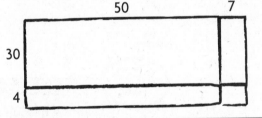

$$\begin{array}{r} 57 \\ \times\ 34 \\ \hline 1,500 \\ 210 \end{array}$$

← Multiply the tens by the ones.
4 × 5 tens = 20 tens

STEP 4

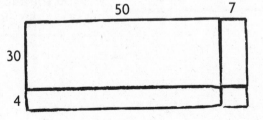

$$\begin{array}{r} 57 \\ \times\ 34 \\ \hline 1,500 \\ 210 \\ 200 \\ + \end{array}$$

← Multiply the ones by the ones.
4 × 7 ones = 28 ones
← Add the partial products.

So, 34 × 57 = 1,938. Since 1,938 is close to the estimate of 1,800, it is reasonable.

Math Talk

Math Processes and Practices ⑧

Use Repeated Reasoning You can write 10 × 4 ones = 40 ones as 10 × 4 = 40. What is another way to write 10 × 3 tens = 30 tens?

ⓘ Example

The apples from each tree in an orchard can fill 23 bushel baskets. If 1 row of the orchard has 48 trees, how many baskets of apples can be filled?

Multiply. 48 × 23   **Estimate.** 50 × 20 = _____

	THINK		RECORD

STEP 1

Multiply the tens by the tens.

$$\begin{array}{r} 23 \\ \times\ 48 \\ \hline \end{array}$$

← 40 × _____ tens = _____ tens

STEP 2

Multiply the ones by the tens.

$$\begin{array}{r} 23 \\ \times\ 48 \\ \hline 800 \\ \end{array}$$

← 40 × _____ ones = _____ ones

STEP 3

Multiply the tens by the ones.

$$\begin{array}{r} 23 \\ \times\ 48 \\ \hline 800 \\ 120 \\ \end{array}$$

← 8 × _____ tens = _____ tens

STEP 4

Multiply the ones by the ones. Then add the partial products.

$$\begin{array}{r} 23 \\ \times\ 48 \\ \hline 800 \\ 120 \\ 160 \\ + \\ \hline \end{array}$$

← 8 × _____ ones = _____ ones

So, 1,104 baskets can be filled.

Math Talk

Math Processes and Practices ①

Evaluate Reasonableness How do you know your answer is reasonable?

Share and Show MATH BOARD

1. Find 24 × 34.

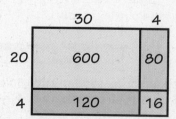

	30	4
20	600	80
4	120	16

$$\begin{array}{r} 3\ 4 \\ \times\ 2\ 4 \\ \hline \end{array}$$

Record the product.

2.　12
　×12

3.　31
　×24

☑4.　25
　×43

☑5.　37
　×26

Math Talk

Math Processes and Practices ④

Model Mathematics How would you model and record 74×25?

On Your Own

Record the product.

6.　54
　×15

7.　87
　×16

8.　62
　×56

9.　49
　×63

Practice: Copy and Solve **Record the product.**

10. 38×47

11. 46×27

12. 72×53

13. 98×69

14. 53×68

15. 76×84

16. 92×48

17. 37×79

Math Processes and Practices ② **Reason Abstractly** **Algebra** Find the unknown digits. Complete the problem.

18.　　6
　×　4
　1,400
　　120
　　280
　+　24
　_____

19.　　2
　×　7
　7,200
　　180
　　560
　+　14
　_____

20.　　6
　×5
　1,500
　　300
　　90
　+　18
　_____

21.　3
　×　8
　600
　80
　240
　+　32
　_____

Problem Solving • Applications

Use the picture graph for 22–24.

22. **Math Processes and Practices ④ Use Graphs** A fruit-packing warehouse is shipping 15 boxes of grapefruit to a store in Santa Rosa, California. What is the total weight of the shipment?

_____

23. **GO DEEPER** How much less do 13 boxes of tangelos weigh than 18 boxes of tangerines?

_____

24. What is the weight of 12 boxes of oranges?

_____

Pounds of Citrus Fruit per Box

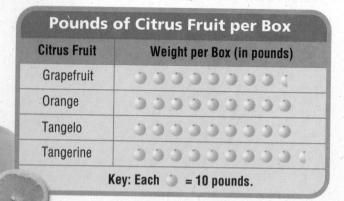

Citrus Fruit	Weight per Box (in pounds)
Grapefruit	
Orange	
Tangelo	
Tangerine	

Key: Each 🟠 = 10 pounds.

WRITE *Math* • **Show Your Work**

25. **THINK SMARTER** Each person in the United States eats about 65 fresh apples each year. Based on this estimate, how many apples do 3 families of 4 eat each year?

_____

26. **GO DEEPER** The product 26 × 93 is greater than 25 × 93. How much greater? Explain how you know without multiplying.

_____

_____

_____

27. **THINK SMARTER** Margot wants to use partial products to find 22 × 17. Write the numbers in the boxes to show 22 × 17.

$$(\boxed{} \times \boxed{}) + (\boxed{} \times \boxed{}) + (\boxed{} \times \boxed{}) + (\boxed{} \times \boxed{})$$

Multiply Using Partial Products

Learning Objective You will use partial products and place value understanding to multiply two 2-digit numbers.

Record the product.

1.
```
    23
×   79
 1,400
   210
   180
+   27
 1,817
```

2.
```
   56
× 32
```

3.
```
   87
× 64
```

4.
```
   33
× 25
```

5.
```
   94
× 12
```

6.
```
   51
× 77
```

7.
```
   69
× 49
```

Problem Solving

8. Evelyn drinks 8 glasses of water a day, which is 56 glasses of water a week. How many glasses of water does she drink in a year? (1 year = 52 weeks)

9. Joe wants to use the Hiking Club's funds to purchase new walking sticks for each of its 19 members. The sticks cost $26 each. The club has $480. Is this enough money to buy each member a new walking stick? If not, how much more money is needed?

10. **WRITE** ▸Math Explain why it works to break apart a number by place values to multiply.

_____

_____

_____

_____

Lesson Check

1. A carnival snack booth made $76 selling popcorn in one day. It made 22 times as much selling cotton candy. How much money did the snack booth make selling cotton candy?

2. List the partial products of 42×28.

Spiral Review

3. Last year, the city library collected 117 used books for its shelves. This year, it collected 3 times as many books. How many books did it collect this year?

4. Washington Elementary has 232 students. Washington High has 6 times as many students. How many students does Washington High have?

5. List the partial products of 35×7.

6. Shelby has ten $5 bills and thirteen $10 bills. How much money does Shelby have in all?

FOR MORE PRACTICE
GO TO THE
Personal Math Trainer

Name _____

✓ Mid-Chapter Checkpoint

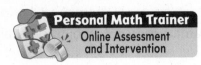

Concepts and Skills

1. Explain how to find 40 × 50 using mental math.

   _____

   _____

2. What is the first step in estimating 56 × 27?

   _____

Choose a method. Then find the product.

3. 35 × 10 _____   4. 19 × 20 _____   5. 12 × 80 _____

6. 70 × 50 _____   7. 58 × 40 _____   8. 30 × 40 _____

9. 14 × 60 _____   10. 20 × 30 _____   11. 16 × 90 _____

Estimate the product. Choose a method.

12. 81 × 38 _____   13. 16 × $59 _____   14. 43 × 25 _____

15. 76 × 45 _____   16. 65 × $79 _____   17. 92 × 38 _____

18. 37 × 31 _____   19. 26 × $59 _____   20. 54 × 26 _____

21. 52 × 87 _____   22. 39 × 27 _____   23. 63 × 58 _____

24. Ms. Traynor's class is taking a field trip to the zoo. The trip will cost $26 for each student. There are 22 students in her class. What is a good estimate for the cost of the students' field trip?

25. Tito wrote the following on the board. What is the unknown number?

$$50 \times 80 = 50 \times (8 \times 10)$$
$$= (50 \times 8) \times 10$$
$$= ? \times 10$$
$$= 4,000$$

26. What are the partial products that result from multiplying 15×32?

27. GO DEEPER A city bus company sold 39 one-way tickets and 20 round-trip tickets from West Elmwood to East Elmwood. One-way tickets cost $14. Round trip tickets cost $25. How much money did the bus company collect?

© Houghton Mifflin Harcourt Publishing Company

Multiply with Regrouping

Essential Question How can you use regrouping to multiply 2-digit numbers?

Learning Objective You will use place value understanding and regrouping to multiply two 2-digit numbers.

 Unlock the Problem Real World

By 1914, Henry Ford had streamlined his assembly line to make a Model T Ford car in 93 minutes. How many minutes did it take to make 25 Model Ts?

 Use place value and regrouping.

Multiply. 93 × 25   **Estimate.** 90 × 30 = _____

▲ The first production Model T Ford was assembled on October 1, 1908.

THINK	RECORD
STEP 1 • Think of 93 as 9 tens and 3 ones. • Multiply 25 by 3 ones.	$\begin{array}{r} \overset{1}{25} \\ \times\ 93 \\ \hline \end{array}$ ← 3 × 25
STEP 2 • Multiply 25 by 9 tens.	$\begin{array}{r} \overset{4}{\cancel{1}} \\ 25 \\ \times\ 93 \\ \hline 75 \\ \end{array}$ ← 90 × 25
STEP 3 • Add the partial products.	$\begin{array}{r} \overset{4}{\cancel{1}} \\ 25 \\ \times\ 93 \\ \hline 75 \\ 2,250 \\ \hline \end{array}$

So, 93 × 25 is 2,325. Since _____ is close

to the estimate of _____, the answer is reasonable.

 Math Talk

Math Processes and Practices ⑧

Use Repeated Reasoning Why do you get the same answer whether you multiply 93 × 25 or 25 × 93?

Different Ways to Multiply You can use different ways to multiply and still get the correct answer. Shawn and Patty both solved 67 × 40 correctly, but they used different ways.

Look at Shawn's paper.

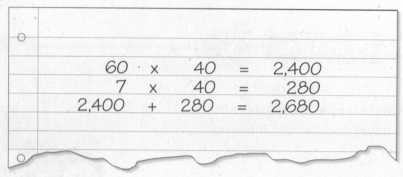

60 ×	40	=	2,400
7 ×	40	=	280
2,400 +	280	=	2,680

So, Shawn's answer is 67 × 40 = 2,680.

Look at Patty's paper.

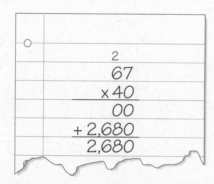

```
    2
   67
 × 40
   00
+2,680
 2,680
```

So, Patty also found 67 × 40 = 2,680.

1. What method did Shawn use to solve the problem?

_____

2. What method did Patty use to solve the problem?

_____

Share and Show MATH BOARD

1. Look at the problem. Complete the sentences.

Multiply _____ and _____ to get 0.

Multiply _____ and _____ to get 1,620.

Add the partial products.

0 + 1,620 = _____

```
   4
  27
 ×60
   0
+1,620
```

Name _____

Estimate. Then find the product.

2. Estimate: _____

$$68 \times 53$$

3. Estimate: _____

$$61 \times 54$$

4. Estimate: _____

$$90 \times 27$$

Math Talk

Math Processes and Practices 8

Generalize Why can you omit zeros of the first partial product when you multiply 20×34?

On Your Own

Estimate. Then find the product.

5. Estimate: _____

$$30 \times 47$$

6. Estimate: _____

$$78 \times 56$$

7. Estimate: _____

$$27 \times 25$$

Practice: Copy and Solve Estimate. Then find the product.

8. 34×65 **9.** $42 \times \$13$ **10.** 60×17 **11.** 62×45 **12.** $57 \times \$98$

Math Processes and Practices 7 **Look for a Pattern** **Algebra** Write a rule for the pattern.
Use your rule to find the unknown numbers.

13.

Hours	h	5	10	15	20	25
Minutes	m	300	600	900		

Rule: _____

14. **GO DEEPER** Owners of a summer camp are buying new cots for their cabins. There are 16 cabins. Each cabin needs 6 cots. Each cot costs $92. How much will the new cots cost?

_____

15. **GO DEEPER** A theater has 28 rows of 38 seats downstairs and 14 rows of 26 seats upstairs. How many seats does the theater have?

_____

Unlock the Problem

16. **THINK SMARTER** Machine A can label 11 bottles in 1 minute. Machine B can label 12 bottles in 1 minute. How many bottles can both machines label in 15 minutes?

a. What do you need to know? _____

_____

b. What numbers will you use? _____

c. Tell why you might use more than one operation to solve the problem.

_____

_____

_____

d. Solve the problem.

So, both machines can label _____ bottles

in _____ minutes.

17. **Math Processes and Practices ①** **Make Sense of Problems**
A toy company makes wooden blocks. A carton holds 85 blocks. How many blocks can 19 cartons hold?

18. **GO DEEPER** A company is packing cartons of candles. Each carton can hold 75 candles. So far, 50 cartons have been packed, but only 30 cartons have been loaded on a truck. How many more candles are left to load on the truck?

Personal Math Trainer

19. **THINK SMARTER +** Mr. Garcia's class raised money for a field trip to the zoo. There are 23 students in his class. The cost of the trip will be $17 for each student. What is the cost for all the students? Explain how you found your answer.

_____

_____

Multiply with Regrouping

Learning Objective You will use place value understanding and regrouping to multiply two 2-digit numbers.

Estimate. Then find the product.

1. Estimate: ____2,700____

   $$
   \begin{array}{r}
   \overset{2}{\overset{1}{}} \\
   87 \\
   \times\ 32 \\
   \hline
   174 \\
   +\ 2,610 \\
   \hline
   2,784
   \end{array}
   $$

   Think: 87 is close to 90 and 32 is close to 30.

   $$90 \times 30 = 2,700$$

2. Estimate: _____

   $$
   \begin{array}{r}
   73 \\
   \times\ 28 \\
   \hline
   \end{array}
   $$

3. Estimate: _____

   $$
   \begin{array}{r}
   48 \\
   \times\ 38 \\
   \hline
   \end{array}
   $$

4. Estimate: _____

   $$
   \begin{array}{r}
   59 \\
   \times\ 52 \\
   \hline
   \end{array}
   $$

Problem Solving Real World

5. Baseballs come in cartons of 84 baseballs. A team orders 18 cartons of baseballs. How many baseballs does the team order?

6. There are 16 tables in the school lunch room. Each table can seat 22 students. How many students can be seated at lunch at one time?

_____

_____

7. **WRITE** ▸ *Math* Write about which method you prefer to use to multiply two 2-digit numbers—regrouping, partial products, or breaking apart a model. Explain why.

_____

_____

_____

_____

Lesson Check

1. The art teacher has 48 boxes of crayons. There are 64 crayons in each box. How many crayons does the teacher have?

2. A basketball team scored an average of 52 points in each of 15 games. Based on the average, how many points did the team score in all?

Spiral Review

3. One Saturday, an orchard sold 83 bags of apples. There are 27 apples in each bag. How many apples were sold?

4. Hannah has a grid of squares that has 12 rows with 15 squares in each row. She colors 5 rows of 8 squares in the middle of the grid blue. She colors the rest of the squares red. How many squares does Hannah color red?

5. Gabriella has 4 times as many erasers as Leona. Leona has 8 erasers. How many erasers does Gabriella have?

6. Phil has 3 times as many rocks as Peter. Together, they have 48 rocks. How many more rocks does Phil have than Peter?

FOR MORE PRACTICE
GO TO THE
Personal Math Trainer

Name _____

Choose a Multiplication Method

Essential Question How can you find and record products of two 2-digit numbers?

Learning Objective You will choose a method to find and record products of two 2-digit numbers.

¶ Unlock the Problem Real World

Did you know using math can help prevent you from getting a sunburn?

The time it takes to burn without sunscreen multiplied by the SPF, or sun protection factor, is the time you can stay in the sun safely with sunscreen.

If today's UV index is 8, Erin will burn in 15 minutes without sunscreen. If Erin puts on lotion with an SPF of 25, how long will she be protected?

- Underline the sentence that tells you how to find the answer.
- Circle the numbers you need to use. What operation will you use?

  _____

🔑 One Way Use partial products to find 15 × 25.

```
      25
    × 15
  _____
  _____   ← 10 × 2 tens  =  20 tens
  _____   ← 10 × 5 ones  =  50 ones
  _____   ←  5 × 2 tens  =  10 tens
+ _____   ←  5 × 5 ones  =  25 ones
  _____   ← Add.
```

▲ Sunscreen helps to prevent sunburn.

✏️ **Draw a picture to check your work.**

So, if Erin puts on lotion with an SPF of 25, she will be protected for 375 minutes.

Math Talk

Math Processes and Practices ⑥

Explain how it was easier to find the product using partial products.

🔑 Another Way Use regrouping to find 15 × 25.

Estimate. 20 × 20 = _____

STEP 1

Think of 15 as 1 ten 5 ones.
Multiply 25 by 5 ones, or 5.

$$
\begin{array}{r}
\overset{2}{25} \\
\times\ 15 \\
\hline
\boxed{} \quad \leftarrow 5 \times 25
\end{array}
$$

STEP 2

Multiply 25 by 1 ten, or 10.

$$
\begin{array}{r}
\overset{2}{25} \\
\times\ 15 \\
\hline
125 \\
\boxed{} \quad \leftarrow 10 \times 25
\end{array}
$$

STEP 3

Add the partial products.

$$
\begin{array}{r}
\overset{2}{25} \\
\times\ 15 \\
\hline
125 \\
+\ 250 \\
\hline
\boxed{}
\end{array}
$$

Try This! Multiply. 57 × $43

Estimate. 57 × $43	Use partial products.	Use regrouping.
	$ 4 3 × 5 7	$ 4 3 × 5 7

1. How do you know your answer is reasonable?

_____

_____

2. Look at the partial products and regrouping methods above. How
   are the partial products 2,000 and 150 related to 2,150?

_____

   How are the partial products 280 and 21 related to 301?

_____

Name _____

1. Find the product.

		5	4
×		2	9

Math Talk Math Processes and Practices ⑧

Draw Conclusions Why do you begin with the ones place when you use the regrouping method to multiply?

Estimate. Then choose a method to find the product.

2. Estimate: _____

36
× 14

3. Estimate: _____

63
× 42

✔**4.** Estimate: _____

84
× 53

✔**5.** Estimate: _____

71
× 13

On Your Own

Practice: Copy and Solve Estimate. Find the product.

6. 29 × $82

7. 57 × 79

8. 80 × 27

9. 32 × $75

10. 55 × 48

11. 19 × $82

12. 25 × $25

13. 41 × 98

Math Processes and Practices ⑦ **Identify Relationships** **Algebra** Use mental math to find the number.

14. 30 × 14 = 420, so 30 × 15 = _____.

15. 25 × 12 = 300, so 25 × _____ = 350.

16. Math Processes and Practices ⑥ The town conservation manager bought 16 maple trees for $26 each. She paid with five $100 bills. How much change will the manager receive? **Explain**.

_____

_____

17. GO DEEPER Each of 25 students in Group A read for 45 minutes. Each of 21 students in Group B read for 48 minutes. Which group read for more minutes? Explain.

_____

Unlock the Problem (Real World)

18. **THINK SMARTER** Martin collects stamps. He counted 48 pages in his collector's album. The first 20 pages each have 35 stamps in 5 rows. The rest of the pages each have 54 stamps. How many stamps does Martin have in his album?

a. What do you need to know? _____

_____

b. How will you use multiplication to find the number of stamps? _____

_____

c. Tell why you might use addition and subtraction to help solve the problem.

_____

_____

d. Show the steps to solve the problem.

e. Complete the sentences.

   Martin has a total of _____ stamps on the first 20 pages.

   There are _____ more pages after the first 20 pages in Martin's album.

   There are _____ stamps on the rest of the pages.

   There are _____ stamps in the album.

19. **THINK SMARTER** Select the expressions that have the same product as 35 × 17. Mark all that apply.

○ (30 × 10) + (30 × 7) + (5 × 10) + (5 × 7)   ○ (30 × 17) + (5 × 17)

○ (35 × 30) + (35 × 5) + (35 × 10) + (35 × 7)   ○ (35 × 10) + (35 × 7)

○ (35 × 10) + (30 × 10) + (5 × 10) + (5 × 7)   ○ (35 × 30) + (35 × 5)

Name _____

Choose a Multiplication Method

Learning Objective You will choose a method to find and record products of two 2-digit numbers.

Estimate. Then choose a method to find the product.

1. Estimate: _1,200_

$$
\begin{array}{r}
31 \\
\times\ 43 \\
\hline
93 \\
+\ 1,240 \\
\hline
1,333
\end{array}
$$

2. Estimate: _____

$$
\begin{array}{r}
67 \\
\times\ 85 \\
\hline
\end{array}
$$

3. Estimate: _____

$$
\begin{array}{r}
68 \\
\times\ 38 \\
\hline
\end{array}
$$

4. Estimate: _____

$$
\begin{array}{r}
95 \\
\times\ 17 \\
\hline
\end{array}
$$

5. Estimate: _____

$$
\begin{array}{r}
49 \\
\times\ 54 \\
\hline
\end{array}
$$

6. Estimate: _____

$$
\begin{array}{r}
91 \\
\times\ 26 \\
\hline
\end{array}
$$

7. Estimate: _____

$$
\begin{array}{r}
82 \\
\times\ 19 \\
\hline
\end{array}
$$

Problem Solving · Real World

8. A movie theatre has 26 rows of seats. There are 18 seats in each row. How many seats are there?

_____

9. Each class at Briarwood Elementary collected at least 54 cans of food during the food drive. If there are 29 classes in the school, what was the least number of cans collected?

_____

10. **WRITE** ▸*Math* How is multiplication using partial products different from multiplication using regrouping? How are they similar?

_____

_____

_____

Lesson Check

1. A choir needs new robes for each of its 46 singers. Each robe costs $32. What will be the total cost for all 46 robes?

2. A wall on the side of a building is made up of 52 rows of bricks with 44 bricks in each row. How many bricks make up the wall?

Spiral Review

3. Write an expression that shows how to multiply 4 × 362 using place value and expanded form.

4. Use the model below. What is the product 4 × 492?

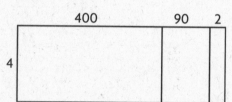

5. What is the sum 13,094 + 259,728?

6. During the 2008–2009 season, there were 801,372 people who attended the home hockey games in Philadelphia. There were 609,907 people who attended the home hockey games in Phoenix. How much greater was the home attendance in Philadelphia than in Phoenix that season?

FOR MORE PRACTICE
GO TO THE
Personal Math Trainer

Name _____

Problem Solving • Multiply 2-Digit Numbers

Essential Question How can you use the strategy *draw a diagram* to solve multistep multiplication problems?

Learning Objective You will use the strategy *draw a diagram* to solve multistep multiplication problems.

Unlock the Problem

During the 2010 Great Backyard Bird Count, an average of 42 bald eagles were counted in each of 20 locations throughout Alaska. In 2009, an average of 32 bald eagles were counted in each of 26 locations throughout Alaska. Based on this data, how many more bald eagles were counted in 2010 than in 2009?

Use the graphic organizer to help you solve the problem.

Read the Problem	Solve the Problem
What do I need to find? I need to find _____ bald eagles were counted in 2010 than in 2009.	• First, find the total number of bald eagles counted in 2010. _____ × _____ = _____ bald eagles counted in 2010
What information do I need to use? In 2010, _____ locations counted an average of _____ bald eagles each. In 2009 _____ locations counted an average of _____ bald eagles each.	• Next, find the total number of bald eagles counted in 2009. = _____ × _____ = _____ bald eagles counted in 2009
How will I use the information? I can solve simpler problems. Find the number of bald eagles counted in _____. Find the number of bald eagles counted in _____. Then draw a bar model to compare the _____ count to the _____ count.	• Last, draw a bar model. I need to subtract. 840 bald eagles in 2010 832 bald eagles in 2009 ? 840 − 832 = _____ So, there were _____ more bald eagles counted in 2010 than in 2009.

Chapter 3   183

🔓 Try Another Problem

Prescott Valley, Arizona, reported a total of 29 mourning doves in the Great Backyard Bird Count. Mesa, Arizona, reported 20 times as many mourning doves as Prescott Valley. If Chandler reported a total of 760 mourning doves, how many more mourning doves were reported in Chandler than in Mesa?

Mourning dove ▲

Read the Problem	Solve the Problem
What do I need to find?	
What information do I need to use?	
	760 mourning doves in Chandler
How will I use the information?	580 mourning doves in Mesa ?

- Is your answer reasonable? Explain. _____

_____

_____

Math Talk

Math Processes and Practices ②

Reason Abstractly What is another way you could solve this problem?

© Houghton Mifflin Harcourt Publishing Company • (t) ©William Leaman/Alamy Images

Name _____

1. An average of 74 reports with bird counts were turned in each day in June. An average of 89 were turned in each day in July. How many reports were turned in for both months? (Hint: There are 30 days in June and 31 days in July.)

First, write the problem for June.

_____

Next, write the problem for July.

_____

WRITE ▸ *Math* · **Show Your Work**

Last, find and add the two products.

_____ reports were turned in for both months.

2. What if an average of 98 reports were turned in each day for the month of June? How many reports were turned in for June? Describe how your answer for June would be different.

_____

_____

_____

3. **GO DEEPER** There are 48 crayons in a box. There are 12 boxes in a carton. Mr. Johnson ordered 6 cartons of crayons for the school. How many crayons did he get?

_____

4. **Math Processes and Practices ①** **Make Sense of Problems** Each of 5 bird-watchers reported seeing 15 roseate spoonbills in a day. If they each reported seeing the same number of roseate spoonbills over 14 days, how many would be reported?

_____

© Houghton Mifflin Harcourt Publishing Company

On Your Own

5. **THINK SMARTER** On each of Maggie's bird-watching trips, she has seen at least 24 birds. If she has taken 4 of these trips each year over the past 16 years, at least how many birds has Maggie seen?

_____

6. **Math Processes and Practices ①** **Make Sense of Problems**
There are 12 inches in a foot. In September, Mrs. Harris orders 32 feet of ribbon for the Crafts Club. In January, she orders 9 feet less. How many inches of ribbon does Mrs. Harris order? Explain how you found your answer.

_____

_____

7. **GO DEEPER** Lydia is having a party on Saturday. She decides to write a riddle on her invitations to describe her house number on Cypress Street. Use the clues to find Lydia's address.

_____

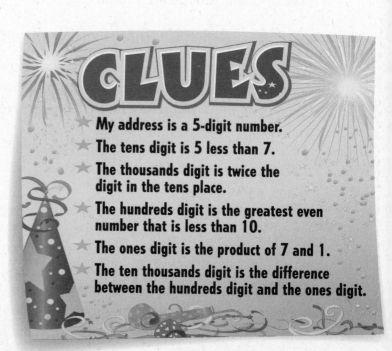

CLUES

★ My address is a 5-digit number.
★ The tens digit is 5 less than 7.
★ The thousands digit is twice the digit in the tens place.
★ The hundreds digit is the greatest even number that is less than 10.
★ The ones digit is the product of 7 and 1.
★ The ten thousands digit is the difference between the hundreds digit and the ones digit.

Personal Math Trainer

8. **THINK SMARTER +** A school is adding 4 rows of seats to the auditorium. There are 7 seats in each row. Each new seat costs $99. What is the total cost for the new seats? Show your work.

_____

Problem Solving • Multiply 2-Digit Numbers

Learning Objective You will use the strategy *draw a diagram* to solve multistep multiplication problems.

Solve each problem. Use a bar model to help.

1. Mason counted an average of 18 birds at his bird feeder each day for 20 days. Gloria counted an average of 21 birds at her bird feeder each day for 16 days. How many more birds did Mason count at his feeder than Gloria counted at hers?

360 birds counted by Mason

336 birds counted by Gloria

   ?

   Birds counted by Mason: **18 × 20 = 360**

   Birds counted by Gloria: **21 × 16 = 336**

   Draw a bar model to compare.

   Subtract. **360 − 336 = 24**

   So, Mason counted ___24___ more birds.

2. The 24 students in Ms. Lee's class each collected an average of 18 cans for recycling. The 21 students in Mr. Galvez's class each collected an average of 25 cans for recycling. How many more cans were collected by Mr. Galvez's class than Ms. Lee's class?

3. At East School, each of the 45 classrooms has an average of 22 students. At West School, each of the 42 classrooms has an average of 23 students. How many more students are at East School than at West School?

4. **WRITE** ▸*Math* Draw a bar model that shows how the number of hours in March compares with the number of hours in February of this year.

Lesson Check

1. Ace Manufacturing ordered 17 boxes with 85 ball bearings each. They also ordered 15 boxes with 90 springs each. How many more ball bearings than springs did they order?

2. Elton hiked 16 miles each day on a 12-day hiking trip. Lola hiked 14 miles each day on her 16-day hiking trip. In all, how many more miles did Lola hike than Elton hiked?

Spiral Review

3. An orchard has 24 rows of apple trees. There are 35 apple trees in each row. How many apple trees are in the orchard?

4. An amusement park reported 354,605 visitors last summer. What is this number rounded to the nearest thousand?

5. Attendance at the football game was 102,653. What is the value of the digit 6?

6. Jill's fish weighs 8 times as much as her parakeet. Together, the pets weigh 63 ounces. How much does the fish weigh?

FOR MORE PRACTICE
GO TO THE
Personal Math Trainer

✓ Chapter 3 Review/Test

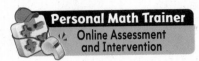

Personal Math Trainer
Online Assessment
and Intervention

1. Explain how to find 40×50 using mental math.

2. Mrs. Traynor's class is taking a field trip to the zoo. The trip will cost $26 for each student. There are 22 students in her class.

   Part A

   Round each factor to estimate the total cost of the students' field trip.

   Part B

   Use compatible numbers to estimate the total cost of the field trip.

   Part C

   Which do you think is the better estimate? Explain.

3. For numbers 3a–3e, select Yes or No to show if the answer is correct.

3a. $35 \times 10 = 350$ ○ Yes   ○ No

3b. $19 \times 20 = 380$ ○ Yes   ○ No

3c. $12 \times 100 = 120$ ○ Yes   ○ No

3d. $70 \times 100 = 7,000$ ○ Yes   ○ No

3e. $28 \times 30 = 2,100$ ○ Yes   ○ No

4. There are 23 boxes of pencils in Mr. Shaw's supply cabinet. Each box contains 100 pencils. How many pencils are in the supply cabinet?

_____ pencils

5. Which would provide a reasonable estimate for each product? Write the estimate beside the product. An estimate may be used more than once.

| 50×20 | 25×40 | 30×30 |

23×38 [ ] 46×18 [ ]

31×32 [ ] 39×21 [ ]

6. There are 26 baseball teams in the league. Each team has 18 players. Write a number sentence that will provide a reasonable estimate for the number of players in the league. Explain how you found your estimate.

7. The model shows 48×37. Write the partial products.

190

© Houghton Mifflin Harcourt Publishing Company

8. Jess made this model to find the product 32 × 17. Her model is incorrect.

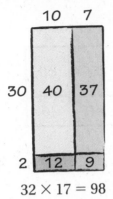

32 × 17 = 98

Part A

What did Jess do wrong?

Part B

Redraw the model so that it is correct.

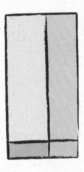

Part C

What is the actual product 32 × 17?

_____

9. Tatum wants to use partial products to find 15 × 32. Write the numbers in the boxes to show 15 × 32.

$$\left(\boxed{} \times \boxed{} \right) + \left(\boxed{} \times \boxed{} \right) + \left(\boxed{} \times \boxed{} \right) + \left(\boxed{} \times \boxed{} \right)$$

10. Which product is shown by the model? Write the letter of the product on the line below the model.

(A) 17 × 36   (B) 24 × 14   (C) 13 × 13

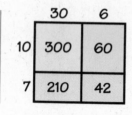

	10	3
10	100	30
3	30	9

	30	6
10	300	60
7	210	42

	10	4
20	200	80
4	40	16

_____   _____   _____

11. **GO DEEPER** Mrs. Jones places 3 orders for school T-shirts. Each order has 16 boxes of shirts and each box holds 17 shirts. How many T-shirts does Mrs. Jones order? Use partial products to help you.

12. Write the unknown digits. Use each digit exactly once.

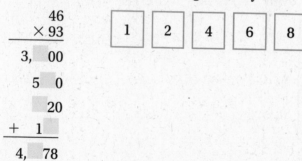

```
      46
    × 93
   _____
   3,  00
     5 0
      20
 +   1
   _____
   4,  78
```

| 1 | 2 | 4 | 6 | 8 |

13. Mike has 16 baseball cards. Niko has 17 times as many baseball cards as Mike does. How many baseball cards does Niko have?

_____ baseball cards

14. Multiply.

36 × 28 = _____

15. A farmer planted 42 rows of tomatoes with 13 plants in each row. How many tomato plants did the farmer grow?

42 × 13 = _____ tomato plants

16. Select another way to show 25 × 18. Mark all that apply.

○ (20 × 10) + (20 × 8) + (5 × 10) + (5 × 8)

○ (25 × 20) + (25 × 5) + (25 × 10) + (25 × 8)

○ (20 × 18) + (5 × 10) + (5 × 8)

○ (25 × 10) + (25 × 8)

○ (25 × 20) + (25 × 5)

17. Terrell runs 15 sprints. Each sprint is 65 meters. How many meters does Terrell run? Show your work.

18.  THINK SMARTER ✚   There are 3 new seats in each row in a school auditorium. There are 15 rows in the auditorium. Each new seat cost $74. What is the cost for the new seats? Explain how you found your answer.

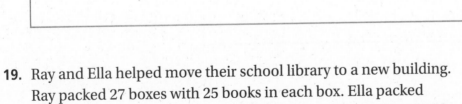

19. Ray and Ella helped move their school library to a new building. Ray packed 27 boxes with 25 books in each box. Ella packed 23 boxes with 30 books in each box. How many more books did Ella pack? Show your work.

20. Julius and Walt are finding the product of 25 and 16.

	Julius	Walt
	25	25
	× 16	× 16
	150	200
	+ 250	50
	500	120
		+ 300
		670

Part A

Julius' answer is incorrect. What did Julius do wrong?

Part B

What did Walt do wrong?

Part C

What is the correct product?

21. A clothing store sells 26 shirts and 22 pairs of jeans. Each item of clothing costs $32.

Part A

What is a reasonable estimate for the total cost of the clothing? Show or explain how you found your answer.

Part B

What is the exact answer for the total cost of the clothing? Show or explain how you found your answer.

Divide by 1-Digit Numbers

✓ Show What You Know

Check your understanding of important skills.

Name _____

▶ **Use Arrays to Divide** **Draw to complete each array.**
Then complete the number sentence.

1. ■ ■ ■ ■

    8 ÷ 4 = _____

2. ■
   ■
   ■

    21 ÷ 3 = _____

▶ **Multiples** **Write the first six multiples of the number.**

3. 4: _____

4. 10: _____

▶ **Subtract Through 4-Digit Numbers** **Find the difference.**

5. 626
    −   8

6. 744
    − 36

7. 5,413
    −2,037

8. 8,681
    − 422

**Each digit in the division example has
been replaced with the same letter
throughout. (r stands for remainder.)
The digits used were 1, 2, 3, 4, 5, 7, and 9.
Find the numbers. Clue: U is 5.**

```
      SU rE
  U)CAN
   −CU
    IN
   −IU
     E
```

▶ **Visualize It** ••••••••••••••••••••••••••••••••••••

Sort the words into the Venn diagram.

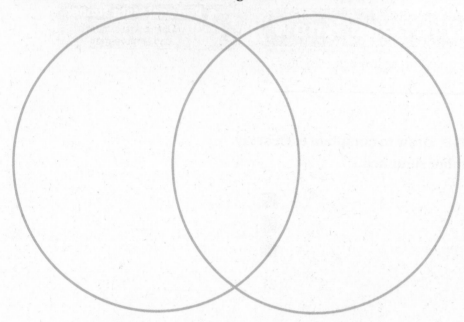

Multiplication Words   Division Words

Review Words

Distributive Property

divide

dividend

division

divisor

factor

multiplication

product

quotient

Preview Words

compatible numbers

multiple

partial quotient

remainder

▶ **Understand Vocabulary** •••••••••••••••••••••••••••••

Write the word that answers the riddle.

1. I am the method of dividing in which multiples of the divisor are subtracted from the dividend and then the quotients are added together.

   _____

2. I am the number that is to be divided in a division problem.

   _____

3. I am the amount left over when a number cannot be

   divided equally. _____

4. I am the number that divided the dividend.

   _____

• **Interactive Student Edition**
• **Multimedia eGlossary**

Chapter 4 Vocabulary

compatible numbers

números compatibles

15

Distributive Property

propiedad distributiva

23

dividend

dividendo

24

divisor

divisor

26

multiple

múltiplo

55

partial quotient

cociente parcial

62

quotient

cociente

75

remainder

residuo

79

The property that states that multiplying a sum by a number is the same as multiplying each addend by the number and then adding the products

Example: $5 \times (10 + 6) = (5 \times 10) + (5 \times 6)$

Numbers that are easy to compute mentally

Example: Estimate. $176 \div 8$

160 divides easily by 8

↑
compatible number

The number that divides the dividend

Example: $15 \div 3 = 5$

↑
divisor

The number that is to be divided in a division problem

Example: $36 \div 6 = 6$

↑
dividend

A method of dividing in which multiples of the divisor are subtracted from the dividend and then the quotients are added together

Example:

```
      5)125         Partial Quotients
       -50    10 × 5      10
        75
       -50    10 × 5      10
        25
       -25    5 × 5      +5
         0               25
```

The product of a number and a counting number is called a multiple of the number

Example:

$$\begin{array}{cccc} 3 & 3 & 3 & 3 \\ \times 1 & \times 2 & \times 3 & \times 4 \\ \hline 3 & 6 & 9 & 12 \end{array}$$

← counting numbers
← multiples of 3

The amount left over when a number cannot be divided equally

Example:
```
     4 R2
  3)14
```
↑
remainder

The number, not including the remainder, that results from dividing

Example: $35 \div 7 = 5$

↑
quotient

Pick It

For 3 to 4 players

Materials

- 4 sets of word cards.

How to Play

1. Each player is dealt 5 cards. The remaining cards are a draw pile.

2. To take a turn, ask any player if he or she has a word that matches one of your word cards.

3. If the player has the word, he or she gives the card to you, and you must define the word.
   - If you are correct, keep the card and put the matching pair in front of you. Take another turn.
   - If you are wrong, return the card. Your turn is over.

4. If the player does not have the word, he or she answers, "Pick it." Then you take a card from the draw pile.

5. If the card you draw matches one of your word cards, follow the directions for Step 3 above. If it does not, your turn is over.

6. The game is over when one player has no cards left. The player with the most pairs wins.

Word Box

compatible
  numbers
Distributive
  Property
dividend
divisor
multiple
partial quotient
quotient
remainder

The Write Way

Reflect

Choose one idea. Write about it.

- Write a paragraph that uses at least three of these words.

  dividend   divisor   multiple   quotient   remainder

- Explain how you know that the quotient of $143 \div 5$ has a remainder.

- Think about what you learned about division in math class today. Complete one of these sentences.

  I learned that _____.

  I was surprised that _____.

  I noticed that _____.

  I discovered that _____.

Name _____

Estimate Quotients Using Multiples

Essential Question How can you use multiples to estimate quotients?

Learning Objective You will use multiples to estimate quotients.

🔑 Unlock the Problem

The bakery made 110 pumpkin muffins. They will be packed in boxes with 8 muffins in each box. About how many boxes will there be?

You can use multiples to estimate.

A **multiple** of a number is the product of a number and a counting number. 1, 2, 3, 4, and so on, are counting numbers.

 Estimate. 110 ÷ 8

Think: What number multiplied by 8 is about 110?

STEP 1 List the multiples of 8 until you reach 110 or greater.

Counting number	1	2	3	4	5	6	7	8	9	10	11	12	13	14
Multiple of 8	8	16	24	32			56	64				96		112

STEP 2 Find the multiples of 8 that 110 is between.

13 × 8 = _____

14 × 8 = _____

110 is between _____ and _____, so 110 ÷ 8 is between 13 and 14.

110 is closest to _____, so 110 ÷ 8 is about _____.

So, there will be about _____ boxes.

Math Processes and Practices ⑦

Identify Relationships
When estimating a quotient, how do you know which two numbers it is between?

Try This!

List the next 8 multiples of 10.

10, 20, _____

List the next 7 multiples of 100.

100, 200, _____

Chapter 4 197

🔑 Example Estimate. 196 ÷ 4

Think: What number times 4 is about 196?

STEP 1 List the next 6 multiples of 4.

4, 8, 12, 16, _____

Are any multiples close to 196? _____

_____

Think: If I multiply by multiples of 10, the products will be greater. Using multiples of 10 will get me to 196 faster.

STEP 2 Multiply 4 by multiples of 10.

$10 \times 4 = 40$

$20 \times 4 = 80$

$30 \times 4 =$ _____

$40 \times 4 =$ _____

$50 \times 4 =$ _____

The quotient is between 40 and 50.

_____ × 4 is closest to _____, so 196 ÷ 4 is about _____.

Share and Show MATH BOARD

1. A restaurant has 68 chairs. There are six chairs at each table. About how many tables are in the restaurant?

   Estimate. 68 ÷ 6

   Think: What number times 6 is about 68?

   $10 \times 6 =$ _____

   $11 \times 6 =$ _____

   $12 \times 6 =$ _____

   68 is closest to _____, so the best estimate is

   about _____ tables are in the restaurant.

Math Talk

Math Processes and Practices ⑤

Communicate When do you multiply the divisor by multiples of 10 to estimate a quotient? Explain.

Name _____

Find two numbers the quotient is between. Then estimate the quotient.

✓ **2.** 41 ÷ 3

✓ **3.** 192 ÷ 5

_____   _____

_____   _____

On Your Own

Find two numbers the quotient is between. Then estimate the quotient.

4. 90 ÷ 7

_____

_____

5. 67 ÷ 4

_____

_____

6. 281 ÷ 9

_____

_____

7. 102 ÷ 7

_____

_____

8. 85 ÷ 6

_____

_____

9. 220 ÷ 8

_____

_____

Decide whether the actual quotient is greater than or less than the estimate given. Write < or >.

10. 83 ÷ 8 ◯ 10

11. 155 ÷ 4 ◯ 40

12. 70 ÷ 6 ◯ 11

13. **What's the Question?** A dolphin's heart beats 688 times in 6 minutes. Answer: about 100 times.

_____

_____

14. **Math Processes and Practices ①** **Analyze** A mother bottlenose dolphin ate about 278 pounds of food in one week. About how much food did she eat in a day?

_____

_____

15. **GO DEEPER** Tanya has $42 to spend at the Dolphin Island store. T-shirts sell for $7 each and a pair of sunglasses sells for $6. Tanya buys 3 T-shirts. How many pairs of sunglasses can she buy with the amount of money she has left?

_____

Problem Solving • Applications

16. **THINK SMARTER** If a bottlenose dolphin can eat 175 pounds of fish, squid, and shrimp in a week, about how many pounds of food does it eat in a day? Milo says the answer is about 20 pounds. Leah says the answer is about 30 pounds. Who is correct? Explain.

_____

_____

_____

_____

17. **GO DEEPER** Four families went out for lunch. The total food bill came to $167. The families also left a $30 tip for the waitress. If each family spent the same amount, about how much did each family spend on dinner? Explain how you found your answer.

WRITE *Math*
Show Your Work

_____

_____

_____

_____

18. **THINK SMARTER** There are 6 showings of a film about Van Gogh at the Art Museum. A total of 459 people saw the film. The same number of people were at each showing. About how many people were at each showing? Circle the numbers the quotient is between. Then explain how you found your answer.

40   50   60   70   80

_____

_____

Estimate Quotients Using Multiples

Learning Objective You will use multiples to estimate quotients.

Find two numbers the quotient is between. Then estimate the quotient.

1. $175 \div 6$

   between 20 and _____

   30 about 30

   Think: $6 \times 20 = 120$ and $6 \times 30 = 180$.
   So, $175 \div 6$ is between 20 and 30. Since 175 is closer to 180 than to 120, the quotient is about 30.

2. $53 \div 3$

   _____

   _____

3. $75 \div 4$

   _____

   _____

4. $215 \div 9$

   _____

   _____

5. $284 \div 5$

   _____

   _____

6. $191 \div 3$

   _____

   _____

7. $100 \div 7$

   _____

   _____

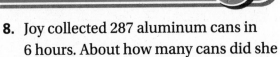

Problem Solving · Real World

8. Joy collected 287 aluminum cans in 6 hours. About how many cans did she collect per hour?

   _____

9. Paul sold 162 cups of lemonade in 5 hours. About how many cups of lemonade did he sell each hour?

   _____

10. **WRITE** ▸*Math* Write a word problem that you can solve using multiples to estimate the quotient. Include a solution.

    _____

    _____

    _____

Lesson Check

1. Abby did 121 sit-ups in 8 minutes. Estimate the number of sit-ups she did in 1 minute.

2. The Garibaldi family drove 400 miles in 7 hours. Estimate the number of miles they drove in 1 hour.

Spiral Review

3. Twelve boys collected 16 aluminum cans each. Fifteen girls collected 14 aluminum cans each. How many more cans did the girls collect than the boys?

4. George bought 30 packs of football cards. There were 14 cards in each pack. How many cards did George buy?

5. Sarah made a necklace using 5 times as many blue beads as white beads. She used a total of 30 beads. How many blue beads did Sarah use?

6. This year, Ms. Webster flew 145,000 miles on business. Last year, she flew 83,125 miles on business. How many more miles did Ms. Webster fly on business this year?

© Houghton Mifflin Harcourt Publishing Company

FOR MORE PRACTICE
GO TO THE
Personal Math Trainer

Name _____

Remainders

Essential Question How can you use models to divide whole numbers that do not divide evenly?

Learning Objective You will use models to find whole-number quotients and remainders with up to 2-digit dividends and 1-digit divisors.

Investigate

Materials ■ counters

Andrea and 2 friends are playing a game of dominoes. There are 28 dominoes in the set. Andrea wants each player to receive the same number of dominoes. Can she divide them equally among the 3 players? Why or why not?

You can use division to find the number of dominoes each player will receive.

A. Use 28 counters to represent the 28 dominoes. Then draw 3 circles to represent the 3 players.

B. Share the counters equally among the 3 groups by placing them in the circles.

> **Draw a quick picture to show your work.**
>
>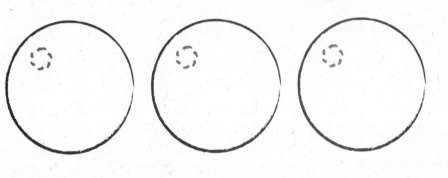

C. Find the number of counters in each group and the number of counters left over. Record your answer.

_____ counters in each group

_____ counter left over

© Houghton Mifflin Harcourt Publishing Company • Image Credits: (t) ©Houghton Mifflin Harcourt

Chapter 4   203

Draw Conclusions

1. How many dominoes does each player receive? _____

   How many dominoes are left over? _____

2. **THINK SMARTER** Explain how the model helped you find the number of dominoes each player receives. Why is 1 counter left outside the equal groups?

   _____

   _____

   _____

3. Use counters to represent a set of 28 dominoes. How many players can play dominoes if each player receives 9 dominoes? Will any dominoes be left over? Explain.

   _____

   _____

Make Connections

When a number cannot be divided evenly, the amount left over is called the **remainder**.

Use counters to find 39 ÷ 5.

• Use 39 counters.

• Share the counters equally among 5 groups. The number of counters left over is the remainder.

Draw a quick picture to show your work.

For 39 ÷ 5, the quotient is _____ and the remainder

is _____, or 7 r4.

Math Talk

Math Processes and Practices ⑧

Generalize How do you know when there will be a remainder in a division problem?

Name _____

Use counters to find the quotient and remainder.

1. $10 \div 3$ **2.** $28 \div 5$ **3.** $15 \div 6$ **4.** $11 \div 3$

_____   _____   _____   _____

5. $29 \div 4$ **6.** $34 \div 5$ **7.** $25 \div 3$ ✓**8.** $7\overline{)20}$

_____   _____   _____   _____

Divide. Draw a quick picture to help.

9. $4\overline{)35}$ ✓**10.** $23 \div 8$

_____   _____

11. **Math Processes and Practices 6** **Explain** how you use a quick picture to find the quotient and remainder.

_____

_____

_____

_____

12. **GO DEEPER**   Alyson has 46 beads to make bracelets. Each bracelet has 5 beads. How many more beads does Alyson need so that all the beads she has are used? Explain.

_____

_____

13. **THINK SMARTER**   For 13a–13d, choose Yes or No to tell whether the division expression has a remainder.

13a. $36 \div 9$ ○ Yes   ○ No

13b. $23 \div 3$ ○ Yes   ○ No

13c. $82 \div 9$ ○ Yes   ○ No

13d. $28 \div 7$ ○ Yes   ○ No

What's the Error?

14. **THINK SMARTER** Macy, Kayley, Maddie, and Rachel collected
13 marbles. They want to share the marbles equally. How many
marbles will each of the 4 girls get? How many marbles will be
left over?

Oscar used a model to solve this problem. He says his
model represents $4\overline{)13}$. What is his error?

Look at the way Oscar solved this problem. Find and describe his error.

Draw a correct model and solve the problem.

So, each of the 4 girls will get _____ marbles

and _____ marble will be left over.

Name _____

Remainders

Learning Objective You will use models to find whole-number quotients and remainders with up to 2-digit dividends and 1-digit divisors.

Use counters to find the quotient and remainder.

1. $13 \div 4$

_____3 r1_____

2. $24 \div 7$

_____

3. $39 \div 5$

_____

4. $36 \div 8$

_____

5. $6\overline{)27}$

_____

6. $25 \div 9$

_____

7. $3\overline{)17}$

_____

8. $26 \div 4$

_____

Divide. Draw a quick picture to help.

9. $14 \div 3$

10. $5\overline{)29}$

_____

_____

Problem Solving Real World

11. Mark drew the following model and said it represented the problem $21 \div 4$. Is Mark's model correct? If so, what is the quotient and remainder? If not, what is the correct quotient and remainder?

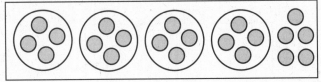

_____

_____

12. **WRITE** *Math* Describe a real-life situation where you would have a remainder.

_____

_____

_____

Lesson Check

1. What is the quotient and remainder for 32 ÷ 6?

2. What is the remainder in the division problem modeled below?

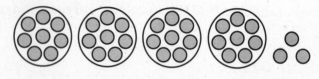

_____

Spiral Review

3. Each kit to build a castle contains 235 parts. How many parts are in 4 of the kits?

4. In 2010, the population of Alaska was about 710,200. What is this number written in word form?

_____

5. At the theater, one section of seats has 8 rows with 12 seats in each row. In the center of each of the first 3 rows are 4 broken seats that cannot be used. How many seats can be used in the section?

6. What partial products are shown by the model below?

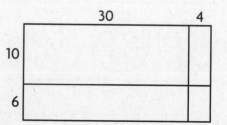

_____

FOR MORE PRACTICE
GO TO THE
Personal Math Trainer

Name _____

Interpret the Remainder

Essential Question How can you use remainders in division problems?

 Unlock the Problem Real World

Magda has some leftover wallpaper 73 inches long. She wants to cut it into 8 pieces to use around the photos in her scrapbook. Each piece will have equal length. How long will each piece be?

When you solve a division problem with a remainder, the way you interpret the remainder depends on the situation and the question.

One Way Write the remainder as a fraction.

The divisor is _____ pieces.

The _____ is 73 inches.

Divide to find the quotient and remainder. $8\overline{)73}$ has quotient 9 r1

The remainder represents 1 inch left over, which can also be divided into 8 equal parts and written as a fraction.

$$\frac{\text{remainder}}{\text{divisor}} = \underline{\quad}$$

Write the quotient with the remainder written as a fraction. _____

So, each piece will be _____ inches long.

Remember
You can use multiples, counters, or draw a quick picture to divide.

Try This!

Daniel made 32 ounces of soup for 5 people. How many ounces will each person get? Complete the division.

$5\overline{)32}$ _____

Each person gets _____ ounces.

Math Talk

Math Processes and Practices ⑦

Explain what the 2 in the answer represents.

Chapter 4   209

🔑 Other Ways

Ⓐ Use only the quotient.

Ben is a tour guide at a glass-blowing studio. He can take no more than 7 people at a time on a tour. If 80 people want to see the glass-blowing demonstration, how many groups of 7 people will Ben show around?

First, divide to find the quotient and remainder.
Then, decide how to use the quotient and remainder.

The quotient is _____.

$$\begin{array}{r} 11 \text{r} \\ 7\overline{)80} \end{array}$$

The remainder is _____.

Ben can give tours to 7 people at a time. The quotient is the number of tour groups of exactly 7 people he can show around.

So, Ben gives tours to _____ groups of 7 people.

Ⓑ Add 1 to the quotient.

If Ben gives tours to all 80 people, how many tours will he give? A tour can have no more than 7 people. To show all 80 people around, Ben will have to give 1 more tour.

So, Ben will give _____ tours in all for 80 people.

Ⓒ Use only the remainder.

Ben gives tours to all 80 people. After he completes the tours for groups of 7 people, how many people are in his last tour?

The remainder is 3.

So, Ben's last tour will have _____ people.

Math Talk

Math Processes and Practices ⑧

Use Repeated Reasoning Why would you not write the remainder as a fraction when you found the number of vans needed?

Try This!

Students are driven to soccer games in vans. Each van holds 9 students. How many vans are needed for 31 students?

Divide. $31 \div 9$ _____

Since there are _____ students left over, _____ vans are needed to carry 31 students.

Name _____

1. Olivia baked 53 mini-loaves of banana bread to be sliced for snacks at a craft fair. She will place an equal number of loaves in 6 different locations. How many loaves will be at each location?

   a. Divide to find the quotient and remainder.

   b. Decide how to use the quotient and remainder to answer the question.

   $$6\overline{)53}r$$

   _____

Interpret the remainder to solve.

☑ 2. What if Olivia wants to put only whole loaves at each location? How many loaves will be at each location?

   _____

☑ 3. Ed carves 22 small wooden animals to sell at the craft fair. He displays them in rows with 4 animals in a row. How many animals will not be in equal rows?

   _____

On Your Own

Interpret the remainder to solve.

4. Myra has a 17-foot roll of crepe paper to make 8 streamers to decorate for a party. How long will each streamer be if she cuts the roll into equal pieces?

   _____

5. **THINK SMARTER** Juan has a piano recital next month. Last week he practiced for 8 hours in the morning and 7 hours in the afternoon. Each practice session is 2 hours long. How many full practice sessions did Juan complete?

   _____

6. **GO DEEPER** A total of 25 students sign up to be hosts on Parent's Night. Teams of 3 students greet parents. How many students cannot be on a team? Explain.

   _____

   _____

   _____

Problem Solving • Applications

Use the picture for 7–9.

7. Teresa is making sock puppets just like the one in the picture. If she has 53 buttons, how many puppets can she make?

_____

8. 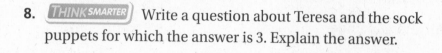 Write a question about Teresa and the sock puppets for which the answer is 3. Explain the answer.

_____

_____

_____

_____

9. 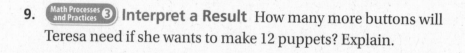 **Interpret a Result** How many more buttons will Teresa need if she wants to make 12 puppets? Explain.

_____

_____

_____

_____

WRITE Math
Show Your Work

10. 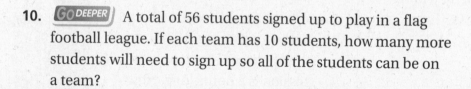 A total of 56 students signed up to play in a flag football league. If each team has 10 students, how many more students will need to sign up so all of the students can be on a team?

_____

Personal Math Trainer

11. _THINK SMARTER +_ A teacher plans for groups of her students to eat lunch at tables. She has 34 students in her class. Each group will have 7 students. How many tables will she need? Explain how to use the quotient and remainder to answer the question.

_____

_____

Interpret the Remainder

Interpret the remainder to solve.

1. Hakeem has 100 tomato plants. He wants to plant them in rows of 8. How many full rows will he have?

Think: $100 \div 8$ is 12 with a remainder of 4. The question asks "how many full rows," so use only the quotient.

_____ 12 full rows _____

2. A teacher has 27 students in her class. She asks the students to form as many groups of 4 as possible. How many students will not be in a group?

_____

3. A sporting goods company can ship 6 footballs in each carton. How many cartons are needed to ship 75 footballs?

_____

Problem Solving · Real World

4. Joanna has 70 beads. She uses 8 beads for each bracelet. She makes as many bracelets as possible. How many beads will Joanna have left over?

_____

5. A teacher wants to give 3 markers to each of her 25 students. Markers come in packages of 8. How many packages of markers will the teacher need?

_____

6. **WRITE** ▸ *Math* Write word problems that represent each way you can use a remainder in a division problem. Include solutions.

_____

_____

_____

Lesson Check

1. Marcus sorts his 85 baseball cards into stacks of 9 cards each. How many stacks of 9 cards can Marcus make?

2. A minivan can hold up to 7 people. How many minivans are needed to take 45 people to a basketball game?

Spiral Review

3. Mrs. Wilkerson cut some oranges into 20 equal pieces to be shared by 6 friends. How many pieces did each person get and how many pieces were left over?

4. A school bought 32 new desks. Each desk cost $24. Estimate how much the school spent on the new desks.

5. Kris has a box of 8 crayons. Sylvia's box has 6 times as many crayons as Kris's box. How many crayons are in Sylvia's box?

6. Yesterday, 1,743 people visited the fair. Today, there are 576 more people at the fair than yesterday. How many people are at the fair today?

FOR MORE PRACTICE
GO TO THE
Personal Math Trainer

Name _____

Divide Tens, Hundreds, and Thousands

Essential Question How can you divide numbers through thousands by whole numbers to 10?

Learning Objective You will use place value to divide tens, hundreds, and thousands.

Unlock the Problem

Dustin is packing apples in gift boxes. Each gift box holds 4 apples. How many boxes can Dustin pack with 120 apples?

You can divide using basic facts and place value.

Example 1 Divide. 120 ÷ 4

STEP 1 Identify the basic fact.   12 ÷ 4

_____

STEP 2 Use place value.   120 = _____ tens

_____

STEP 3 Divide.   12 tens ÷ 4 = _____ tens   ← **Think:** 4 × 3 tens = 12 tens

= _____

120 ÷ 4 = 30

So, Dustin can pack _____ boxes.

Example 2 Divide. 1,200 ÷ 4

STEP 1 Identify the basic fact.   12 ÷ 4

_____

STEP 2 Use place value.   1,200 = _____ hundreds

_____

STEP 3 Divide.   12 hundreds ÷ 4 = _____ hundreds   ← **Think:** 4 × 3 hundreds = 12 hundreds

= _____

1,200 ÷ 4 = 300

Math Talk

Math Processes and Practices ⑦

Look for a Pattern What pattern do you notice in the place value of the dividends and quotients?

• **Math Processes and Practices ⑥** **Explain** how to use a basic fact and place value to divide 4,000 ÷ 5.

_____

_____

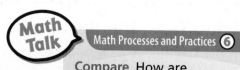
Math Talk

Math Processes and Practices 6

Compare How are Exercises 1 and 2 alike and how are they different?

1. Divide. 2,800 ÷ 7

What basic fact can you use? _____

2,800 = 28 _____

28 hundreds ÷ 7 = _____

2,800 ÷ 7 = _____

2. Divide. 280 ÷ 7

What basic fact can you use? _____

280 = 28 _____

28 tens ÷ _____ = 4 _____

280 ÷ 7 = _____

Use basic facts and place value to find the quotient.

3. 360 ÷ 6 = _____

4. 2,000 ÷ 5 = _____

5. 4,500 ÷ 9 = _____

On Your Own

Use basic facts and place value to find the quotient.

6. 560 ÷ 8 = _____

7. 6,400 ÷ 8 = _____

8. 3,500 ÷ 7 = _____

Math Processes and Practices 5 **Use Patterns** **Algebra** **Find the unknown number.**

9. 420 ÷ ■ = 60 _____

10. ■ ÷ 4 = 30 _____

11. 810 ÷ ■ = 90 _____

12. **THINK SMARTER** Divide 400 ÷ 40. Explain how patterns and place value can help.

_____

_____

13. **GO DEEPER** Eileen collected 98 empty cans to recycle, and Carl collected 82 cans. They packed an equal number of cans into each of three boxes to take to the recycling center. How many cans were in each box?

_____

14. **GO DEEPER** It costs a baker $18 to make a small cake. He sells 8 small cakes for $240. How much more is the selling price of each cake than the cost?

_____

Name _____

15. Jamal put 600 pennies into 6 equal rolls. How many pennies were in each roll?

_____

16. Sela has 6 times as many coins now as she had 4 months ago. If Sela has 240 coins now, how many coins did she have 4 months ago?

_____

17. **THINK SMARTER** Chip collected 2,090 dimes. Sue collected 1,910 dimes. They divided all their dimes into 8 equal stacks. How many dimes are in each stack?

_____

_____

18. **Math Processes and Practices 5** **Communicate** Mr. Roberts sees a rare 1937 penny. The cost of the penny is $210. If he saves $3 each week, will Mr. Roberts have enough money to buy the penny in one year? Explain.

WRITE *Math* **Show Your Work**

_____

_____

_____

19. **GO DEEPER** Mrs. Fletcher bought 5 coins for $32 each. Later, she sold all the coins for $300. How much more did Mrs. Fletcher receive for each coin than she paid? Explain.

_____

_____

_____

20. **THINK SMARTER** Which quotients are equal to 20? Mark all that apply.

Ⓐ 600 ÷ 2

Ⓓ 140 ÷ 7

Ⓑ 1,200 ÷ 6

Ⓔ 500 ÷ 5

Ⓒ 180 ÷ 9

Connect to Science

Insect Flight

True flight is shared only by insects, bats, and birds. Flight in insects varies from the clumsy flight of some beetles to the acrobatic moves of dragonflies.

The wings of insects are not moved by muscles attached to the wings. Muscles in the middle part of the body, or thorax, move the wings. The thorax changes shape as the wings move.

Insect Wing Beats in 3 Minutes

Insect	Approximate Number of Wing Beats
Aeschnid Dragonfly	6,900
Damselfly	2,700
Large White Butterfly	2,100
Scorpion Fly	5,000

21. About how many times does a damselfly's wings beat in 1 minute?

_____

22. About how many times do a scorpion fly's wings beat in 6 minutes?

_____

23. **THINK SMARTER** In one minute, about how many more times do a damselfly's wings beat than a large white butterfly's wings?

_____

24. **What's the Question?** The answer is about 2,300 times.

_____

_____

Divide Tens, Hundreds, and Thousands

Learning Objective You will use place value to divide tens, hundreds, and thousands.

Use basic facts and place value to find the quotient.

1. $3,600 \div 4 =$ _____900_____

   Think: 3,600 is 36 hundreds.

   Use the basic fact $36 \div 4 = 9$.

   So, 36 hundreds $\div 4 = 9$ hundreds, or 900.

2. $240 \div 6 =$ _____

3. $5,400 \div 9 =$ _____

4. $300 \div 5 =$ _____

5. $4,800 \div 6 =$ _____

6. $420 \div 7 =$ _____

7. $150 \div 3 =$ _____

8. $6,300 \div 7 =$ _____

9. $1,200 \div 4 =$ _____

10. $360 \div 6 =$ _____

Problem Solving

11. At an assembly, 180 students sit in 9 equal rows. How many students sit in each row?

    _____

12. Hilary can read 560 words in 7 minutes. How many words can Hilary read in 1 minute?

    _____

13. A company produces 7,200 gallons of bottled water each day. The company puts 8 one-gallon bottles in each carton. How many cartons are needed to hold all the one-gallon bottles produced in one day?

    _____

14. An airplane flew 2,400 miles in 4 hours. If the plane flew the same number of miles each hour, how many miles did it fly in 1 hour?

    _____

15. **WRITE** ▸*Math* Explain how your knowledge of place value helps you divide a number in the thousands by whole numbers to 10. Give an example to support your explanation.

    _____

    _____

Lesson Check

1. A baseball player hits a ball 360 feet to the outfield. It takes the ball 4 seconds to travel this distance. How many feet does the ball travel in 1 second?

_____

2. Sebastian rides his bike 2,000 meters in 5 minutes. How many meters does he bike in 1 minute?

_____

Spiral Review

3. A full container of juice holds 64 fluid ounces. How many 7-fluid ounce servings of juice are in a full container?

_____

_____

4. Paolo pays $244 for 5 identical calculators. About how much does Paolo pay for one calculator?

_____

_____

5. A football team paid $28 per jersey. They bought 16 jerseys. How much money did the team spend on jerseys?

_____

6. Suzanne bought 50 apples at the apple orchard. She bought 4 times as many red apples as green apples. How many more red apples than green apples did Suzanne buy?

_____

FOR MORE PRACTICE
GO TO THE
Personal Math Trainer

Name _____

Estimate Quotients Using Compatible Numbers

Essential Question How can you use compatible numbers to estimate quotients?

Learning Objective You will use compatible numbers to estimate quotients.

 Unlock the Problem

A horse's heart beats 132 times in 3 minutes. About how many times does it beat in 1 minute?

You can use compatible numbers to estimate quotients.

Compatible numbers are numbers that are easy to compute mentally.

- Will a horse's heart beat more or fewer than 132 times in 1 minute?

  _____

- What operation will you use to solve the problem?

  _____

Example 1 Estimate. 132 ÷ 3

STEP 1 Find a number close to 132 that divides easily by 3. Use basic facts.

12 ÷ 3 is a basic fact. 120 divides easily by 3.

15 ÷ 3 is a basic fact. 150 divides easily by 3.

Think: Choose 120 because it is closer to 132.

STEP 2 Use place value.

120 = _____ tens

12 ÷ 3 = _____

12 tens ÷ 3 = _____ tens

120 ÷ 3 = _____

So, a horse's heart beats about _____ times a minute.

Example 2 Use compatible numbers to find two estimates that the quotient is between. 1,382 ÷ 5

STEP 1 Find two numbers close to 1,382 that divide easily by 5.

_____ ÷ 5 is a basic fact. 1,000 divides easily by 5.

_____ ÷ 5 is a basic fact. 1,500 divides easily by 5.

1,382 is between _____ and _____.

So, 1,382 ÷ 5 is between _____ and _____.

STEP 2 Divide each number by 5. Use place value.

1,000 ÷ 5

_____ hundreds ÷ 5 = _____ hundreds, or _____

1,500 ÷ 5

_____ hundreds ÷ 5 = _____ hundreds, or _____

 Math Talk

Math Processes and Practices 6

Explain which estimate you think is more reasonable.

Share and Show

1. Estimate. 1,718 ÷ 4   **Think:** What number close to 1,718 is easy to divide by 4?

_____ is close to 1,718.   What basic fact can you use? _____ ÷ 4

_____ is close to 1,718.   What basic fact can you use? _____ ÷ 4

Choose 1,600 because _____.

16 ÷ 4 = _____

1,600 ÷ _____ = _____

1,718 ÷ 4 is about _____

Math Talk Math Processes and Practices ③

Apply How might your estimate change if the problem were 1,918 ÷ 4?

Use compatible numbers to estimate the quotient.

2. 455 ÷ 9

_____

3. 1,509 ÷ 3

_____

✅ 4. 176 ÷ 8

_____

✅ 5. 2,795 ÷ 7

_____

On Your Own

Use compatible numbers to find two estimates that the quotient is between.

6. 5,321 ÷ 6

_____

7. 1,765 ÷ 6

_____

8. 1,189 ÷ 3

_____

9. 2,110 ÷ 4

_____

Math Processes and Practices ② **Reason Abstractly** **Algebra** Estimate to compare. Write <, >, or =.

10. 613 ÷ 3 ◯ 581 ÷ 2

_____   _____
estimate   estimate

11. 364 ÷ 4 ◯ 117 ÷ 6

_____   _____
estimate   estimate

12. 2,718 ÷ 8 ◯ 963 ÷ 2

_____   _____
estimate   estimate

13. **GO DEEPER** If Cade shoots 275 free throw baskets in 2 hours, about how many can he shoot in 5 hours?

_____

_____

14. **GO DEEPER** A carpenter has 166 doorknobs in his workshop. Of those doorknobs, 98 are round and the rest are square. If he wants to place 7 square doorknobs in each bin, about how many bins would he need?

_____

Problem Solving • Applications

Use the table for 15–17.

Animal Heartbeats in 5 Minutes	
Animal	**Number of Heartbeats**
Whale	31
Cow	325
Pig	430
Dog	520
Chicken	1,375

15. About how many times does a chicken's heart beat in 1 minute?

_____

16. **GO DEEPER** About how many times does a cow's heart beat in 2 minutes?

_____

17. **Math Processes and Practices ②** **Use Reasoning** About how many times faster does a cow's heart beat than a whale's?

_____

WRITE ▸Math ・ **Show Your Work**

18. **THINK SMARTER** Martha had 154 stamps and her sister had 248 stamps. They combined their collections and put the stamps in an album. If they want to put 8 stamps on each page, about how many pages would they need?

_____

19. Jamie and his two brothers divided a package of 125 toy cars equally. About how many cars did each of them receive?

_____

20. **THINK SMARTER** Harold and his brother collected 2,019 cans over a 1-year period. Each boy collected the same number of cans. About how many cans did each boy collect? Explain how you found your answer.

_____

_____

_____

Cause and Effect

The reading skill *cause and effect* can help you understand how one detail in a problem is related to another detail.

Chet wants to buy a new bike that costs $276. Chet mows his neighbor's lawn for $15 each week. Since Chet does not have money saved, he needs to decide which layaway plan he can afford to buy the new bike.

Bike Shop Layaway Plans	
Plan A	3 months (3 equal payments)
Plan B	6 months (6 equal payments)

Cause:	**Effect:**
Chet does not have money saved to purchase the bike.	Chet will have to decide which layaway plan he can afford to purchase the bike.

→

Which plan should Chet choose?

3-month layaway:

$276 ÷ 3

Estimate.

$270 ÷ 3 _____

6-month layaway:

$276 ÷ 6

Estimate.

$300 ÷ 6 _____

Chet earns $15 each week. Since there are usually 4 weeks in a month, multiply to see which payment he can afford.

$15 × 4 = _____

So, Chet can afford the _____ layaway plan.

Use estimation to solve.

21. Sofia wants to buy a new bike that costs $214. Sofia helps her grandmother with chores each week for $18. Estimate to find which layaway plan Sofia should choose and why.

_____

_____

_____

22. **WRITE** *Math* Describe a situation when you have used cause and effect to help you solve a math problem.

_____

_____

_____

_____

Name _____

Estimate Quotients Using Compatible Numbers

Learning Objective You will use compatible numbers to estimate quotients.

Use compatible numbers to estimate the quotient.

1. $389 \div 4$

$\underline{400 \div 4 = 100}$

2. $358 \div 3$

3. $784 \div 8$

4. $179 \div 9$

5. $315 \div 8$

6. $2{,}116 \div 7$

7. $4{,}156 \div 7$

8. $474 \div 9$

Use compatible numbers to find two estimates that the quotient is between.

9. $1{,}624 \div 3$

10. $2{,}593 \div 6$

11. $1{,}045 \div 2$

12. $1{,}754 \div 9$

Problem Solving · Real World

13. A CD store sold 3,467 CDs in 7 days. About the same number of CDs were sold each day. About how many CDs did the store sell each day?

14. Marcus has 731 books. He puts about the same number of books on each of 9 shelves in his bookcase. About how many books are on each shelf?

15. WRITE *Math* How can you estimate $1{,}506 \div 2$ so that it is close to the actual answer of 753?

Lesson Check

1. Jamal is planting seeds for a garden nursery. He plants 9 seeds in each container. If Jamal has 296 seeds to plant, about how many containers will he use?

2. Winona purchased a set of vintage beads. There are 2,140 beads in the set. If she uses the beads to make bracelets that have 7 beads each, about how many bracelets can she make?

Spiral Review

3. A train traveled 360 miles in 6 hours. How many miles per hour did the train travel?

4. An orchard has 12 rows of pear trees. Each row has 15 pear trees. How many pear trees are there in the orchard?

5. Megan rounded 366,458 to 370,000. To which place did Megan round the number?

6. Mr. Jessup, an airline pilot, flies 1,350 miles a day. How many miles will he fly in 8 days?

© Houghton Mifflin Harcourt Publishing Company

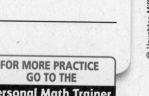

FOR MORE PRACTICE
GO TO THE
Personal Math Trainer

Name _____

Division and the Distributive Property

Essential Question How can you use the Distributive Property to find quotients?

Learning Objective You will use a model and the Distributive Property to find whole number quotients with up to 3-digit dividends and 1-digit divisors.

Investigate

Materials ■ color pencils ■ grid paper

You can use a model and the Distributive Property to break apart numbers to make them easier to divide.

To use the Distributive Property with division, find the quotient each smaller rectangle represents. Then find the sum of the quotients.

A. Outline a rectangle on a grid to model $69 \div 3$.

Shade columns of 3 until you have 69 squares.

How many groups of 3 can you make? _____

B. Think of 69 as $60 + 9$. Break apart the model into two rectangles to show $(60 + 9) \div 3$. Label and shade the smaller rectangles. Use two different colors.

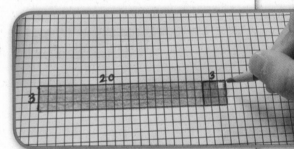

C. Each rectangle models a division.

$69 \div 3 = ($ _____ $\div 3) + ($ _____ $\div 3)$

$\qquad = $ _____ $+$ _____

$\qquad = $ _____

D. Outline another model to show $68 \div 4$.

How many groups of 4 can you make? _____

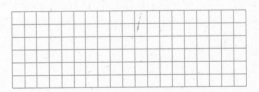

E. Think of 68 as $40 + 28$. Break apart the model, label, and shade to show two divisions.

$68 \div 4 = ($ _____ $\div 4) + ($ _____ $\div 4)$

$\qquad = $ _____ $+$ _____

$\qquad = $ _____

Draw Conclusions

1. Explain how each small rectangle models a quotient and a product in Step C.

_____

_____

_____

2. Compare your answer in Step A to the final quotient in Step C. What can you conclude?

_____

_____

3. **THINK SMARTER** To find the quotient 91 ÷ 7, would you break up the dividend into 90 + 1 or 70 + 21? Explain.

_____

_____

Make Connections

Math Talk

Math Processes and Practices ⑦

Look for Structure
Describe another way you could use the Distributive Property to solve 68 ÷ 4.

You can also model 68 ÷ 4 using base-ten blocks.

STEP 1 Model 68.

68 = _____ + _____

STEP 2 Share the tens equally among 4 groups with 2 tens left. Regroup 2 tens as 20 ones. Share them equally among the 4 groups.

60 ÷ 4 = _____

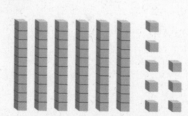

STEP 3 Share the 8 ones equally among the 4 equal groups.

8 ÷ 4 = _____

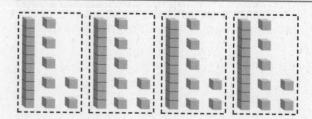

So, 68 ÷ 4 = (60 ÷ 4) + (8 ÷ 4) = _____ + _____ = _____

228

Name _____

Model the division on the grid.

☑ **1.** $26 \div 2 = ($ _____ $\div 2) + ($ _____ $\div 2)$

   $=$ _____ $+$ _____

   $=$ _____

2. $45 \div 3 = ($ _____ $\div 3) + ($ _____ $\div 3)$

   $=$ _____ $+$ _____

   $=$ _____

Find the quotient.

☑ **3.** $86 \div 2$

   $= ($ _____ $\div 2) + ($ _____ $\div 2)$

   $=$ _____ $+$ _____

   $=$ _____

4. $208 \div 4$

   $= ($ _____ $\div 4) + ($ _____ $\div 4)$

   $=$ _____ $+$ _____

   $=$ _____

Use base-ten blocks to model the quotient.
Then record the quotient.

5. $88 \div 4 =$ _____

6. $36 \div 3 =$ _____

7. $186 \div 6 =$ _____

Problem Solving • Applications Real World

8. WRITE ▸Math Explain how you can model finding quotients using the Distributive Property.

_____
_____
_____
_____
_____

9. GO DEEPER Justin earned $50 mowing lawns and $34 washing cars. He wants to divide his money into 3 equal accounts. How much will he put in each account? Explain.

_____
_____
_____
_____
_____

Pose a Problem

10. **THINK SMARTER** Christelle went to a gift shop. The shop sells candles in a variety of sizes and colors. The picture shows a display of candles.

Write a problem that can be solved using the picture.

Pose a problem.

Solve your problem.

- **Math Processes and Practices ❶** **Describe** how you could change the problem by changing the number of rows of candles. Then solve the problem.

_____

_____

_____

_____

11. **THINK SMARTER** For 11a–11d, choose Yes or No to indicate if the expression shows a way to break apart the dividend to find the quotient $147 \div 7$.

11a. $(135 \div 7) + (10 \div 7)$ ○ Yes   ○ No

11b. $(147 \div 3) + (147 \div 4)$ ○ Yes   ○ No

11c. $(140 \div 7) + (7 \div 7)$ ○ Yes   ○ No

11d. $(70 \div 7) + (77 \div 7)$ ○ Yes   ○ No

Name _____

Division and the Distributive Property

Learning Objective You will use a model and the Distributive Property to find whole number quotients with up to 3-digit dividends and 1-digit divisors.

Find the quotient.

1. $54 \div 3 = ($ __30__ $\div 3) + ($ __24__ $\div 3)$

    $= $ __10__ $+$ __8__

    $= $ __18__

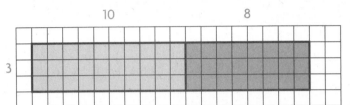

2. $81 \div 3 = $ _____

3. $232 \div 4 = $ _____

4. $305 \div 5 = $ _____

5. $246 \div 6 = $ _____

6. $69 \div 3 = $ _____

7. $477 \div 9 = $ _____

Problem Solving

8. Cecily picked 219 apples. She divided the apples equally into 3 baskets. How many apples are in each basket?

    _____

9. Jordan has 260 basketball cards. He divides them into 4 equal groups. How many cards are in each group?

    _____

10. The Wilsons drove 324 miles in 6 hours. If they drove the same number of miles each hour, how many miles did they drive in 1 hour?

    _____

11. Phil has 189 stamps to put into his stamp album. He puts the same number of stamps on each of 9 pages. How many stamps does Phil put on each page?

    _____

12. **WRITE** ▸*Math* Explain how to use the Distributive Property to solve $48 \div 3$. Include a model to support your explanation.

    _____

    _____

Lesson Check

1. A landscaping company planted 176 trees in 8 equal rows in the new park. How many trees did the company plant in each row?

2. Arnold can do 65 push-ups in 5 minutes. How many push-ups can he do in 1 minute?

Spiral Review

3. Last Saturday, there were 1,486 people at the Cineplex. There were about the same number of people in each of the 6 theaters. Between which two numbers does the number of people in each theater fall?

4. Nancy walked 50 minutes each day for 4 days last week. Gillian walked 35 minutes each day for 6 days last week. How does the total number of minutes that Gillian walked compare to the total number of minutes that Nancy walked?

5. Three boys share 28 toy cars equally. How many cars did each boy get and how many were left over?

6. An airplane flies at a speed of 474 miles per hour. How many miles does the plane fly in 5 hours?

© Houghton Mifflin Harcourt Publishing Company

FOR MORE PRACTICE
GO TO THE
Personal Math Trainer

Name _____

✓ Mid-Chapter Checkpoint

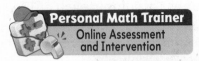 **Personal Math Trainer**
Online Assessment
and Intervention

Vocabulary

Choose the best term from the box to complete the sentence.

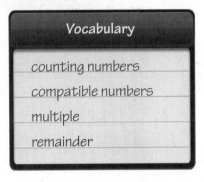

Vocabulary
counting numbers
compatible numbers
multiple
remainder

1. A number that is the product of a number and a counting

   number is called a _____ . (p. 197)

2. Numbers that are easy to compute mentally are called

   _____ . (p. 221)

3. When a number cannot be divided evenly, the amount

   left over is called the _____ . (p. 204)

Concepts and Skills

Divide. Draw a quick picture to help.

4. 26 ÷ 3 _____   5. 19 ÷ 4 _____

Use basic facts and place value to find the quotient.

6. 810 ÷ 9 = _____   7. 210 ÷ 7 = _____   8. 3,000 ÷ 6 = _____

Use compatible numbers to estimate the quotient.

9. 635 ÷ 9   10. 412 ÷ 5   11. 490 ÷ 8

   _____   _____   _____

Use grid paper or base-ten blocks to model the quotient. Then record the quotient.

12. 63 ÷ 3 = _____   13. 85 ÷ 5 = _____   14. 168 ÷ 8 = _____

© Houghton Mifflin Harcourt Publishing Company

15. Ana has 296 coins in her coin collection. She put the same number of coins in each of 7 jars. About how many coins are in each jar?

_____

16. Which two estimates is the quotient 345 ÷ 8 between?

_____

17. **Go DEEPER** A total of 8,644 people went to the football game. Of those people, 5,100 sat on the home side and the rest sat on the visitor's side. If the people sitting on the visitor's side filled 8 equal-sized sections, about how many people sat in each of the sections?

_____

18. There are 4 students on a team for a relay race. How many teams can be made from 27 students?

_____

19. Eight teams of high school students helped clean up trash in the community. Afterwards, they shared 23 pizzas equally. How many pizzas did each team get?

_____

Name _____

Divide Using Repeated Subtraction

Essential Question How can you use repeated subtraction and multiples to find quotients?

Learning Objective You will use repeated subtraction and multiples to find quotients.

Investigate

Materials ■ counters ■ grid paper

John is building a backyard pizza oven with an arch opening. He has 72 bricks. He will place 6 bricks at a time as he builds the oven. If he arranges the bricks in piles of 6, how many piles will he have?

You can use repeated subtraction to divide $72 \div 6$.

A. Begin with 72 counters. Subtract 6 counters.

How many are left? _____

B. Record the subtraction on grid paper as shown. Record the number of counters left and the number of times you subtracted.

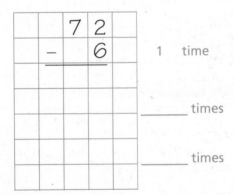

    1   time

_____ times

_____ times

C. Can you reach zero evenly? Explain.

_____

_____

D. Count the number of times you subtracted 6 counters. _____

So, there are _____ piles of 6 bricks.

1. Explain the relationship between the divisor, the dividend, the quotient, and the number of times you subtracted the divisor from the dividend.

_____

_____

2. What happens if you subtract multiples of 6? Complete the example at the right.

$$6\overline{)72}$$
$$-60 \leftarrow \boxed{} \times 6 \quad 10$$
$$\boxed{}$$
$$-12 \leftarrow \boxed{} \times 6 + \boxed{}$$
$$\boxed{}$$

   • What multiples of 6 did you use? How did you use them?

   _____

   _____

   • What numbers did you add? Why?

   _____

   _____

   • How did using multiples of the divisor help you?

   _____

   _____

3. **THINK SMARTER** Why should you subtract 10×6 and not 9×6 or 20×6?

   _____

   _____

   _____

Math Talk

Math Processes and Practices ④

Use Models How does subtracting counters and counting back on a number line help you divide?

Make Connections

Another way to divide by repeated subtraction is to use a number line. Count back by 4s from 52 to find $52 \div 4$.

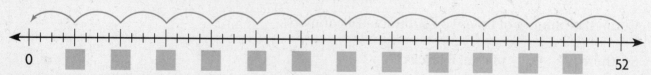

How many equal groups of 4 did you subtract? _____

So, $52 \div 4 =$ _____.

Name _____

Use repeated subtraction to divide.

1. 84 ÷ 7 _____

2. 60 ÷ 4 _____

3. 91 ÷ 8 _____

Draw a number line to divide.

4. 65 ÷ 5 = _____

Problem Solving • Applications Real World

5. Math Processes and Practices ⑤ **Use Appropriate Tools** Can you divide 32 by 3 evenly? Use the number line to explain your answer.

0   32

_____

_____

_____

6. GO DEEPER John has $40 to spend at the yard sale. He buys 6 books for $2 each. He would like to spend the rest of his money on model cars for his collection. If the cars cost $7 each, how many can he buy? Explain.

_____

_____

_____

Unlock the Problem

7. **THINK SMARTER** A new playground will be 108 feet long. Builders need to allow 9 feet of space for each piece of climbing equipment. They want to put as many climbers along the length of the playground as possible. How many climbers can they place?

a. What are you asked to find?

_____

b. How can you use repeated subtraction to solve the problem?

_____

_____

c. Tell why you might use multiples of the divisor to solve the problem.

_____

_____

d. Show steps to solve the problem.

e. Complete the sentences.

There are _____ equal parts of the

playground, each _____ feet long.

So, _____ climbers can fit along the length of the playground.

8. **THINK SMARTER** Which model matches each expression? Write the letter on the line next to the model.

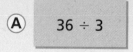

(A) 36 ÷ 3

0   36

_____

(B) 36 ÷ 2

0   36

_____

Name _____

Divide Using Repeated Subtraction

Learning Objective You will use repeated subtraction and multiples to find quotients.

Use repeated subtraction to divide.

1. $42 \div 3 =$ ___14___

2. $72 \div 4 =$ _____

3. $93 \div 3 =$ _____

$$
\begin{array}{r}
3)\overline{42} \\
-30 \quad \leftarrow 10 \times 3 \quad 10 \\
\hline
12 \\
-12 \quad \leftarrow 4 \times 3 \quad +4 \\
\hline
0 \qquad\qquad 14
\end{array}
$$

4. $35 \div 4$ _____

5. $93 \div 10$ _____

6. $86 \div 9$ _____

Draw a number line to divide.

7. $70 \div 5 =$ _____

Problem Solving Real World

8. Gretchen has 48 small shells. She uses 2 shells to make one pair of earrings. How many pairs of earrings can she make?

9. **WRITE** *Math* Show how you can use repeated subtraction to find $84 \div 6$.

Lesson Check

1. Randall collects postcards that his friends send him when they travel. He can put 6 cards on one scrapbook page. How many pages does Randall need to fit 42 postcards?

_____

2. Ari stocks shelves at a grocery store. He puts 35 cans of juice in each display case. The case has 4 shelves with an equal number of cans, and one shelf with only 3 cans. How many cans are on each of the equal shelves?

_____

Spiral Review

3. Fiona sorted her CDs into separate bins. She placed 4 CDs in each bin. If she has 160 CDs, how many bins did she fill?

_____

4. Eamon is arranging 39 books on 3 shelves. If he puts the same number of books on each shelf, how many books will there be on each shelf?

_____

5. A newborn boa constrictor measures 18 inches long. An adult boa constrictor measures 9 times the length of the newborn plus 2 inches. How long is the adult?

_____

6. Madison has 6 rolls of coins. Each roll has 20 coins. How many coins does Madison have?

_____

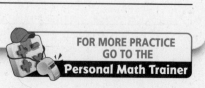

FOR MORE PRACTICE
GO TO THE
Personal Math Trainer

Name _____

Divide Using Partial Quotients

Essential Question How can you use partial quotients to divide by 1-digit divisors?

Learning Objective You will use partial quotients to divide by 1-digit divisors.

⚷ Unlock the Problem

At camp, there are 5 players on each lacrosse team. If there are 125 people on lacrosse teams, how many teams are there?

- Underline what you are asked to find.
- Circle what you need to use.
- What operation can you use to find the number of teams?

_____

🔒 One Way Use partial quotients.

In the **partial quotient** method of dividing, multiples of the divisor are subtracted from the dividend and then the partial quotients are added together.

Divide. $125 \div 5$ **Write.** $5\overline{)125}$

STEP 1

Start by subtracting a greater multiple, such as 10 times the divisor. For example, you know that you can make at least 10 teams of 5 players.

Continue subtracting until the remaining number is less than the multiple, 50.

STEP 2

Subtract smaller multiples, such as 5, 2, or 1 times the divisor until the remaining number is less than the divisor. In other words, keep subtracting multiples until you no longer have enough players to make a team.

Then add the partial quotients to find the quotient.

So, there are _____ lacrosse teams.

Partial Quotients

$$5\overline{)125} \quad \downarrow$$

$-\;\rule{1.5em}{0.1em}\quad 10 \times \rule{1.5em}{0.1em} \qquad 10$

$-\;\rule{1.5em}{0.1em}\quad 10 \times \rule{1.5em}{0.1em} \qquad 10$

$-\;\rule{1.5em}{0.1em}\quad 5 \times \rule{1.5em}{0.1em} \qquad + 5$

Math Talk

Math Processes and Practices ⑧

Use Repeated Reasoning How did you use partial quotients to solve the problem?

🔒 Another Way Use rectangular models to record the partial quotients.

Jarod and Ana also found the number of teams using partial quotients. They recorded the partial quotients using rectangular models. They each still had 25 as the quotient.

Jarod

5 | 125 |

10
5 | 50 | 75 | $\begin{array}{r} 125 \\ - \boxed{} \\ \hline 75 \end{array}$

10   10
5 | 50 | 50 | 25 | $\begin{array}{r} 75 \\ - \boxed{} \\ \hline 25 \end{array}$

10   10   5
5 | 50 | 50 | 25 | $\begin{array}{r} 25 \\ - \boxed{} \\ \hline 0 \end{array}$

10 + 10 + 5 = _____

Ana

5 | 125 |

20
5 | 100 | 25 | $\begin{array}{r} 125 \\ - \boxed{} \\ \hline 25 \end{array}$

20   5
5 | 100 | 25 | $\begin{array}{r} 25 \\ - \boxed{} \\ \hline 0 \end{array}$

20 + 5 = _____

Math Talk

Math Processes and Practices ②

Reason Abstractly Why might you prefer to use one method rather than the other?

Share and Show 🖊 MATH BOARD

1. Lacrosse is played on a field 330 ft long. How many yards long is a lacrosse field? (3 feet = 1 yard)

Divide. Use partial quotients.

$3\overline{)330}$

$- \boxed{}$ $100 \times \boxed{}$ 100

$\boxed{}$

$\boxed{}$ $10 \times \boxed{}$ $+ 10$

$\boxed{}$

So, the lacrosse field is _____ yards long.

Name _____

Divide. Use partial quotients.

2. 3)225

Divide. Use rectangular models to record the partial quotients.

3. 428 ÷ 4 = _____

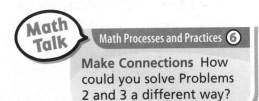

Math Talk Math Processes and Practices ⑥

Make Connections How could you solve Problems 2 and 3 a different way?

On Your Own

Divide. Use partial quotients.

4. 7)224

5. 7)259

6. 8)864

7. 6)738

Divide. Use rectangular models to record the partial quotients.

8. 328 ÷ 2 = _____

9. 475 ÷ 5 = _____

10. 219 ÷ 3 = _____

11. 488 ÷ 4 = _____

12. Math Processes and Practices ② **Use Reasoning** What is the least number you can divide by 5 to get a three-digit quotient? Explain how you found your answer.

_____

_____

_____

Problem Solving • Applications

Use the table for 13–15.

13. Rob wants to put 8 baseball cards on each page in an album. How many pages will he fill?

_____

14. **GO DEEPER** Rob filled 5 plastic boxes with hockey cards. There were the same number of cards in each box. How many cards did he put in each box? How many cards were left over?

_____

15. **THINK SMARTER** Rob filled 3 fewer plastic boxes with football cards than basketball cards. He filled 9 boxes with basketball cards. How many boxes did he fill with football cards? How many football cards were in each box?

_____

16. **GO DEEPER** Marshall can buy 5 T-shirts for $60. If each shirt costs the same amount, what is the cost of 4 T-shirts?

_____

17. **THINK SMARTER** Use partial quotients. Fill in the blanks.

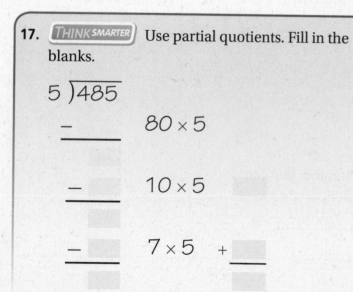

$5 \overline{)485}$

$- \quad 80 \times 5$

$- \quad 10 \times 5$

$- \quad 7 \times 5 \quad + $

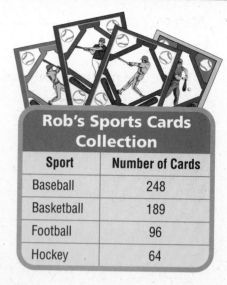

Rob's Sports Cards Collection

Sport	Number of Cards
Baseball	248
Basketball	189
Football	96
Hockey	64

Math on the Spot

WRITE *Math* • **Show Your Work**

Name _____

Divide Using Partial Quotients

Learning Objective You will use partial quotients to divide by 1-digit divisors.

Divide. Use partial quotients.

1. 8)184
    −80 10 × 8 10
    104
    −80 10 × 8 10
    24
    −24 3 × 8 +3
    0   23

2. 6)258

3. 5)630

Divide. Use rectangular models to record the partial quotients.

4. 246 ÷ 3 = _____

5. 126 ÷ 2 = _____

6. 605 ÷ 5 = _____

Divide. Use either way to record the partial quotients.

7. 492 ÷ 3 = _____

8. 198 ÷ 9 = _____

9. 692 ÷ 4 = _____

Problem Solving · Real World

10. Allison took 112 photos on vacation. She wants to put them in a photo album that holds 4 photos on each page. How many pages can she fill?

    _____

11. **WRITE** ▸ *Math* Explain how to use partial quotients to divide 235 by 5.

    _____

    _____

© Houghton Mifflin Harcourt Publishing Company

Lesson Check

1. Annaka used partial quotients to divide 145 ÷ 5. What could be the partial quotients Annaka used?

_____

_____

2. Mel used partial quotients to find the quotient of 378 ÷ 3. What could be the partial quotients that Mel found?

_____

_____

Spiral Review

3. What are the partial products of 42 × 5?

_____

4. Mr. Watson buys 4 gallons of paint that cost $34 per gallon. How much does Mr. Watson spend on paint?

_____

5. Use the area model to find the product of 28 × 32.

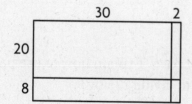

_____

6. An adult male lion eats about 108 pounds of meat per week. About how much meat does an adult male lion eat in one day?

_____

FOR MORE PRACTICE
GO TO THE
Personal Math Trainer

Name _____

Model Division with Regrouping

Essential Question How can you use base-ten blocks to model division with regrouping?

Learning Objective You will use base-ten blocks and draw quick pictures to model division with regrouping.

Investigate

Materials ■ base-ten blocks

The librarian wants to share 54 books equally among 3 classes. How many books will she give to each class?

A. Draw 3 circles to represent the classes. Then use base-ten blocks to model 54. Show 54 as 5 tens 4 ones.

B. Share the tens equally among the 3 groups.

C. If there are any tens left, regroup them as ones. Share the ones equally among the 3 groups.

D. There are _____ ten(s) and _____ one(s) in each group.

So, the librarian will give _____ books to each class.

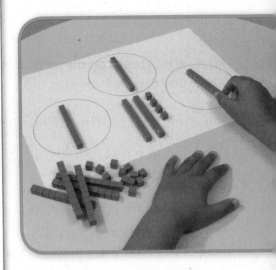

Draw Conclusions

1. **THINK SMARTER** Explain why you needed to regroup in Step C.

_____

_____

2. How you can use base-ten blocks to find the quotient of 92 ÷ 4?

_____

_____

_____

_____

Make Connections

Use the quick picture at the bottom of the page to help you divide.
Record each step.

Find 76 ÷ 3.

STEP 1
Model 76 as 7 tens 6 ones.
Draw three circles to represent equal groups.

$$3\overline{)76}$$

STEP 2
Share the 7 tens equally among the 3 groups.
Cross out the tens you use.

There are _____ tens in each group.

_____ tens were used. There is _____ ten left over.

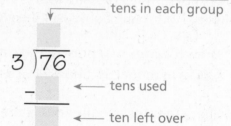

tens in each group

tens used

ten left over

STEP 3
One ten cannot be shared among 3 groups
without regrouping.
Regroup 1 ten by drawing 10 ones.

There are now _____ ones to share.

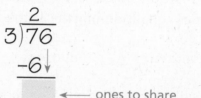

ones to share

STEP 4
Share the ones equally among the 3 groups.
Cross out the ones you use.

There are _____ ones in each group.

_____ ones were used. There is _____ one left over.

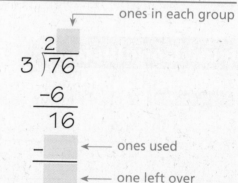

ones in each group

ones used

one left over

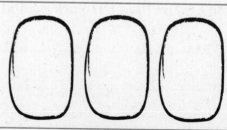

There are 3 groups of _____ and _____ left over.

So, for 76 ÷ 3, the quotient is _____ and the remainder is _____.

This can be written as _____.

Math Talk

Math Processes and Practices ④

Interpret a Result Why
do you share tens equally
among groups before
sharing ones?

Name _____

Share and Show MATH BOARD

Divide. Use base-ten blocks.

1. 48 ÷ 3 _____

2. 84 ÷ 4 _____

3. 72 ÷ 5 _____

4. Divide. Draw a quick picture. Record the steps.

84 ÷ 3 _____

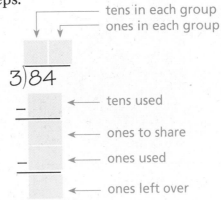

tens in each group
ones in each group

$3\overline{)84}$

tens used

ones to share

ones used

ones left over

Problem Solving • Applications Real World

5. WRITE ▸Math Explain why you did not need to regroup in Exercise 2.

_____

6. GO DEEPER Mindy is preparing fruit boxes for gifts. She divides 36 apples evenly into 6 boxes. Then she divided 54 bananas evenly into the same 6 boxes. How many pieces of fruit are in each of Mindy's boxes?

_____

7. THINK SMARTER Ami needs to divide these base-ten blocks among 4 equal groups.

Describe a model that would show how many are in each group.

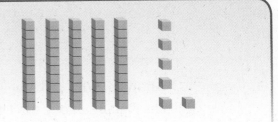

_____

Sense or Nonsense?

8. **THINK SMARTER** Angela and Zach drew quick pictures to find 68 ÷ 4. Whose quick picture makes sense? Whose quick picture is nonsense? Explain your reasoning.

I drew 1 ten and 2 ones in each group.

I drew 1 ten and 7 ones in each group.

Angela's Quick Picture

_____

_____

_____

_____

Zach's Quick Picture

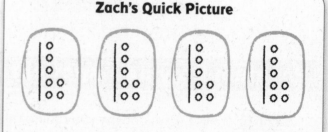

_____

_____

_____

_____

9. **Math Processes and Practices 1 Analyze** What did Angela forget to do after she shared the tens equally among the 4 groups?

_____

_____

Name _____

Model Division with Regrouping

Learning Objective You will use base-ten blocks and draw quick pictures to model division with regrouping.

Divide. Use base-ten blocks.

1. $63 \div 4$ ___15 r3___

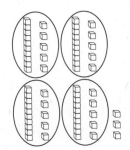

2. $83 \div 3$ _____

Divide. Draw quick pictures. Record the steps.

3. $85 \div 5$ _____

4. $97 \div 4$ _____

Problem Solving Real World

5. Tamara sold 92 cold drinks during her 2-hour shift at a festival food stand. If she sold the same number of drinks each hour, how many cold drinks did she sell each hour?

6. **WRITE** ▸ *Math* Write a division problem that has a 2-digit dividend and a 1-digit divisor. Show how to solve it by drawing a quick picture.

_____   _____

Lesson Check

1. Gail bought 80 buttons to put on the shirts she makes. She uses 5 buttons for each shirt. How many shirts can Gail make with the buttons she bought?

_____

2. Marty counted how many breaths he took in 3 minutes. In that time, he took 51 breaths. He took the same number of breaths each minute. How many breaths did Marty take in one minute?

_____

Spiral Review

3. Kate is solving brain teasers. She solved 6 brain teasers in 72 minutes. How long did she spend on each brain teaser?

_____

4. Jenny works at a package delivery store. She puts mailing stickers on packages. Each package needs 5 stickers. How many stickers will Jenny use if she is mailing 105 packages?

_____

5. The Puzzle Company packs standard-sized puzzles into boxes that hold 8 puzzles. How many boxes would it take to pack up 192 standard-sized puzzles?

_____

6. Mt. Whitney in California is 14,494 feet tall. Denali in Alaska is 5,826 feet taller than Mt. Whitney. How tall is Denali?

_____

FOR MORE PRACTICE
GO TO THE
Personal Math Trainer

Name _____

Place the First Digit

Essential Question How can you use place value to know where to place the first digit in the quotient?

Learning Objective You will use place value to determine where to place the first digit in the quotient.

Unlock the Problem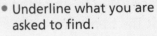

Victor took 144 photos on a digital camera.
The photos are to be placed equally in 6 photo albums.
How many photos will be in each album?

* Underline what you are asked to find.
* Circle what you need to use.

Example 1 Divide. 144 ÷ 6

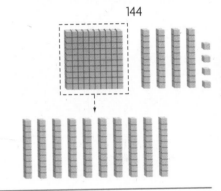

144

STEP 1 Use place value to place the first digit.
Look at the hundreds in 144.
1 hundred cannot be shared among 6 groups
without regrouping.
Regroup 1 hundred as 10 tens.

Now there are _____ tens to share among 6 groups.

The first digit of the quotient will be in the _____ place.

STEP 2 Divide the tens.

$$6\overline{)144}$$ with 2 above

Divide. 14 tens ÷ 6

Multiply. 6 × 2 tens

Subtract. 14 tens − 12 tens
Check. 2 tens cannot be shared among
6 groups without regrouping.

STEP 3 Divide the ones.
Regroup 2 tens as 20 ones.

Now there are _____ ones to share among 6 groups.

$$6\overline{)144} \quad 24$$
$$-12\downarrow$$
$$\quad 24$$

Divide. _____ ones ÷ _____

Multiply. _____ × _____ ones

Subtract. _____ ones − _____ ones
Check. 0 ones cannot be shared among 6 groups.

Math Idea
After you divide each place, the remainder should be less than the divisor.

Math Talk Math Processes and Practices ③

Apply How would the answer change if Victor had 146 photos?

So, there will be _____ photos in each album.

Example 2 Divide. 287 ÷ 2

Omar has 287 photographs of animals. If he wants to put the photos into 2 groups of the same size, how many photos will be in each group?

STEP 1

Use place value to place the first digit.
Look at the hundreds in 287.
2 hundreds can be shared between 2 groups.

So, the first digit of the quotient will be in the _____ place.

STEP 2

Divide the hundreds.

Divide. 2 hundreds ÷ 2

Multiply. 2 × 1 hundred

Subtract. 2 hundreds − 2 hundreds.

0 hundreds are left.

STEP 3

Divide the tens.

$$\begin{array}{r} 14 \\ 2\overline{)287} \\ -2 \\ \hline 0 \\ \end{array}$$

Divide. _____ tens ÷ _____

Multiply. _____ × _____ tens

Subtract. _____ tens − _____ tens 0 tens are left.

STEP 4

Divide the ones.

$$\begin{array}{r} 143\,r1 \\ 2\overline{)287} \\ -2 \\ \hline 08 \\ -8 \\ \hline 07 \\ \end{array}$$

Divide. _____ ones ÷ _____

Multiply. _____ × _____ ones

Subtract. _____ ones − _____ ones 1 one cannot be equally shared between 2 groups.

So, there will be _____ photos in each group with 1 photo left.

Name _____

1. There are 452 pictures of dogs in 4 equal groups. How many pictures are in each group? Explain how you can use place value to place the first digit in the quotient.

_____

_____

$4\overline{)452}$

Divide.

✓ 2. $4\overline{)166}$ ✓ 3. $5\overline{)775}$

Math Talk

Math Processes and Practices ⑦

Look for Structure How did you know where to place the first digit of the quotient in Exercise 2?

On Your Own

Divide.

4. $4\overline{)284}$ 5. $5\overline{)394}$ 6. $3\overline{)465}$ 7. $8\overline{)272}$

Practice: Copy and Solve Divide.

8. $516 \div 2$ 9. $516 \div 3$ 10. $516 \div 4$ 11. $516 \div 5$

12. (Math Processes and Practices ⑥) Look back at your answers to Exercises 8–11. What happens to the quotient when the divisor increases? **Explain**.

_____

_____

13. **GO DEEPER** Reggie has 192 pictures of animals. He wants to keep half and then divide the rest equally among three friends. How many pictures will each friend get?

_____

14. **GO DEEPER** There are 146 students, 5 teachers, and 8 chaperones going to the theater. To reserve their seats, they need to reserve entire rows. Each row has 8 seats. How many rows must they reserve?

_____

Unlock the Problem

15. **THINK SMARTER**   Nan wants to put 234 pictures in an album with a blue cover. How many full pages will she have in her album?

Photo Albums

Color of cover	Pictures per page
Blue	4
Green	6
Red	8

a. What do you need to find?

_____

b. How will you use division to find the number of full pages?

_____

_____

_____

c. Show the steps you will use to solve the problem.

d. Complete the following sentences.

Nan has _____ pictures.

She wants to put the pictures in an album

with pages that each hold _____ pictures.

She will have an album with _____ full

pages and _____ pictures on another page.

16. **GO DEEPER**   Mr. Parsons bought 293 apples to make pies for his shop. Six apples are needed for each pie. If Mr. Parsons makes the greatest number of apple pies possible, how many apples will be left?

_____

17. **THINK SMARTER**   Carol needs to divide 320 stickers equally among 4 classes. In which place is the first digit of the quotient? Choose the word that completes the sentence.

The first digit of the quotient is in

the | ones / tens / hundreds / thousands | place.

Place the First Digit

Learning Objective You will use place value to determine where to place the first digit in the quotient.

Divide.

1.
$$\begin{array}{r} 62 \\ 3\overline{)186} \\ -18\!\downarrow \\ \hline 06 \\ -6 \\ \hline 0 \end{array}$$

2. $4\overline{)298}$

3. $3\overline{)461}$

4. $9\overline{)315}$

5. $2\overline{)988}$

6. $4\overline{)604}$

7. $6\overline{)796}$

8. $5\overline{)449}$

Problem Solving · Real World

9. There are 132 projects in the science fair. If 8 projects can fit in a row, how many full rows of projects can be made? How many projects are in the row that is not full?

10. There are 798 calories in six 10-ounce bottles of apple juice. How many calories are there in one 10-ounce bottle of apple juice?

_____

11. **WRITE** ▸*Math* Write a division problem that will have a 2-digit quotient and another division problem that will have a 3-digit quotient. Explain how you chose the divisors and dividends.

_____

_____

_____

Lesson Check

1. To divide 572 ÷ 4, Stanley estimated to place the first digit of the quotient. In which place is the first digit of the quotient?

2. Onetta biked 325 miles in 5 days. If she biked the same number of miles each day, how far did she bike each day?

Spiral Review

3. Mort makes beaded necklaces that he sells for $32 each. About how much will Mort make if he sells 36 necklaces at the local art fair?

4. Estimate the product of 54 × 68.

5. Ms. Eisner pays $888 for 6 nights in a hotel. How much does Ms. Eisner pay per night?

6. What division problem does the model show?

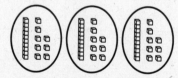

FOR MORE PRACTICE
GO TO THE
Personal Math Trainer

Name _____

Divide by 1-Digit Numbers

Essential Question How can you divide multidigit numbers and check your answers?

Learning Objective You will find whole-number quotients and remainders with up to 4-digit dividends and 1-digit divisors.

 Unlock the Problem

Students in the third, fourth, and fifth grades made 525 origami animals to display in the library. Each grade made the same number of animals. How many animals did each grade make?

Example 1 Divide. 525 ÷ 3

STEP 1 Use place value to place the first digit. Look at the hundreds in 525. 5 hundreds can be shared among 3 groups without regrouping. The first digit of the quotient will be in the _____ place.

Math Talk Math Processes and Practices ⑧

Use Repeated Reasoning At the checking step, what would you do if the number is greater than the divisor?

STEP 2 Divide the hundreds.

$$3\overline{)525}$$ with 1 above

Divide. Share _____ hundreds equally among _____ groups.

Multiply. _____ × _____

Subtract. _____ − _____ .

Check. _____ hundreds cannot be shared among 3 groups without regrouping.

STEP 3 Divide the tens.

$$3\overline{)525}$$ with 17 above, −3, 22

Divide. Share _____ equally among _____ groups.

Multiply. _____

Subtract. _____ − _____

Check. _____

_____

_____ .

STEP 4 Divide the ones.

$$3\overline{)525}$$ with 175 above, −3, 22, −21, 15

Divide. Share _____ equally among _____ groups.

Multiply. _____

Subtract. _____ − _____

Check. _____ are left.

So, each class made _____ origami animals.

There are 8,523 sheets of origami paper to be divided equally among 8 schools. How many sheets of origami paper will each school get?

Example 2 Divide. 8,523 ÷ 8

STEP 1 Use place value to place the first digit.

Look at the thousands in 8,523.
8 thousands can be shared among
8 groups without regrouping.

The first digit of the quotient will be

in the _____ place.

STEP 2 Divide the thousands.

STEP 3 Divide the hundreds.

STEP 4 Divide the tens.

STEP 5 Divide the ones.

So, each school will get _____ sheets of origami paper.

There will be _____ sheets left.

$$8\overline{)8{,}5\ 2\ 3}$$

 ERROR Alert

Place a zero in the quotient when a place in the dividend cannot be divided by the divisor.

CONNECT Division and multiplication are inverse operations. You can use multiplication to check your answer to a division problem.

Multiply the quotient by the divisor. If there is a remainder, add it to the product. The result should equal the dividend.

Divide.

quotient →   1,065 r3   ← remainder
divisor → 8)8,523   ← dividend

Check.

$$
\begin{array}{r}
1{,}065 \quad \leftarrow \text{quotient}\\
\times \qquad 8 \quad \leftarrow \text{divisor}\\
\hline
8{,}520 \qquad\qquad\\
+ \qquad 3 \quad \leftarrow \text{remainder}\\
\hline
8{,}523 \quad \leftarrow \text{dividend}
\end{array}
$$

The check shows that the division is correct.

Name _____

1. Ollie used 852 beads to make 4 bracelets. He put the same number of beads on each bracelet. How many beads does each bracelet have? Check your answer.

Divide.

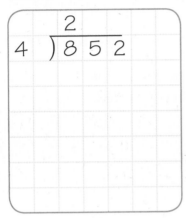

```
      2
  4 ) 8 5 2
```

Check.

Math Talk | Math Processes and Practices ⑦

Identify Relationships
How could you check to see if your quotient is correct?

So, each bracelet has _____ beads.

Divide and check.

2. 2) 394

✔ 3. 2) 803

✔ 4. 4) 3,448

On Your Own

Divide and check.

5. 2) 816

6. 4) 709

7. 3) 267

8. GO DEEPER The flower shop received a shipment of 248 pink roses and 256 red roses. The shop owner uses 6 roses to make one arrangement. How many arrangements can the shop owner make if he uses all the roses?

_____

Problem Solving · Applications (Real World)

Use the table for 9–11.

The Craft Store

Item	Price
Origami Book	$24 each
Origami Paper	$6 per pack
Origami Kit	$8 each

9. **THINK SMARTER**   Four teachers bought 10 origami books and 100 packs of origami paper for their classrooms. They will share the cost of the items equally. How much should each teacher pay?

_____

10. **Math Processes and Practices 5** **Communicate**   Six students shared equally the cost of 18 of one of the items in the chart. Each student paid $24. What item did they buy? Explain how you found your answer.

_____

_____

_____

_____

11. Ms. Alvarez has $1,482 to spend on origami paper. How many packs can she buy?

_____

12. **GO DEEPER**   Evan made origami cranes with red, blue, and yellow paper. The number of cranes in each color is the same. If there are 342 cranes, how many of them are blue or yellow?

_____

13. **THINK SMARTER**   On Monday 336 fourth graders went on a field trip to a local park. The teachers divided the students into 8 groups.

Use a basic fact. Estimate the number of students in each group. Show your work.

_____

_____

WRITE ▶ Math
Show Your Work

262

Divide by 1-Digit Numbers

Learning Objective You will find
whole-number quotients and remainders
with up to 4-digit dividends and 1-digit
divisors.

Divide and check.

1.
$$\begin{array}{r} 318 \\ 2\overline{)636} \\ -6 \\ \hline 03 \\ -2 \\ \hline 16 \\ -16 \\ \hline 0 \end{array}$$

$$\begin{array}{r} 318 \\ \times\ \ 2 \\ \hline 636 \end{array}$$

2. $4\overline{)631}$

3. $8\overline{)906}$

Problem Solving · Real World

Use the table for 4 and 5.

4. The Briggs rented a car for 5 weeks. What
was the cost of their rental car per week?

_____

5. The Lees rented a car for 4 weeks. The
Santos rented a car for 2 weeks. Whose
weekly rental cost was lower? **Explain**.

Rental Car Costs	
Family	**Total Cost**
Lee	$632
Brigg	$985
Santo	$328

_____

_____

6. **WRITE** ▸*Math* Josey got an answer of 167 r4 for $3\overline{)505}$. Explain
and correct Josey's error.

_____

_____

_____

_____

Lesson Check

1. Write an expression that can be used to check the quotient of 646 ÷ 3.

_____

_____

2. There are 8 volunteers at the telethon. The goal for the evening is to raise $952. If each volunteer raises the same amount, what is the minimum amount each needs to raise to meet the goal?

_____

Spiral Review

3. What product is shown by the model?

_____

4. The computer lab at a high school ordered 26 packages of CDs. There were 50 CDs in each package. How many CDs did the computer lab order?

_____

5. Write a division problem whose quotient has its first digit in the hundreds place.

_____

6. Sharon has 64 fluid ounces of juice. She is going to use the juice to fill as many 6-ounce glasses as possible. She will drink the leftover juice. How much juice will Sharon drink?

_____

FOR MORE PRACTICE
GO TO THE
Personal Math Trainer

Name _____

Problem Solving • Multistep Division Problems

Essential Question How can you use the strategy *draw a diagram* to solve multistep division problems?

Learning Objective You will use the strategy *draw a diagram* to solve multistep division problems.

Unlock the Problem

Lucia picked 3 times as much corn as Eli. Together, they picked 96 ears of corn. Eli wants to divide the number of ears he picked equally among 8 bags. How many ears of corn will Eli put in each of the 8 bags?

Read the Problem

What do I need to find?

I need to find the number of _____ that will go in each bag.

What information do I need to use?

Lucia picked _____ times as much corn as Eli.

Together they picked _____ ears of corn. The

number of ears Eli picked are divided equally

among _____ bags.

How will I use the information?

I will make a bar model for each step to

visualize the information. Then I will _____

to find the number of ears Eli picked and

_____ to find the number for each bag.

Solve the Problem

I can draw bar models to visualize the information given.

First, I will model and compare to find the number of ears of corn that Eli picked.

Lucia's

Eli's

96

96 ÷ 4 = _____

↑ number of parts

Then I will model and divide to find how many ears of corn Eli will put in each bag.

24

---

1. How many ears of corn will Eli put in each bag? _____

2. How can you check your answers? _____

_____

🔑 Try Another Problem

There are 8 dinner rolls in a package. How many packages will be needed to feed 64 people if each person has 2 dinner rolls?

Read the Problem	Solve the Problem
What do I need to find?	
What information do I need to use?	
How will I use the information?	

3. How many packages of rolls will be needed? _____

4. How did drawing a bar model help you solve the problem?

_____

_____

_____

Math Talk

Math Processes and Practices ①

Analyze What other method could you have used to solve the problem?

Name _____

Share and Show MATH BOARD

✓ Use the Problem Solving MathBoard.
✓ Underline important facts.
✓ Choose a strategy you know.

1. A firehouse pantry has 52 cans of vegetables and 74 cans of soup. Each shelf holds 9 cans. What is the least number of shelves needed for all the cans?

   First, draw a bar model for the total number of cans.

   Next, add to find the total number of cans.

   Then, draw a bar model to show the number of shelves needed.

   Finally, divide to find the number of shelves needed.

Math Talk   Math Processes and Practices ①

Evaluate How could you check to see that your answer is correct?

So, _____ shelves are needed to hold all of the cans.

2. **THINK SMARTER** What if 18 cans fit on a shelf? What is the least number of shelves needed? Describe how your answer would be different.

   _____

   _____

   _____

WRITE Math
Show Your Work

3. Julio's dad bought 10 dozen potatoes. The potatoes were equally divided into 6 bags. How many potatoes are in each bag?

   _____

4. At the garden shop, each small tree costs $125 and each large tree costs $225. How much will 3 small trees and 1 large tree cost?

   _____

On Your Own

5. **THINK SMARTER** Ms. Johnson bought 6 bags of balloons. Each bag has 25 balloons. She fills all the balloons and puts 5 balloons in each bunch. How many bunches can she make?

_____

6. **THINK SMARTER** An adult's dinner costs $8. A family of 2 adults and 2 children pays $26 for their dinners. How much does a child's dinner cost? Explain.

_____

_____

_____

_____

7. **Math Processes and Practices 5** **Communicate** Use the table at the right. Maria bought 80 ounces of apples. She needs 10 apples to make a pie. How many apples will be left over? Explain.

_____

_____

_____

_____

Fruit	Average weight
Peach	6 ounces
Apple	5 ounces
Plum	2 ounces

8. **GO DEEPER** Taylor has 16 tacks. She buys 2 packages of 36 tacks each. How many garage sale posters can she put up if she uses 4 tacks for each poster?

_____

Personal Math Trainer

9. **THINK SMARTER +** Ryan bought 8 dozen bandages for the track team first-aid kit. The bandages were divided equally into 4 boxes.

How many bandages are in each box?

_____

Problem Solving • Multistep Division Problems

Learning Objective You will use the strategy *draw a diagram* to solve multistep division problems.

Solve. Draw a diagram to help you.

1. There are 3 trays of eggs. Each tray holds 30 eggs. How many people can be served if each person eats 2 eggs?

   Think: What do I need to find? How can I draw a diagram to help?

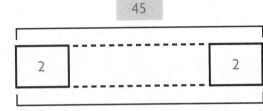

   Multiply to find the total number of eggs.

   Divide to find how many people can be served 2 eggs.

   _____ 45 people can be served. _____   90

2. There are 8 pencils in a package. How many packages will be needed for 28 children if each child gets 4 pencils?

   _____

3. There are 3 boxes of tangerines. Each box has 93 tangerines. The tangerines will be divided equally among 9 classrooms. How many tangerines will each classroom get?

   _____

4. | WRITE ▸ *Math* Write a two-step problem that you can solve using the strategy *draw a diagram*. Explain how you can use the strategy to find the solution.

   _____

   _____

Lesson Check

1. Gavin buys 89 blue pansies and 86 yellow pansies. He will plant the flowers in 5 rows with an equal number of plants in each row. Draw a bar model to help you find how many plants will be in each row.

2. A pet store receives 7 boxes of cat food. Each box has 48 cans. The store wants to put the cans in equal stacks of 8 cans. Draw a bar model to help you find how many stacks can be formed.

Spiral Review

3. What product does the model show?

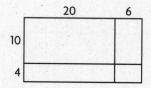

4. Mr. Hatch bought 4 round-trip airplane tickets for $417 each. He also paid $50 in baggage fees. How much did Mr. Hatch spend?

5. Mae read 976 pages in 8 weeks. She read the same number of pages each week. How many pages did she read each week?

6. Yolanda and her 3 brothers shared a box of 156 toy dinosaurs. About how many dinosaurs did each child get?

FOR MORE PRACTICE
GO TO THE
Personal Math Trainer

✓ Chapter 4 Review/Test

Personal Math Trainer
Online Assessment
and Intervention

1. There are 9 showings of a film about endangered species at the science museum. A total of 459 people saw the film. The same number of people were at each showing. About how many people were at each showing? Select the numbers the quotient is between.

(A) 40   (B) 50   (C) 60   (D) 70   (E) 80

2. Between which two numbers is the quotient of 87 ÷ 5? Write the numbers in the boxes.

5   10   15   20   25

The quotient is between ☐ and ☐.

3. Look at the model. What division does it show?

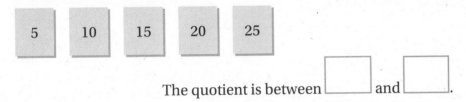

_____ ÷ _____ → _____ r _____

4. For 4a–4d, choose Yes or No to tell whether the division expression has a remainder.

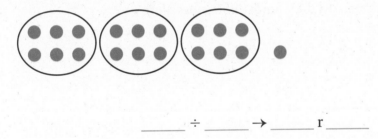

		Yes	No
4a.	28 ÷ 4	○ Yes	○ No
4b.	35 ÷ 2	○ Yes	○ No
4c.	40 ÷ 9	○ Yes	○ No
4d.	45 ÷ 5	○ Yes	○ No

GO DIGITAL Assessment Options
Chapter Test

5. A park guide plans the swan boat rides for 40 people. Each boat can carry 6 people at a time. What is the best way to interpret the remainder in this situation so that everyone gets a ride?

_____

6. Nolan divides his 88 toy cars into boxes. Each box holds 9 cars. How many boxes does Nolan need to store all of his cars?

_____ boxes

7. A group of 140 tourists are going on a tour. The tour guide rents 15 vans. Each van holds 9 tourists.

Part A

Write a division problem that can be used to find the number of vans needed to carry the tourists. Then solve.

Part B

What does the remainder mean in the context of the problem?

Part C

How can you use your answer to determine if the tour guide rented enough vans? Explain.

8. Solve.

$3{,}200 \div 8 =$ _____

9. Which quotients are equal to 300? Mark all that apply.

   Ⓐ 1,200 ÷ 4   Ⓒ 2,400 ÷ 8   Ⓔ 90 ÷ 3

   Ⓑ 180 ÷ 9   Ⓓ 2,100 ÷ 7   Ⓕ 3,000 ÷ 3

10. Margo estimated 188 ÷ 5 to be between 30 and 40. Which basic facts did she use to help her estimate? Mark all that apply.

   Ⓐ 10 ÷ 5   Ⓑ 15 ÷ 5   Ⓒ 20 ÷ 5   Ⓓ 25 ÷ 5

11. Mathias and his brother divided 2,029 marbles equally. About how many marbles did each of them receive?

   ┌───┐
   │   │
   │   │
   │   │
   └───┘

12. For 12a–12d, choose Yes or No to show how to use the Distributive Property to break apart the dividend to find the quotient 132 ÷ 6.

   12a. (115 ÷ 6) + (17 ÷ 6)   ○ Yes   ○ No

   12b. (100 ÷ 6) + (32 ÷ 6)   ○ Yes   ○ No

   12c. (90 ÷ 6) + (42 ÷ 6)   ○ Yes   ○ No

   12d. (72 ÷ 6) + (60 ÷ 6)   ○ Yes   ○ No

13. There are 136 people waiting for a river raft ride. Each raft holds 8 people. Silvia used the work below to find the number of rafts needed. Explain how Silvia's work can be used to find the number of rafts needed.

$$
\begin{array}{r}
8\overline{)136} \\
-80 \\
\hline
56 \\
-56 \\
\hline
0
\end{array}
$$

   ┌───┐
   │   │
   │   │
   │   │
   │   │
   │   │
   │   │
   │   │
   └───┘

14. A traveling circus brings along everything it needs for a show in big trucks.

Part A

The circus sets up chairs in rows with 9 seats in each row. How many rows will need to be set up if 513 people are expected to attend the show?

_____ rows

Part B

Can the rows be divided into a number of equal sections? Explain how you found your answer.

Part C

Circus horses eat about 250 pounds of horse food per week. About how many pounds of food does a circus horse eat each day? Explain.

15. Hilda wants to save 825 digital photographs in an online album. Each folder of the album can save 6 photographs. She uses division to find out how may full folders she will have. In what place is the first digit of the quotient?

_____

© Houghton Mifflin Harcourt Publishing Company

Name _____

16. Which model matches each expression? Write the letter in the box next to the model.

(A) $60 \div 5$ (B) $72 \div 4$ (C) $60 \div 4$ (D) $72 \div 6$

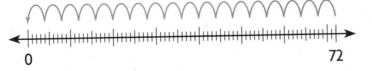

0   72   □

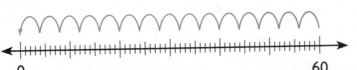

0   60   □

0   72   □

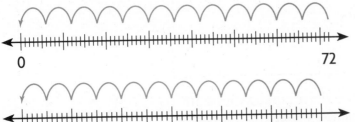

0   60   □

17. Popcorn was donated for the school fair by 3 different popcorn vendors. They donated a total of 636 bags of popcorn. Each vendor donated the same number of bags. How many bags of popcorn did each vendor donate?

_____ bags

18. Use partial quotients. Fill in the blanks.

$$8 \overline{)832}$$

$-$ _____ 100×8

$-$ _____ 4×8

19. Zack needs to divide these base-ten blocks into 3 equal groups.

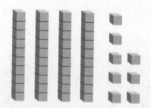

Draw or describe a model to show how many are in each group.

20. Jim needs to divide 750 coupon books equally among 9 stores. In which place is the first digit of the quotient? Choose the word that makes the sentence true.

The first digit of the quotient is in the

| ones |
| tens |
| hundreds |
| thousands |

place.

---

21. **THINK** SMARTER **+** Ursula bought 9 dozen rolls of first aid tape for the health office. The rolls were divided equally into 4 boxes. How many rolls are in each box?

_____ rolls

22. **GO DEEPER** There are 112 seats in the school auditorium. There are 7 seats in each row. There are 70 people seated, filling up full rows of seats. How many rows are empty?

_____ rows

Factors, Multiples, and Patterns

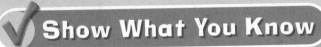 **Show What You Know**

 **Personal Math Trainer**
Online Assessment and Intervention

Check your understanding of important skills.

Name _____

▶ **Skip-Count** **Skip-count to find the unknown numbers.**

1. Skip count by 3s.

___3___ , _____ , _____ , _____

2. Skip count by 5s.

___5___ , _____ , _____ , _____

0 1 2 3 4 5 6 7 8 9 10 11 12 13 14 15 16 17 18 19 20

▶ **Arrays** **Use the array to find the product.**

3.

_____ rows of _____ = _____

4.

_____ rows of _____ = _____

▶ **Multiplication Facts** **Find the product.**

5. $4 \times 5 =$ _____

6. $9 \times 4 =$ _____

7. $6 \times 7 =$ _____

 **Math in the Real World**

Recycled plastic helps keep people warm. Some factories use recycled plastic, combined with other fabrics, to make winter jackets. A warehouse has 46 truckloads of recycled plastic. They use 8 truckloads each day. When there are fewer than 16 truckloads, more needs to be ordered. Figure out how many truckloads will be left after 2 days. After 3 days. When will more need to be ordered?

Vocabulary Builder

▶ **Visualize It** ∙∙∙

Complete the flow map by using the words with a ✓.

Multiplying

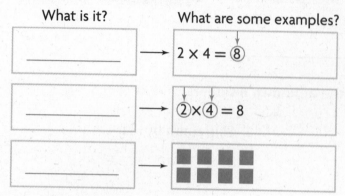

What is it?

What are some examples?

$2 \times 4 = ⑧$

$②\times④ = 8$

▶ **Understand Vocabulary** ∙∙∙∙∙∙∙∙∙∙∙∙∙∙∙∙∙∙∙∙∙∙∙∙∙∙∙∙∙∙∙∙∙∙∙∙

Complete the sentences by using preview words.

1. A number that is a factor of two or more numbers is a

   _____.

2. A number that is a multiple of two or more numbers is a

   _____.

3. A number that has exactly two factors, 1 and itself, is a

   _____.

4. A number that has more than two factors is a

   _____.

5. A number is _____ by another number if the
   quotient is a counting number and the remainder is 0.

6. An ordered set of numbers or objects is a _____.

7. Each number in a pattern is called a _____.

GO DIGITAL • Interactive Student Edition
• Multimedia eGlossary

Chapter 5 Vocabulary

common factor

factor común

10

common multiple

múltiplo común

11

composite number

número compuesto

16

divisible

divisible

25

factor

factor

33

pattern

patrón

63

prime number

número primo

71

term

término

90

A number that is a multiple of two or more numbers

A number that is a factor of two or more numbers

$$
\begin{array}{ccc}
8 & & 6 \\
2 \times 2 \times \textcircled{2} \leftarrow \text{common factor} \rightarrow \textcircled{2} \times 3
\end{array}
$$

factors

A number is divisible by another number if the quotient is a counting number and the remainder is zero

Example: 18 is divisible by 3.

A number having more than two factors

Example: 6 is a composite number. Its factors are 1, 2, 3, and 6.

An ordered set of numbers or objects; the order helps you predict what will come next

Examples: 2, 4, 6, 8, 10

A number that is multiplied by another number to find a product

Example: $4 \times 5 = 20$

factor   factor

A number or object in a pattern

A number that has exactly two factors: 1 and itself

Examples: 2, 3, 5, 7, 11, 13, 17, and 19 are prime numbers. 1 is not a prime number.

Game

Guess the Word

Word Box

common factor

common multiple

composite number

divisible

factor

prime number

pattern

term

For 3 to 4 players

Materials

- timer

How to Play

1. Take turns to play.

2. Choose a math term, but do not say it aloud.

3. Set the timer for 1 minute.

4. Give a one-word clue about your term. Give each player one chance to guess the term.

5. If nobody guesses correctly, repeat Step 4 with a different clue. Repeat until a player guesses the term or time runs out.

6. The player who guesses your term gets 1 point. If the player can use the word in a sentence, he or she gets 1 more point. Then that player gets a turn.

7. The first player to score 10 points wins.

The Write Way

Reflect

Choose one idea. Write about it.

- Which solution to finding the common factors of 6 and 8 is correct? Explain how you know.

  Eli's solution: 1 and 2

  Fiona's solution: 1, 2, 3, 4, 6, and 8

- Summarize the differences between prime numbers and composite numbers.

- Write about a time you were confused learning the ideas in this chapter. What did you do to get help? How did you figure out what was confusing to you?

Name _____

Model Factors

Essential Question How can you use models to find factors?

Learning Objective You will make arrays using square tiles to find and record all the factors of a whole number.

🔑 Unlock the Problem Real World

A **factor** is a number multiplied by another number to find a product. Every whole number greater than 1 has at least two factors, that number and 1.

$18 = 1 \times 18$ $7 = 7 \times 1$ $342 = 1 \times 342$

     ↑   ↑

   factor   factor

Many numbers can be broken into factors in different ways.

$16 = 1 \times 16$ $16 = 4 \times 4$ $16 = 2 \times 8$

🔓 Activity Model and record the factors of 24.

Materials ■ square tiles

Use all 24 tiles to make as many different arrays as you can. Record the arrays in the grid, and write the factors modeled.

Math Idea

When you are asked to find factors of a whole number, only list factors that are also whole numbers.

$2 \times 12 = 24$

Factors: _____, _____

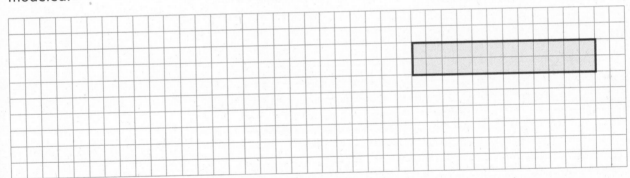

_____ × _____ = 24   _____ × _____ = 24   _____ × _____ = 24

Factors: _____, _____   Factors: _____, _____   Factors: _____, _____

The factors of 24, from least to greatest, are

_____, _____, _____, _____, _____, _____, _____, and _____.

Two factors that make a product are sometimes called a factor pair. How many factor pairs does 24 have? Explain.

_____

Math Talk   Math Processes and Practices ②

Reason Abstractly Can you arrange the tiles in each array another way and show the same factors? Explain.

Chapter 5   279

1. Use the arrays to name the factors of 12.

_____ × _____ = 12   _____ × _____ = 12   _____ × _____ = 12

The factors of 12 are 1, _____, 3, _____, 6, and _____.

Use tiles to find all the factors of the product. Record the arrays and write the factors shown.

Math Talk

Math Processes and Practices ⑥

Use Math Vocabulary
Explain how the numbers 3 and 12 are related. Use the word *factor* in your explanation.

2. 5: _____

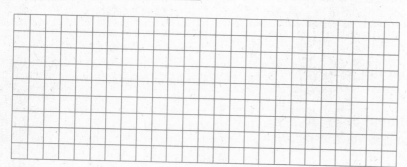

3. 20: _____

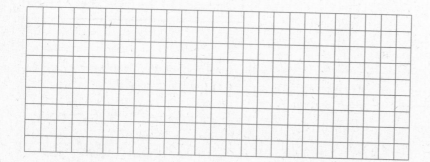

4. 25: _____

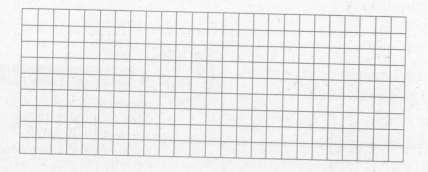

Name _____

On Your Own

Practice: Copy and Solve Use tiles to find all the factors of the product. Record the arrays on grid paper and write the factors shown.

5. 9 **6.** 21 **7.** 17 **8.** 18

Problem Solving • Applications

Use the diagram for 9–10.

Pablo's Tiles

9. **Math Processes and Practices 6** Pablo is using 36 tiles to make a patio. Can he arrange the tiles in another way and show the same factors? Draw a quick picture and **explain**.

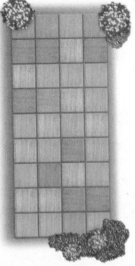

10. **THINK SMARTER** How many different rectangular arrays can Pablo make with all 36 tiles, so none of the arrays show the same factors?

_____

11. If 6 is a factor of a number, what other numbers must be factors of the number?

_____

12. **GO DEEPER** Jean spent $16 on new T-shirts. If each shirt cost the same whole-dollar amount, how many could she have bought?

_____

Unlock the Problem (Real World)

13. **Go DEEPER** Carmen has 18 connecting cubes. She wants to model a house shaped like a rectangle. If the model has a height of one connecting cube, how many different ways can Carmen model the house using all 18 connecting cubes and none of the models show the same side lengths?

a. What do you need to know? _____

_____

b. How is finding the number of ways to model a rectangular house

related to finding factor pairs? _____

_____

_____

c. Why is finding the factor pairs only the first step in solving the problem? _____

_____

_____

d. Show the steps you used to solve the problem.

_____

_____

_____

_____

e. Complete the sentences. Factor pairs for

18 are _____

_____

There are _____ different ways Carmen can arrange the cubes to model the house.

14. **THINK SMARTER** Sarah was organizing vocabulary words using index cards. She arranged 40 index cards in the shape of a rectangle on a poster. For 14a–14e, choose Yes or No to tell whether a possible arrangement of cards is shown.

14a. 4 rows of 10 cards   ○ Yes   ○ No   14d. 40 rows of 1 card   ○ Yes   ○ No

14b. 6 rows of 8 cards   ○ Yes   ○ No   14e. 35 rows of 5 cards   ○ Yes   ○ No

14c. 20 rows of 2 cards   ○ Yes   ○ No

Name _____

Model Factors

Learning Objective You will make arrays using square tiles to find and record all the factors of a whole number.

Use tiles to find all the factors of the product.
Record the arrays on grid paper and write the factors shown.

1. 15

$1 \times 15 = 15$
_____
$3 \times 5 = 15$
1, 3, 5, 15

2. 30

_____

_____

3. 45

_____

_____

4. 19

_____

_____

5. 40

_____

_____

_____

6. 36

_____

_____

_____

7. 22

_____

_____

_____

8. 4

_____

_____

_____

Problem Solving

9. Brooke has to set up 70 chairs in equal rows for the class talent show. But, there is not room for more than 20 rows. What are the possible number of rows that Brooke could set up?

_____

10. Eduardo thinks of a number between 1 and 20 that has exactly 5 factors. What number is he thinking of?

_____

11. | WRITE | ▸*Math* Have students write the answer to the Essential Question and draw examples to explain their answer.

_____

_____

_____

_____

Lesson Check

1. List all the factors of 24.

2. Natalia has 48 tiles. Write a factor pair for the number 48.

Spiral Review

3. The Pumpkin Patch is open every day. If it sells 2,750 pounds of pumpkins each day, about how many pounds does it sell in 7 days?

4. What is the remainder in the division problem modeled below?

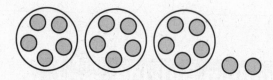

5. Represent the model shown below using a multiplication equation.

6. Channing jogs 10 miles a week. How many miles will she jog in 52 weeks?

284

FOR MORE PRACTICE
GO TO THE
Personal Math Trainer

Name _____

Factors and Divisibility

Essential Question How can you tell whether one number is a factor of another number?

Learning Objective You will use a list of factor pairs and divisibility rules to tell whether one number is a factor of another number for whole numbers in the range 1–100.

🔑 Unlock the Problem (Real World)

Students in Carlo's art class painted 32 square tiles for a mosaic. They will arrange the tiles to make a rectangle. Can the rectangle have 32 tiles arranged into 3 equal rows, without gaps or overlaps?

🔑 One Way Draw a model.

Think: Try to arrange the tiles into 3 equal rows to make a rectangle.

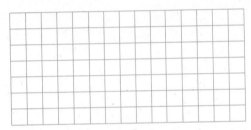

A rectangle _____ have 32 tiles arranged into 3 equal rows.

🔑 Another Way Use division.

If 3 is a factor of 32, then the unknown factor in $3 \times \blacksquare = 32$ is a whole number.

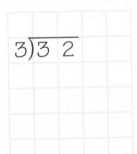

Think: Divide to see whether the unknown factor is a whole number.

> **Math Idea**
> A factor of a number divides the number evenly. This means the quotient is a whole number and the remainder is 0.

▲ Mosaics are decorative patterns made with pieces of glass or other materials.

The unknown factor in $3 \times \blacksquare = 32$ _____ a whole number.

So, a rectangle _____ have 32 tiles arranged in 3 rows.

• Explain how you can tell if 4 is a factor of 30.

_____

_____

Math Talk

Math Processes and Practices ④

Interpret a Result How does the model relate to the quotient and remainder for 32 ÷ 3?

© Houghton Mifflin Harcourt Publishing Company • Image Credits: (t) ©artville/Getty Images

Divisibility Rules A number is **divisible** by another number if the quotient is a counting number and the remainder is 0.

Some numbers have a divisibility rule. You can use a divisibility rule to tell whether one number is a factor of another.

 Is 6 a factor of 72?

Think: If 72 is divisible by 6, then 6 is a factor of 72.

Test for divisibility by 6:

Is 72 even? _____

What is the sum of the digits of 72?

_____ + _____ = _____

Is the sum of the digits divisible by 3?

_____

72 is divisible by _____.

So, 6 is a factor of 72.

Divisibility Rules	
Number	**Divisibility Rule**
2	The number is even.
3	The sum of the digits is divisible by 3.
5	The last digit is 0 or 5.
6	The number is even and divisible by 3.
9	The sum of the digits is divisible by 9.

Try This! List all the factor pairs for 72 in the table.

Complete the table.

Factors of 72	
1 × 72 = 72	1, 72
____ × ____ = ____	____ , ____
____ × ____ = ____	____ , ____
____ × ____ = ____	____ , ____
____ × ____ = ____	____ , ____
____ × ____ = ____	____ , ____

Show your work.

Math Talk

Identify Relationships How are divisibility and factors related? Explain.

- How did you check if 7 is a factor of 72? Explain.

_____

_____

Name _____

1. Is 4 a factor of 28? Draw a model to help.

Think: Can you make a rectangle with 28 squares in 4 equal rows?

4 _____ a factor of 28.

Is 5 a factor of the number? Write *yes* or *no*.

2. 27

☑ **3.** 30

4. 36

☑ **5.** 53

Math Talk Math Processes and Practices ③

Use Counterexamples If 3 is a factor of a number, is 6 always a factor of the number? If not, give an example.

On Your Own

Is 9 a factor of the number? Write *yes* or *no*.

6. 54

7. 63

8. 67

9. 93

List all the factor pairs in the table.

10.

Factors of 24	
___ × ___ = ___	___ , ___
___ × ___ = ___	___ , ___
___ × ___ = ___	___ , ___
___ × ___ = ___	___ , ___

11.

Factors of 39	
___ × ___ = ___	___ , ___
___ × ___ = ___	___ , ___

Practice: Copy and Solve List all the factor pairs for the number. Make a table to help.

12. 56

13. 64

Problem Solving • Applications (Real World)

Use the table to solve 14–15.

Stamps Sets	
Country	**Number of stamps**
Germany	90
Sweden	78
Japan	63
Canada	25

14. **THINK SMARTER** Dirk bought a set of stamps. The number of stamps in the set he bought is divisible by 2, 3, 5, 6, and 9. Which set is it?

_____

15. **GO DEEPER** Geri wants to put 6 stamps on some pages in her stamp book and 9 stamps on other pages. Explain how she could do this with the stamp set for Sweden.

_____

_____

_____

_____

16. **Math Processes and Practices ③ Use Counterexamples** George said if 2 and 4 are factors of a number, then 8 is a factor of the number. Is he correct? Explain.

_____

_____

_____

WRITE ✏ *Math* • • • • • • • • • • • • • • • • •
Show Your Work

17. **THINK SMARTER** Classify the numbers. Some numbers may belong in more than one box.

| 27 | 45 | 54 | 72 | 81 | 84 |

Divisible by 5 and 9	Divisible by 3 and 9	Divisible by 2 and 6

Factors and Divisibility

Learning Objective You will use a list of factor pairs and divisibility rules to tell whether one number is a factor of another number for whole numbers in the range 1–100.

Is 6 a factor of the number? Write *yes* or *no*.

1. 36   **2.** 56   **3.** 42   **4.** 66

Think: $6 \times 6 = 36$ _____   _____   _____

yes   _____   _____   _____

Is 5 a factor of the number? Write *yes* or *no*.

5. 38   **6.** 45   **7.** 60   **8.** 39

_____   _____   _____   _____

List all the factor pairs in the table.

9.

Factors of 12	
____ × ____ = ____	____ , ____
____ × ____ = ____	____ , ____
____ × ____ = ____	____ , ____

10.

Factors of 25	
____ × ____ = ____	____ , ____
____ × ____ = ____	____ , ____

11. List all the factor pairs for 48. Make a table to help.

_____

_____

Problem Solving *Real World*

12. Bryson buys a bag of 64 plastic miniature dinosaurs. Could he distribute them equally into six storage containers and not have any left over? **Explain.**

13. **WRITE** ▸*Math* Find the factors of 42. Show and explain your work, and list the factor pairs in a table.

Lesson Check

1. Write three numbers greater than 20 that have 9 as a factor.

   _____

   _____

2. What digit(s) can be in the ones place of a number that has 5 as a factor?

   _____

   _____

Spiral Review

3. Write an expression that can be used to find 4×275 using mental math and properties of numbers.

   _____

   _____

4. Jack broke apart 5×216 as $(5 \times 200) + (5 \times 16)$ to multiply mentally. What strategy did Jack use?

   _____

   _____

5. Jordan has $55. She earns $67 by doing chores. How much money does Jordan have now?

   _____

   _____

6. Trina has 72 collector's stamps. She puts 43 of the stamps into a stamp book. How many stamps are left?

   _____

   _____

FOR MORE PRACTICE
GO TO THE
Personal Math Trainer

Name _____

Problem Solving • Common Factors

Essential Question How can you use the *make a list* strategy to solve problems with common factors?

Learning Objective You will use the strategy *make a list* to find common factors of two or more numbers.

Unlock the Problem

Chuck has a coin collection with 30 pennies, 24 quarters, and 36 nickels. He wants to arrange the coins into rows. Each row will have the same number of coins, and all the coins in a row will be the same. How many coins can he put in each row?

The information in the graphic organizer below will help you solve the problem.

Read the Problem	Solve the Problem
What do I need to find?	I can list all the factors of each number. Then I can circle the factors that are common to all three numbers.
I need to find _____ that can go in each row so that each row has _____ _____ .	Factors of: 30 24 36
What information do I need to use?	
Chuck has _____ _____ . Each row has _____ _____ _____ .	
How will I use the information?	
I can make a list to find all the factors of _____ . Then I can use the list to find the common factors. A **common factor** is a factor of two or more numbers.	The common factors are _____ .

So, Chuck can put _____ , _____ , _____ , or _____ coins in each row.

🔑 Try Another Problem

Ryan collects animal figures. He has 45 elephants, 36 zebras, and 18 tigers. He will arrange the figures into rows. Each row will have the same number of figures, and all the figures in a row will be the same. How many figures can be in each row?

Use the graphic organizer below to help you solve the problem.

Read the Problem	Solve the Problem
What do I need to find?	
What information do I need to use?	
How will I use the information?	

So, Ryan can put _____, _____, or _____ figures in each row.

Math Talk

Math Processes and Practices ⑤

Use Appropriate Tools
How did the strategy help you solve the problem?

Name _____

Share and Show

1. Lucy has 40 bean plants, 32 tomato plants, and 16 pepper plants. She wants to put the plants in rows with only one type of plant in each row. All rows will have the same number of plants. How many plants can Lucy put in each row?

First, read the problem and think about what you need to find. What information will you use? How will you use the information?

_____

_____

Next, make a list. Find the factors for each number in the problem.

_____

_____

Finally, use the list. Circle the common factors.

So, Lucy can put _____ , _____ , _____ , or _____ plants in each row.

2. What if Lucy has 64 bean plants instead of 40 bean plants? How many plants can Lucy put in each row?

_____

3. **THINK SMARTER** One common factor of two numbers is 40. Another common factor is 10. If both numbers are less than 100, what are the two numbers?

_____

4. The sum of two numbers is 136. One number is 51. What is the other number? What are the common factors of these two numbers?

_____

WRITE *Math*. . . . .
Show Your Work

On Your Own

5. (Math Processes and Practices ①) **Analyze** A number is called a *perfect number* if it equals the sum of all of its factors except itself. For instance, 6 is a perfect number because its factors are 1, 2, 3, and 6, and $1 + 2 + 3 = 6$. What is the next greater perfect number?

_____

6. THINK SMARTER Sona knits 10 squares a day for 7 days. Can she sew together the squares to make 5 equal-sized blankets? Explain.

_____

_____

7. Julianne earned $296 working at a grocery store last week. She earns $8 per hour. How many hours did Julianne work?

_____

WRITE ▸ *Math*
Show Your Work

8. GO DEEPER There are 266 students watching a play in the auditorium. There are 10 rows with 20 students in each row and 5 rows with 8 students in each row. How many students are sitting in each of the 2 remaining rows if each of those rows has an equal number of students?

_____

Personal Math Trainer

9. THINK SMARTER + Ben is planting a garden with 36 zinnias, 18 marigolds, and 24 petunias. Each row will have only one type of plant. Ben says he can put 9 plants in each row. He listed the common factors of 36, 18 and 24 below to support his reasoning.

36: 1, 2, 3, 4, 6, 9, 12, 18, 36
18: 1, 2, 3, 6, 8, 9, 18
24: 1, 2, 3, 4, 6, 8, 9, 12, 24

Is he correct? Explain your answer. If his reasoning is incorrect, explain how he should have found the answer.

_____

_____

Problem Solving • Common Factors

Learning Objective You will use the strategy *make a list* to find common factors of two or more numbers.

Solve each problem.

1. Grace is preparing grab bags for her store's open house. She has 24 candles, 16 pens, and 40 figurines. Each grab bag will have the same number of items, and all the items in a bag will be the same. How many items can Grace put in each bag?

   Find the common factors of 24, 16, and 40.

   1, 2, 4, or 8 items

2. Simon is making wreaths to sell. He has 60 bows, 36 silk roses, and 48 silk carnations. He wants to put the same number of items on each wreath. All the items on a wreath will be the same type. How many items can Simon put on each wreath?

   _____

3. Justin has 20 pencils, 25 erasers, and 40 paper clips. He organizes them into groups with the same number of items in each group. All the items in a group will be the same type. How many items can he put in each group?

   _____

4. A food bank has 50 cans of vegetables, 30 loaves of bread, and 100 bottles of water. The volunteers will put the items into boxes. Each box will have the same number of food items and all the items in the box will be the same type. How many items can they put in each box?

   _____

5. **WRITE** ▸*Math* Describe how making a list can help you solve a math problem. Write a problem that could be solved by making a list.

   _____

   _____

   _____

Lesson Check

1. What are all the common factors of 24, 64, and 88?

2. What are all the common factors of 15, 45, and 90?

Spiral Review

3. Dan puts $11 of his allowance in his savings account every week. How much money will he have after 15 weeks?

4. James is reading a book that is 1,400 pages. He will read the same number of pages each day. If he reads the book in 7 days, how many pages will he read each day?

5. Emma volunteered at an animal shelter for a total of 119 hours over 6 weeks. Estimate the number of hours she volunteered each week.

6. Write an expression that can be used to multiply 6 × 198 mentally.

FOR MORE PRACTICE
GO TO THE
Personal Math Trainer

Mid-Chapter Checkpoint

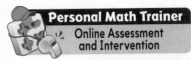

Vocabulary

Vocabulary
common factor
divisible
factor

Choose the best term from the box.

1. A number that is multiplied by another number to find a product

   is called a _____. (p. 279)

2. A number is _____ by another number if the
   quotient is a counting number and the remainder is zero. (p. 286)

Concepts and Skills

List all the factors from least to greatest.

3. 8

   _____

4. 14

   _____

Is 6 a factor of the number? Write _yes_ or _no_.

5. 81   6. 45   7. 42   8. 56

   _____   _____   _____   _____

List all the factor pairs in the table.

9.

Factors of 64		
____ × ____ = ____	____ , ____
____ × ____ = ____	____ , ____
____ × ____ = ____	____ , ____
____ × ____ = ____	____ , ____

10.

Factors of 44		
____ × ____ = ____	____ , ____
____ × ____ = ____	____ , ____
____ × ____ = ____	____ , ____

List the common factors of the numbers.

11. 9 and 18   12. 20 and 50

    _____   _____

13. Sean places 28 tomato plants in rows. All rows contain the same number of plants. There are between 5 and 12 plants in each row. How many plants are in each row?

_____

14. GO DEEPER Ella bought some key chains and spent a total of $24. Each key chain cost the same whole-dollar amount. She bought between 7 and 11 key chains. How many key chains did Ella buy?

_____

15. Sandy has 16 roses, 8 daisies, and 32 tulips. She wants to arrange all the flowers in bouquets. Each bouquet has the same number of flowers and has only one type of flower. What is the greatest number of flowers that could be in each bouquet?

_____

16. Amir arranged 9 photos on a bulletin board. He put the photos in rows. Each row contains the same number of photos. How many photos could be in each row?

_____

© Houghton Mifflin Harcourt Publishing Company

Name _____

Factors and Multiples

Essential Question How are factors and multiples related?

Learning Objective You will describe the relationship between factors and multiples and find common multiples of two or more numbers.

⚷ Unlock the Problem

Toy animals are sold in sets of 3, 5, 10, and 12. Mason wants to make a display with 3 animals in each row. Which sets could he buy, if he wants to display all of the animals?

The product of two numbers is a multiple of each number. Factors and multiples are related.

$$3 \times 4 = 12$$

   ↑   ↑   ↑
factor factor multiple of 3
               multiple of 4

- How many animals will be in each row?

  _____

- How many animals are sold in each set?

  _____

🔑 One Way Find factors.

Tell whether 3 is a factor of each number.

Think: If a number is divisible by 3, then 3 is a factor of the number.

Is 3 a factor of 3? _____

Is 3 a factor of 5? _____

Is 3 a factor of 10? _____

Is 3 a factor of 12? _____

3 is a factor of _____ and _____.

🔑 Another Way Find multiples.

Multiply and make a list.   __3__, _____, _____, _____, _____, ...
                        1 × 3 2 × 3 3 × 3 4 × 3 5 × 3

_____ and _____ are multiples of 3.

So, Mason could buy sets of _____ and _____ toy animals.

Math Talk

Math Processes and Practices ⑥

Explain how you can use what you know about factors to determine whether one number is a multiple of another number.

Common Multiples A **common multiple** is a multiple of two or more numbers.

🔑 Example Find common multiples.

Tony works every 3 days and Amanda works every 5 days. If Tony works June 3 and Amanda works June 5, on what days in June will they work together?

Circle multiples of 3. Draw a box around multiples of 5.

			June			
Sun	**Mon**	**Tue**	**Wed**	**Thu**	**Fri**	**Sat**
	1	2	3	4	5	6
7	8	9	10	11	12	13
14	15	16	17	18	19	20
21	22	23	24	25	26	27
28	29	30				

Think: The common multiples have both a circle and a box.

The common multiples are _____ and _____.

So, Tony and Amanda will work together on June _____ and June _____.

Share and Show MATH BOARD

Math Talk

Math Processes and Practices ⑦

Identify Relationships
Discuss how factors and multiples are related. Give an example.

1. Multiply to list the next five multiples of 4.

   ___4___ , _____ , _____ , _____ , _____ , _____
   1 × 4

Is the number a factor of 6? Write *yes* or *no.*

✓ **2.** 3   **3.** 6   **4.** 16   **5.** 18

_____   _____   _____

Is the number a multiple of 6? Write *yes* or *no.*

✓ **6.** 3   **7.** 6   **8.** 16   **9.** 18

_____   _____   _____

Name _____

On Your Own

Is the number a multiple of 3? Write _yes_ or _no_.

10. 4   **11.** 8   **12.** 24   **13.** 38

_____   _____   _____   _____

14. **List the next nine multiples of each number. Find the common multiples.**

Multiples of 2: 2, _____

Multiples of 8: 8, _____

Common multiples: _____

 Generalize **Algebra** Find the unknown number.

15. 12, 24, 36, _____   **16.** 25, 50, 75, 100, _____

Tell whether 20 is a factor or multiple of the number.
Write _factor, multiple,_ or _neither._

17. 10   **18.** 20   **19.** 30

_____   _____   _____

THINK SMARTER Write _true_ or _false._ Explain.

20. Every whole number is a multiple of 1.   **21.** Every whole number is a factor of 1.

_____   _____

22. **THINK SMARTER** Julio wears a blue shirt every 3 days. Larry wears a blue shirt every 4 days. On April 12, both Julio and Larry wore a blue shirt. What is the next date that they will both wear a blue shirt?

_____

April						
Sun	Mon	Tue	Wed	Thu	Fri	Sat
1	2	3	4	5	6	7
8	9	10	11	12	13	14
15	16	17	18	19	20	21
22	23	24	25	26	27	28
29	30					

Problem Solving · Applications (Real World)

Complete the Venn diagram. Then use it to solve 23–25.

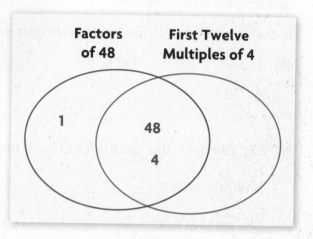

23. What multiples of 4 are not factors of 48?

_____

24. What factors of 48 are multiples of 4?

_____

25. **GO DEEPER** **Pose a Problem** Look back at Problem 24. Write a similar problem by changing the numbers. Then solve.

_____

_____

26. Kia paid $10 for two charms. The price of each charm was a multiple of $2. What are the possible prices of the charms?

_____

27. **Math Processes and Practices 7** **Look for Structure** The answer is 9, 18, 27, 36, 45. What is the question?

_____

28. **WRITE** ▸ *Math* How do you know whether a number is a multiple of another number?

_____

_____

29. **THINK SMARTER** For numbers 29a–29e, select True or False for each statement.

29a. The number 45 is a multiple of 9.   ○ True   ○ False

29b. The number 4 is a multiple of 16.   ○ True   ○ False

29c. The number 28 is a multiple of 4.   ○ True   ○ False

29d. The number 4 is a factor of 28.   ○ True   ○ False

29e. The number 32 is a factor of 8.   ○ True   ○ False

Name _____

Factors and Multiples

Learning Objective You will describe the relationship between factors and multiples and find common multiples of two or more numbers.

Is the number a multiple of 8? Write *yes* or *no*.

1. 4   **2.** 8   **3.** 20   **4.** 40

Think: Since $4 \times 2 = 8$, 4 is a *factor* of 8, not a multiple of 8.

_____ no _____   _____   _____   _____

List the next nine multiples of each number.
Find the common multiples.

5. Multiples of 4: 4, _____

     Multiples of 7: 7, _____

     Common multiples: _____

6. Multiples of 3: 3, _____

     Multiples of 9: 9, _____

     Common multiples: _____

Tell whether 24 is a factor or multiple of the number.
Write *factor*, *multiple*, or *neither*.

7. 6 _____   **8.** 36 _____   **9.** 48 _____

Problem Solving · Real World

10. Ken paid $12 for two magazines. The cost of each magazine was a multiple of $3. What are the possible prices of the magazines?

11. Jodie bought some shirts for $6 each. Marge bought some shirts for $8 each. The girls spent the same amount of money on shirts. What is the least amount they could have spent?

_____   _____

12. **WRITE** ▸*Math* Write a word problem that can be solved by finding the numbers that have 4 as a factor.

_____

_____

Lesson Check

1. Of the numbers listed below, which are NOT multiples of 4?

2, 4, 7, 8, 12, 15, 19, 24, 34

2. What number is a common multiple of 5 and 9?

_____

_____

Spiral Review

3. Jenny has 50 square tiles. She arranges the tiles into a rectangular array of 4 rows. How many tiles will be left over?

4. Jerome added two numbers. The sum was 83. One of the numbers was 45. What was the other number?

_____

_____

5. There are 18 rows of seats in the auditorium. There are 24 seats in each row. How many seats are in the auditorium?

6. The population of Riverdale is 6,735. What is the value of the 7 in the number 6,735?

_____

_____

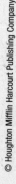

FOR MORE PRACTICE GO TO THE
Personal Math Trainer

Name _____

Prime and Composite Numbers

Essential Question How can you tell whether a number is prime or composite?

Learning Objective You will use divisibility rules to tell whether a number is prime or composite.

Unlock the Problem Real World

Students are arranging square tables to make one larger, rectangular table. The students want to have several ways to arrange the tables. Should they use 12 or 13 tables?

• **What are the factors of 12?**

_____

Use a grid to show all the possible arrangements of 12 and 13 tables.

Draw all of the possible arrangements of 12 tables and 13 tables. Label each drawing with the factors modeled.

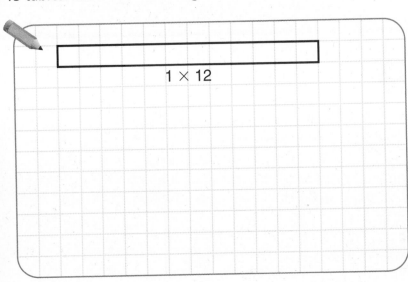

1 × 12

! ERROR Alert

The same factors in a different order should be counted only once. For example, 3 × 4 and 4 × 3 are the same factor pair.

So, there are more ways to arrange _____ tables.

Math Talk Math Processes and Practices 6

Make Connections Explain how knowing whether 12 and 13 are prime or composite could have helped you solve the problem above.

• A **prime number** is a whole number greater than 1 that has exactly two factors, 1 and itself.

• A **composite number** is a whole number greater than 1 that has more than two factors.

Factors of 12: ____ , ____ , ____ , ____ , ____ , ____

Factors of 13: ____ , ____

12 is a _____ number, and 13 is a _____ number.

© Houghton Mifflin Harcourt Publishing Company

Divisibility You can use divisibility rules to help tell whether a number is prime or composite. If a number is divisible by any number other than 1 and itself, then the number is composite.

🔒 Tell whether 51 is *prime* or *composite*.

Is 51 divisible by 2?

_____

Is 51 divisible by 3?

_____

Think: 51 is divisible by a number other than 1 and 51.
51 has more than two factors.

So, 51 is _____ .

> **Math Idea**
> The number 1 is neither prime nor composite, since it has only one factor: 1.

Share and Show MATH BOARD

1. Use the grid to model the factors of 18. Tell whether 18 is *prime* or *composite*.

Factors of 18: _____ , _____ , _____ , _____ , _____ , _____

Think: 18 has more than two factors.

So, 18 is _____ .

Tell whether the number is *prime* or *composite*.

2. 11
   Think: Does 11 have other factors besides 1 and itself?

   _____

3. 73

   _____

✓4. 69

   _____

✓5. 42

   _____

> **Math Talk** Math Processes and Practices ⑦
> **Look for Structure** Is the product of two prime numbers prime or composite? Explain.

Name _____

Tell whether the number is *prime* or *composite*.

6. 18

_____

7. 49

_____

8. 29

_____

9. 64

_____

10. 33

_____

11. 89

_____

12. 52

_____

13. 76

_____

Write *true* or *false* for each statement. Explain or give an example to support your answer.

14. GO DEEPER Only odd numbers are prime numbers.

_____

_____

15. THINK SMARTER A composite number cannot have three factors.

_____

_____

Problem Solving • Applications Real World

16. GO DEEPER I am a number between 60 and 100. My ones digit is two less than my tens digit. I am a prime number. What number am I?

17. Name a 2-digit odd number that is prime. Name a 2-digit odd number that is composite.

_____

_____

18. THINK SMARTER Choose the words that correctly complete the sentence.

The number 9 is
| prime |
| composite |
because it has
| exactly |
| more than |
two factors.

Connect to Social Studies

The Sieve of Eratosthenes

Eratosthenes was a Greek mathematician who lived more than 2,200 years ago. He invented a method of finding prime numbers, which is now called the Sieve of Eratosthenes.

19. Follow the steps below to circle all prime numbers less than 100. Then list the prime numbers.

STEP 1

Cross out 1, since 1 is not prime

STEP 2

Circle 2, since it is prime. Cross out all other multiples of 2.

STEP 3

Circle the next number that is not crossed out. This number is prime. Cross out all the multiples of this number.

STEP 4

Repeat Step 3 until every number is either circled or crossed out.

1	2	3	4	5	6	7	8	9	10
11	12	13	14	15	16	17	18	19	20
21	22	23	24	25	26	27	28	29	30
31	32	33	34	35	36	37	38	39	40
41	42	43	44	45	46	47	48	49	50
51	52	53	54	55	56	57	58	59	60
61	62	63	64	65	66	67	68	69	70
71	72	73	74	75	76	77	78	79	80
81	82	83	84	85	86	87	88	89	90
91	92	93	94	95	96	97	98	99	100

So, the prime numbers less than 100 are

_____

_____

_____

_____

_____

_____

20. **Math Processes and Practices 6** **Explain** why the multiples of any number other than 1 are not prime numbers.

_____

Prime and Composite Numbers

Learning Objective You will use divisibility rules to tell whether a number is prime or composite.

Tell whether the number is *prime* or *composite*.

1. 47

Think: Does 47 have other factors besides 1 and itself?

_____prime_____

2. 68

_____

3. 52

_____

4. 63

_____

5. 75

_____

6. 31

_____

7. 77

_____

8. 59

_____

9. 87

_____

Problem Solving Real World

10. Kai wrote the number 85 on the board. Is 85 prime or composite? **Explain.**

_____

_____

_____

11. Lisa says that 43 is a 2-digit odd number that is composite. Is she correct? **Explain.**

_____

_____

_____

12. **WRITE** ▸*Math* Describe how to decide if 94 is a prime number or composite number.

_____

_____

Lesson Check

1. Is the number 5 prime, composite, or neither?

2. Is the number 1 prime, composite, or neither?

_____

_____

Spiral Review

3. A recipe for a vegetable dish contains a total of 924 calories. The dish serves 6 people. How many calories are in each serving?

4. A store clerk has 45 shirts to pack in boxes. Each box holds 6 shirts. What is the fewest boxes the clerk will need to pack all the shirts?

_____

_____

5. A total of 152,909 people visited a national park during one weekend. What is this number rounded to the nearest hundred thousand?

6. What is the word form of the number 602,107?

_____

_____

_____

_____

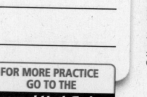

FOR MORE PRACTICE
GO TO THE
Personal Math Trainer

Name _____

Number Patterns

Essential Question How can you make and describe patterns?

Learning Objective You will shade squares to find a number pattern and generate a number pattern that follows a given rule.

Unlock the Problem — Real World

Daryl is making a pattern for a quilt. The pattern shows 40 squares. Every fourth square is blue. How many blue squares are in the pattern?

A **pattern** is an ordered set of numbers or objects. Each number or object in the pattern is called a **term**.

- Underline what you are asked to find.
- Circle what you need to use.

Activity Find a pattern.

Materials ■ color pencils

Shade the squares that are blue.

1	2	3	4	5	6	7	8	9	10
11	12	13	14	15	16	17	18	19	20
21	22	23	24	25	26	27	28	29	30
31	32	33	34	35	36	37	38	39	40

Math Talk Math Processes and Practices ⑦

Look for a Pattern
Describe another number pattern in Daryl's quilt.

Which squares are blue? _____

So, there are _____ blue squares in the pattern.

1. What patterns do you see in the arrangement of the blue squares?

_____

_____

2. What patterns do you see in the numbers of the blue squares?

_____

_____

🔑 **Example** Find and describe a pattern.

The rule for the pattern is *add* 5. The first term in the pattern is 5.

Ⓐ **Use the rule to write the numbers in the pattern.**

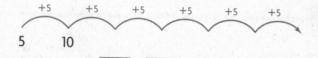

5   10   ___ ___ ___ ___ ___ ___

5, 10, _____, _____, _____, _____, _____, _____, _____, ...

Ⓑ **Describe other patterns in the numbers.**

What do you notice about the digits in the ones place?

_____

_____

Describe the pattern using the words *odd* and *even*.

_____

_____

Describe the pattern using the word *multiples*.

_____

_____

Try This! **Find and describe a pattern.**

The rule for the pattern is *add* 3, *subtract* 1. The first term in the pattern is 6.

Add 3.   Subtract 1.   Add 3.

6   ___ ___ ___ ___ ___ ___ ___

Describe another pattern in the numbers.

_____

_____

_____

Name _____

Math Talk | Math Processes and Practices ⑤

Use Patterns How do you use the first term in a pattern to find the next term?

Use the rule to write the numbers in the pattern.

1. Rule: Subtract 10.   First term: 100

Think: Subtract 10

100

_____ _____ _____ _____

100, _____, _____, _____, _____, ...

**Use the rule to write the numbers in the pattern.
Describe another pattern in the numbers.**

✓ **2.** Rule: Multiply by 2.   First term: 4

4, _____, _____, _____, _____, ...

_____

✓ **3.** Rule: Skip-count by 6.   First term: 12

12, _____, _____, _____, _____, ...

_____

On Your Own

Use the rule to write the first twelve numbers in the pattern. Describe another pattern in the numbers.

4. Rule: Add 7.   First term: 3

_____

_____

5. Rule: Add 2, add 1.   First term: 12

_____

_____

6. **Math Processes and Practices ⑤** **Use Patterns** Marcie likes to collect stickers, but she also likes to give them away. Currently, Marcie has 87 stickers in her collection. If Marcie collects 5 new stickers each week and gives away 3 stickers each week, how many stickers will Marcie have in her collection after 5 weeks?

_____

Problem Solving • Applications (Real World)

7. **THINK SMARTER** John is saving for his trip to see the Alamo. He started with $24 in his savings account. Every week he earns $15 for baby-sitting. Out of that, he spends $8 and saves the rest. John uses the rule *add 7* to find out how much money he has at the end of each week. What are the first 8 numbers in the pattern?

_____

8. **THINK SMARTER +** Draw a check under the column that describes the number.

	Prime	Composite
81		
29		
31		
62		

Pose a Problem

9. **GO DEEPER** An activity at the Math Fair shows two charts.

Numbers
2
3
5
6
10

Operations

addition
subtraction
multiplication

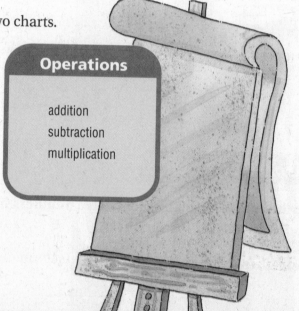

Use at least two of the numbers and an operation from the charts to write a pattern problem. Include the first five terms of your pattern in the solution to your problem.

Pose a problem.	Solve your problem.

- Describe other patterns in the terms you wrote.

_____

Name _____

Number Patterns

Learning Objective You will shade squares to find a number pattern and generate a number pattern that follows a given rule.

Use the rule to write the first twelve numbers in the pattern. Describe another pattern in the numbers.

1. Rule: *Add 8.*   First term: 5

Think: Add 8.

5   13   21   29   37

5, 13, 21, 29, 37, 45, 53, 61, 69, 77, 85, 93 _____

All the terms are odd numbers. _____

2. Rule: *Subtract 7.*   First term: 95

_____

_____

3. Rule: *Add 15, subtract 10.*   First term: 4

_____

_____

Problem Solving (Real World)

4. Barb is making a bead necklace. She strings 1 white bead, then 3 blue beads, then 1 white bead, and so on. Write the numbers for the first eight beads that are white. What is a rule for the pattern?

_____

_____

5. An artist is arranging tiles in rows to decorate a wall. Each new row has 2 fewer tiles than the row below it. If the first row has 23 tiles, how many tiles will be in the seventh row?

_____

_____

6. **WRITE** ▸ *Math* Give an example of a rule for a pattern. List a set of numbers that fit the pattern.

_____

Lesson Check

1. The rule for a pattern is *add 6*. The first term is 5. Write the first five terms in the pattern.

2. What are the next two terms in the pattern 3, 6, 5, 10, 9, 18, 17, . . .?

Spiral Review

3. To win a game, Roger needs to score 2,000 points. So far, he has scored 837 points. How many more points does Roger need to score?

4. Sue wants to use mental math to find 7×53. Write an expression she could use.

5. Pat listed all the numbers that have 15 as a multiple. Write the numbers in Pat's list.

6. Complete the following sentence using the correct term.

   14 is a _____ of 7 and 14.

FOR MORE PRACTICE
GO TO THE
Personal Math Trainer

Name _____

✓ Chapter 5 Review/Test

Personal Math Trainer
Online Assessment
and Intervention

1. List all the factors of the number.

   14: _____

2. Select the numbers that have a factor of 5. Mark all that apply.

   Ⓐ 15   Ⓓ 5

   Ⓑ 3   Ⓔ 50

   Ⓒ 45   Ⓕ 31

3. Jackson was making a poster for his room. He arranged
   50 trading cards in the shape of a rectangle on the poster.
   For 3a–3e, choose Yes or No to tell whether a possible
   arrangement of cards is shown.

3a.	5 rows of 10 cards	○ Yes　　○ No
3b.	7 rows of 8 cards	○ Yes　　○ No
3c.	25 rows of 2 cards	○ Yes　　○ No
3d.	50 rows of 1 card	○ Yes　　○ No
3e.	45 rows of 5 cards	○ Yes　　○ No

4. List all the factor pairs in the table.

Factors of 48	
_____ × _____ = _____	_____ , _____
_____ × _____ = _____	_____ , _____
_____ × _____ = _____	_____ , _____
_____ × _____ = _____	_____ , _____
_____ × _____ = _____	_____ , _____

© Houghton Mifflin Harcourt Publishing Company

GO DIGITAL
Assessment Options
Chapter Test

Chapter 5   **317**

5. Classify the numbers. Some numbers may belong in more than one box.

| 54 | 72 | 84 | 90 | 96 |

Divisible by 5 and 9	Divisible by 6 and 9	Divisible by 2 and 6

6. James works in a flower shop. He will put 36 tulips in vases for a wedding. He must use the same number of tulips in each vase. The number of tulips in each vase must be greater than 1 and less than 10. How many tulips could be in each vase?

_____ tulips

7. Brady has a card collection with 64 basketball cards, 32 football cards, and 24 baseball cards. He wants to arrange the cards in equal piles, with only one type of card in each pile. How many cards can he put in each pile? Mark all that apply.

Ⓐ 1 Ⓑ 2 Ⓒ 3 Ⓓ 4 Ⓔ 8 Ⓕ 32

8. **THINK SMARTER +** The Garden Club is designing a garden with 24 cosmos, 32 pansies, and 36 marigolds. Each row will have only one type of plant in each row. Ben says he can put 6 plants in each row. He listed the common factors of 24, 32, and 36 below to support his reasoning.

24: 1, 2, 3, 4, 6, 8, 12, 24

32: 1, 2, 4, 6, 9, 16, 32

36: 1, 2, 3, 4, 6, 8, 12, 18, 36

Is he correct? Explain your answer. If his reasoning is incorrect, explain how he should have found the answer.

9. The number of pieces of art at a museum is shown in the table.

Art	
Type of Art	**Number of Pieces**
Oil paintings	30
Photographs	24
Sketches	21

Part A

The museum is hosting a show for July that features the oil paintings by different artists. All artists show the same number of paintings and each will show more than 1 painting. How many artists could be featured in the show?

_____ artists

Part B

The museum wants to display all the art pieces in rows. Each row has the same number of pieces and the same type of pieces. How many pieces could be in each row? Explain how you found your answer.

10. Charles was skip counting at the Math Club meeting. He started to count by 8s. He said 8, 16, 24, 32, 40, and 48. What number will he say next?

_____

11. Jill wrote the number 40. If her rule is *add 7*, what is the fourth number in Jill's pattern? How can you check your answer?

12. For numbers 12a–12e, select True or False for each statement.

12a. The number 36 is a multiple of 9. ○ True ○ False

12b. The number 3 is a multiple of 9. ○ True ○ False

12c. The number 54 is a multiple of 9. ○ True ○ False

12d. The number 3 is a factor of 9. ○ True ○ False

12e. The number 27 is a factor of 9. ○ True ○ False

13. What multiple of 7 is also a factor of 7?

_____

14. Manny makes dinner using 1 box of pasta and 1 jar of sauce. If pasta is sold in packages of 6 boxes and sauce is sold in packages of 3 jars, what is the least number of dinners that Manny can make without any supplies leftover?

_____ dinners

15. Serena has several packages of raisins. Each package contains 3 boxes of raisins. Which could be the number of boxes of raisins Serena has? Mark all that apply.

Ⓐ 9 Ⓑ 18 Ⓒ 23 Ⓓ 27 Ⓔ 32

16. Choose the words that make the sentence true.

The number 7 is │ prime / composite │ because it has │ exactly / more than │ two factors.

Name _____

17. Winnie wrote the following riddle: I am a number between 60 and 100. My ones digit is two less than my tens digit. I am a prime number.

Part A

What number does Winnie's riddle describe? Explain.

```



```

Part B

Winnie's friend Marco guessed that her riddle was about the number 79. Why can't 79 be the answer to Winnie's riddle? Explain.

```



```

18. Classify the numbers as prime or composite.

Prime	Composite

37   65

71   82

19. **GO DEEPER** Erica knits 18 squares on Monday. She knits 7 more squares each day from Tuesday through Thursday. How many squares did Erica knit in all by the end of the day on Thursday?

_____ squares

20. Use the rule to write the first five terms of the pattern.

Rule: Add 10, subtract 5   First term: 11

_____

21. Elina had 10 tiles to arrange in a rectangular design. She drew a model of the rectangles she could make with the ten tiles.

Part A

How does Elina's drawing show that the number 10 is a composite number?

Part B

Suppose Elina used 15 tiles to make the rectangular design. How many different rectangles could she make with the 15 tiles? Write a list or draw a picture to show the number and dimensions of the rectangles she could make.

Part C

Elina's friend Luke said that he could make more rectangles with 24 tiles than with Elina's 10 tiles. Do you agree with Luke? Explain.

Glossary

A

acute angle [ə•kyo͞ot′ ang′gəl] **ángulo agudo**
An angle that measures greater than 0° and less than 90°
Example:

acute triangle [ə•kyo͞ot′ trī′ang•gəl]
triángulo acutángulo A triangle with three acute angles
Example:

addend [a′dend] **sumando** A number that is added to another in an addition problem
Example: 2 + 4 = 6;
2 and 4 are addends.

addition [ə•di′shən] **suma** The process of finding the total number of items when two or more groups of items are joined; the opposite operation of subtraction

A.M. [ā•em′] **a.m.** The times after midnight and before noon

analog clock [anəl• ôg kläk] **reloj analógico**
A tool for measuring time, in which hands move around a circle to show hours, minutes, and sometimes seconds
Example:

angle [ang′gəl] **ángulo** A shape formed by two line segments or rays that share the same endpoint
Example:

area [âr′ē•ə] **área** The measure of the number of unit squares needed to cover a surface
Example:

Area = 9 square units

array [ə•rā′] **matriz** An arrangement of objects in rows and columns
Example:

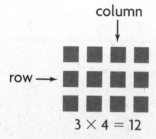

$$3 \times 4 = 12$$

Associative Property of Addition [ə•sō′shē•āt•iv präp′ər•tē əv ə•dish′ən] **propiedad asociativa de la suma** The property that states that you can group addends in different ways and still get the same sum
Example: $3 + (8 + 5) = (3 + 8) + 5$

Associative Property of Multiplication [ə•sō′shē•ə•tiv präp′ər•tē əv mul•tə•pli•kā′shən] **propiedad asociativa de la multiplicación** The property that states that you can group factors in different ways and still get the same product
Example: $3 \times (4 \times 2) = (3 \times 4) \times 2$

bar graph [bär graf] **gráfica de barras** A graph that uses bars to show data
Example:

base [bās] **base** A polygon's side or a two-dimensional shape, usually a polygon or circle, by which a three-dimensional shape is measured or named
Examples:

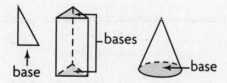

benchmark [bench′märk] **punto de referencia** A known size or amount that helps you understand a different size or amount

calendar [kal′ən•dər] **calendario** A table that shows the days, weeks, and months of a year

capacity [kə•pas′i•tē] **capacidad** The amount a container can hold when filled

Celsius (°C) [sel′sē•əs] **Celsius** A metric scale for measuring temperature

centimeter (cm) [sen′tə•mēt•ər] **centímetro (cm)** A metric unit for measuring length or distance 1 meter = 100 centimeters
Example:

1 centimeter

cent sign (¢) [sent sīn] **símbolo de centavo** A symbol that stands for *cent* or *cents*
Example: 53¢

clockwise [kläk′wīz] **en el sentido de las manecillas del reloj** In the same direction in which the hands of a clock move

closed shape [klōzd shāp] **figura cerrada** A two-dimensional shape that begins and ends at the same point
Examples:

common denominator [käm′ən dē•näm′ə•nāt•ər] **denominador común** A common multiple of two or more denominators
Example: Some common denominators for $\frac{1}{4}$ and $\frac{5}{6}$ are 12, 24, and 36.

common factor [käm′ən fak′tər] **factor común** A number that is a factor of two or more numbers

common multiple [käm′ən mul′tə•pəl] **múltiplo común** A number that is a multiple of two or more numbers

Commutative Property of Addition
[kə·myŌŌt′ə·tiv präp′ər·tē əv ə·dish′ən] **propiedad conmutativa de la suma** The property that states that when the order of two addends is changed, the sum is the same
Example: 4 + 5 = 5 + 4

Commutative Property of Multiplication
[kə·myŌŌt′ə·tiv präp′ər·tē əv mul·tə·pli·kā′shən] **propiedad conmutativa de la multiplicación** The property that states that when the order of two factors is changed, the product is the same
Example: 4 × 5 = 5 × 4

compare [kəm·pâr′] **comparar** To describe whether numbers are equal to, less than, or greater than each other

compatible numbers [kəm·pat′ə·bəl num′bərz] **números compatibles** Numbers that are easy to compute mentally

composite number [kəm·päz′it num′bər] **número compuesto** A number having more than two factors
Example: 6 is a composite number, since its factors are 1, 2, 3, and 6.

corner [kôr′nər] **esquina** See *vertex.*

counterclockwise [kount·er·kläk′wīz] **en sentido contrario a las manecillas del reloj** In the opposite direction in which the hands of a clock move

counting number [kount′ing num′bər] **número natural** A whole number that can be used to count a set of objects (1, 2, 3, 4, . . .)

cube [kyŌŌb] **cubo** A three-dimensional shape with six square faces of the same size
Example:

cup (c) [kup] **taza (tz)** A customary unit used to measure capacity and liquid volume
1 cup = 8 ounces

data [dāt′ə] **datos** Information collected about people or things

decagon [dek′ə·gän] **decágono** A polygon with ten sides and ten angles

decimal [des′ə·məl] **decimal** A number with one or more digits to the right of the decimal point

decimal point [des′ə·məl point] **punto decimal** A symbol used to separate dollars from cents in money amounts, and to separate the ones and the tenths places in a decimal
Example: 6.4
↑ decimal point

decimeter (dm) [des′i·mēt·ər] **decímetro (dm)** A metric unit for measuring length or distance
1 meter = 10 decimeters

degree (°) [di·grē′] **grado (°)** The unit used for measuring angles and temperatures

denominator [dē·näm′ə·nāt·ər] **denominador** The number below the bar in a fraction that tells how many equal parts are in the whole or in the group
Example: $\frac{3}{4}$ ← denominator

diagonal [dī·ag′ə·nəl] **diagonal** A line segment that connects two vertices of a polygon that are not next to each other
Example:

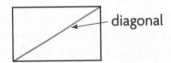

difference [dif′ər·əns] **diferencia** The answer to a subtraction problem

digit [dij′it] **dígito** Any one of the ten symbols 0, 1, 2, 3, 4, 5, 6, 7, 8, or 9 used to write numbers

digital clock [dij′i·təl kläk] **reloj digital** A clock that shows time to the minute, using digits
Example:

dime [dīm] **moneda de 10¢** A coin worth 10 cents and with a value equal to that of 10 pennies; 10¢
Example:

dimension [də•men'shən] **dimensión** A measure in one direction

Distributive Property [di•strib'yōō•tiv präp'ər•tē] **propiedad distributiva** The property that states that multiplying a sum by a number is the same as multiplying each addend by the number and then adding the products
Example: 5 × (10 + 6) = (5 × 10) + (5 × 6)

divide [də•vīd'] **dividir** To separate into equal groups; the opposite operation of multiplication

dividend [dəv'ə•dend] **dividendo** The number that is to be divided in a division problem
Example: 36 ÷ 6; 6)36; the dividend is 36.

divisible [də•viz'ə•bəl] **divisible** A number is divisible by another number if the quotient is a counting number and the remainder is zero
Example: 18 is divisible by 3.

division [də•vi'zhən] **división** The process of sharing a number of items to find how many equal groups can be made or how many items will be in each equal group; the opposite operation of multiplication

divisor [də•vī'zər] **divisor** The number that divides the dividend
Example: 15 ÷ 3; 3)15; the divisor is 3.

dollar [däl'ər] **dólar** Paper money worth 100 cents and equal to 100 pennies; $1.00
Example:

 E

elapsed time [ē•lapst' tīm] **tiempo transcurrido** The time that passes from the start of an activity to the end of that activity

endpoint [end'point] **extremo** The point at either end of a line segment or the starting point of a ray

equal groups [ē'kwəl grōōpz] **grupos iguales** Groups that have the same number of objects

equal parts [ē'kwəl pärts] **partes iguales** Parts that are exactly the same size

equal sign (=) [ē'kwəl sīn] **signo de igualdad** A symbol used to show that two numbers have the same value
Example: 384 = 384

equal to [ē'kwəl tōō] **igual a** Having the same value
Example: 4 + 4 is equal to 3 + 5.

equation [ē•kwā'zhən] **ecuación** A number sentence which shows that two quantities are equal
Example: 4 + 5 = 9

equivalent [ē•kwiv'ə•lənt] **equivalente** Having the same value or naming the same amount

equivalent decimals [ē•kwiv'ə•lənt des'ə•məlz] **decimales equivalentes** Two or more decimals that name the same amount

equivalent fractions [ē•kwiv'ə•lənt frak'shənz] **fracciones equivalentes** Two or more fractions that name the same amount
Example: $\frac{3}{4}$ and $\frac{6}{8}$ name the same amount.

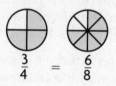

$$\frac{3}{4} = \frac{6}{8}$$

estimate [es'tə•māt] *verb* **estimar** To find an answer that is close to the exact amount

estimate [es'tə•mit] *noun* **estimación** A number that is close to the exact amount

even [ē'vən] **par** A whole number that has a 0, 2, 4, 6, or 8 in the ones place

expanded form [ek•span'did fôrm] **forma desarrollada** A way to write numbers by showing the value of each digit
Example: 253 = 200 + 50 + 3

expression [ek•spresh'ən] **expresión** A part of a number sentence that has numbers and operation signs but does not have an equal sign

fact family [fakt fam′ə•lē] **familia de operaciones** A set of related multiplication and division equations, or addition and subtraction equations
Example: 7 × 8 = 56   8 × 7 = 56
56 ÷ 7 = 8   56 ÷ 8 = 7

factor [fak′tər] **factor** A number that is multiplied by another number to find a product

Fahrenheit (°F) [fâr′ən•hīt] **Fahrenheit** A customary scale for measuring temperature

fluid ounce (fl oz) [floo͞′id ouns] **onza fluida (fl oz)** A customary unit used to measure liquid capacity and liquid volume
1 cup = 8 fluid ounces

foot (ft) [foŏt] **pie (ft)** A customary unit used for measuring length or distance
1 foot = 12 inches

formula [fôr′myoo͞•lə] **fórmula** A set of symbols that expresses a mathematical rule
Example: Area = base × height, or $A = b \times h$

fraction [frak′shən] **fracción** A number that names a part of a whole or part of a group
Example:

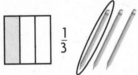

fraction greater than 1 [frak′shən grāt′ər than wun] **fracción mayor que 1** A number which has a numerator that is greater than its denominator

frequency table [frē′kwən•sē tā′bəl] **tabla de frecuencia** A table that uses numbers to record data about how often something happens
Example:

Favorite Color	
Color	Frequency
Blue	10
Red	7
Green	5
Other	3

gallon (gal) [gal′ən] **galón (gal)** A customary unit for measuring capacity and liquid volume
1 gallon = 4 quarts

gram (g) [gram] **gramo (g)** A metric unit for measuring mass
1 kilogram = 1,000 grams

greater than sign (>) [grāt′ər than sīn] **signo de mayor que** A symbol used to compare two quantities, with the greater quantity given first
Example: 6 > 4

grid [grid] **cuadrícula** Evenly divided and equally spaced squares on a shape or flat surface

half gallon [haf gal′ən] **medio galón** A customary unit for measuring capacity and liquid volume
1 half gallon = 2 quarts

half hour [haf our] **media hora** 30 minutes
Example: 4:00 to 4:30 is one half hour.

half-square unit [haf skwâr yoo͞′nit] **media unidad cuadrada** Half of a unit of area with dimensions of 1 unit × 1 unit

height [hīt] **altura** The measure of a perpendicular from the base to the top of a two-dimensional shape

hexagon [hek′sə•gän] **hexágono** A polygon with six sides and six angles
Examples:

horizontal [hôr•i•zänt′l] **horizontal** In the direction from left to right

hour (hr) [our] **hora (hr)** A unit used to measure time
1 hour = 60 minutes

© Houghton Mifflin Harcourt Publishing Company

Glossary H5

hundredth [hun′drədth] **centésimo** One of one hundred equal parts
Example:

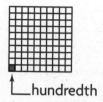

hundredth

Identity Property of Addition [ĭ·den′tə·tē prăp′ər·tē əv ə·dish′ən] **propiedad de identidad de la suma** The property that states that when you add zero to any number, the sum is that number
Example: 16 + 0 = 16

Identity Property of Multiplication [ĭ·den′tə·tē prăp′ər·tē əv mul·tə·pli·kā′shən] **propiedad de identidad de la multiplicación** The property that states that the product of any number and 1 is that number
Example: 9 × 1 = 9

inch (in.) [inch] **pulgada (pulg)** A customary unit used for measuring length or distance
Example:

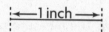

intersecting lines [in·tər·sekt′ing līnz] **líneas secantes** Lines that cross each other at exactly one point
Example:

inverse operations [in′vûrs äp·ə·rā′shənz] **operaciones inversas** Operations that undo each other, such as addition and subtraction or multiplication and division
Example: 6 × 8 = 48 and 48 ÷ 6 = 8

key [kē] **clave** The part of a map or graph that explains the symbols

kilogram (kg) [kil′ō·gram] **kilogramo (kg)** A metric unit for measuring mass
1 kilogram = 1,000 grams

kilometer (km) [kə·läm′ət·ər] **kilómetro (km)** A metric unit for measuring length or distance
1 kilometer = 1,000 meters

length [lengkth] **longitud** The measurement of the distance between two points

less than sign (<) [les <u>th</u>an sīn] **signo de menor que** A symbol used to compare two quantities, with the lesser quantity given first
Example: 3 < 7

line [līn] **línea** A straight path of points in a plane that continues without end in both directions with no endpoints
Example:

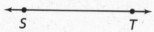

line graph [līn graf] **gráfica lineal** A graph that uses line segments to show how data change over time

line of symmetry [līn əv sim′ə·trē] **eje de simetría** An imaginary line on a shape about which the shape can be folded so that its two parts match exactly
Example:

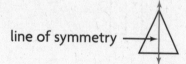

line of symmetry

line plot [līn plöt] **diagrama de puntos** A graph that records each piece of data on a number line
Example:

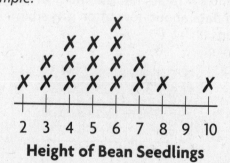

Height of Bean Seedlings

line segment [līn seg′mənt] **segmento** A part of a line that includes two points called endpoints and all the points between them
Example:

A   B

line symmetry [līn sim′ə•trē] **simetría axial** What a shape has if it can be folded about a line so that its two parts match exactly

linear units [lin′ē•ər yoo′nits] **unidades lineales** Units that measure length, width, height, or distance

liquid volume [lik′wid väl′yoom] **volumen de un líquido** The measure of the space a liquid occupies

liter (L) [lēt′ər] **litro (L)** A metric unit for measuring capacity and liquid volume
1 liter = 1,000 milliliters

mass [mas] **masa** The amount of matter in an object

meter (m) [mēt′ər] **metro (m)** A metric unit for measuring length or distance
1 meter = 100 centimeters

midnight [mid′nīt] **medianoche** 12:00 at night

mile (mi) [mīl] **milla (mi)** A customary unit for measuring length or distance
1 mile = 5,280 feet

milliliter (mL) [mil′i•lēt•ər] **mililitro (mL)** A metric unit for measuring capacity and liquid volume
1 liter = 1,000 milliliters

millimeter (mm) [mil′i•mēt•ər] **milímetro (mm)** A metric unit for measuring length or distance
1 centimeter = 10 millimeters

million [mil′yən] **millón** The counting number after 999,999; 1,000 thousands; written as 1,000,000

millions [mil′yənz] **millones** The period after thousands

minute (min) [min′it] **minuto (min)** A unit used to measure short amounts of time
1 minute = 60 seconds

mixed number [mikst num′bər] **número mixto** An amount given as a whole number and a fraction

multiple [mul′tə•pəl] **múltiplo** The product of a number and a counting number is called a multiple of the number
Example:

$$\begin{array}{cccc} 3 & 3 & 3 & 3 \\ \underline{\times\ 1} & \underline{\times\ 2} & \underline{\times\ 3} & \underline{\times\ 4} \leftarrow \text{counting numbers} \\ 3 & 6 & 9 & 12 \leftarrow \text{multiples of 3} \end{array}$$

multiplication [mul•tə•pli•kā′shən] **multiplicación** A process to find the total number of items in equal-sized groups, or to find the total number of items in a given number of groups when each group contains the same number of items; multiplication is the inverse of division

multiply [mul′tə•plī] **multiplicar** To combine equal groups to find how many in all; the opposite operation of division

nickel [nik′əl] **moneda de 5¢** A coin worth 5 cents and with a value equal to that of 5 pennies; 5¢
Example:

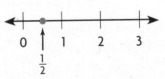

noon [noon] **mediodía** 12:00 in the day

not equal to sign (≠) [not ē′kwəl too sīn] **signo de no igual a** A symbol that indicates one quantity is not equal to another
Example: $12 \times 3 \neq 38$

number line [num′bər līn] **recta numérica** A line on which numbers can be located
Example:

$$\xleftarrow{\quad\underset{\underset{\frac{1}{2}}{\uparrow}}{0}\ \ \ |\ \ 1\ \ \ 2\ \ \ 3\quad}\rightarrow$$

number sentence [num′bər sent′ns] **enunciado numérico** A sentence that includes numbers, operation symbols, and a greater than or less than symbol or an equal sign
Example: $5 + 3 = 8$

numerator [nōō′mər•āt•ər] **numerador** The number above the bar in a fraction that tells how many parts of the whole or group are being considered

Example: $\frac{2}{3}$ ← numerator

obtuse angle [äb•tōōs′ ang′gəl] **ángulo obtuso** An angle that measures greater than 90° and less than 180°
Example:

Word History

The Latin prefix *ob-* means "against." When combined with *-tusus*, meaning "beaten," the Latin word *obtusus*, from which we get *obtuse*, means "beaten against." This makes sense when you look at an obtuse angle, because the angle is not sharp or acute. The angle looks as if it has been beaten against and become blunt and rounded.

obtuse triangle [äb•tōōs′ trī′ang•gəl] **triángulo obtusángulo** A triangle with one obtuse angle

Example:

octagon [äk′tə•gän] **octágono** A polygon with eight sides and eight angles
Examples:

odd [od] **impar** A whole number that has a 1, 3, 5, 7, or 9 in the ones place

one-dimensional [wun də•men′shə•nəl] **unidimensional** Measured in only one direction, such as length
Examples:

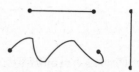

open shape [ō′pən shăp] **figura abierta** A shape that does not begin and end at the same point
Examples:

order [ôr′dər] **orden** A particular arrangement or placement of things one after the other

order of operations [ôr′dər əv äp•ə•rā′shənz] **orden de las operaciones** A special set of rules which gives the order in which calculations are done

ounce (oz) [ouns] **onza (oz)** A customary unit for measuring weight
1 pound = 16 ounces

P

parallel lines [pâr′ə•lel līnz] **líneas paralelas** Lines in the same plane that never intersect and are always the same distance apart
Example:

Word History

Euclid, an early Greek mathematician, was one of the first to explore the idea of parallel lines. The prefix *para-* means "beside or alongside." This prefix helps you understand the meaning of the word *parallel*.

parallelogram [pâr•ə•lel'ə•gram] **paralelogramo** A quadrilateral whose opposite sides are parallel and of equal length
Example:

parentheses [pə•ren'thə•sēz] **paréntesis** The symbols used to show which operation or operations in an expression should be done first

partial product [pär'shəl präd'əkt] **producto parcial** A method of multiplying in which the ones, tens, hundreds, and so on are multiplied separately and then the products are added together

partial quotient [pär'shəl kwō'shənt] **cociente parcial** A method of dividing in which multiples of the divisor are subtracted from the dividend and then the quotients are added together

pattern [pat'ərn] **patrón** An ordered set of numbers or objects; the order helps you predict what will come next
Examples: 2, 4, 6, 8, 10

pattern unit [pat'ərn yōo'nit] **unidad de patrón** The part of a pattern that repeats
Example:

pattern unit

pentagon [pen'tə•gän] **pentágono** A polygon with five sides and five angles
Examples:

perimeter [pə•rim'ə•tər] **perímetro** The distance around a shape

period [pir'ē•əd] **período** Each group of three digits in a multi-digit number; periods are usually separated by commas or spaces.
Example: 85,643,900 has three periods.

perpendicular lines [pər•pən•dik'yōo•lər līnz] **líneas perpendiculares** Two lines that intersect to form four right angles
Example:

picture graph [pik'chər graf] **gráfica con dibujos** A graph that uses symbols to show and compare information
Example:

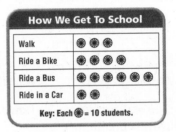

pint (pt) [pīnt] **pinta (pt)** A customary unit for measuring capacity and liquid volume
1 pint = 2 cups

place value [plās val'yōo] **valor posicional** The value of a digit in a number, based on the location of the digit

plane [plān] **plano** A flat surface that extends without end in all directions
Example:

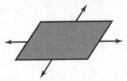

plane shape [plān shāp] **figura plana** See *two-dimensional figure.*

P.M. [pē'em] **p.m.** The times after noon and before midnight

point [point] **punto** An exact location in space

polygon [päl'i•gän] **polígono** A closed two-dimensional shape formed by three or more straight sides that are line segments
Examples:

Polygons   Not Polygons

pound (lb) [pound] **libra (lb)** A customary unit for measuring weight
1 pound = 16 ounces

prime number [prīm num'bər] **número primo** A number that has exactly two factors: 1 and itself
Examples: 2, 3, 5, 7, 11, 13, 17, and 19 are prime numbers. 1 is not a prime number.

prism [priz'əm] **prisma** A solid figure that has two same size, same polygon-shaped bases, and other faces that are all rectangles
Examples:

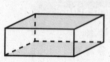
rectangular prism

triangular prism

product [präd'əkt] **producto** The answer to a multiplication problem

protractor [prō'trak•tər] **transportador** A tool for measuring the size of an angle

Q

quadrilateral [kwä•dri•lat'ər•əl] **cuadrilátero** A polygon with four sides and four angles

quart (qt) [kwôrt] **cuarto (ct)** A customary unit for measuring capacity and liquid volume
1 quart = 2 pints

quarter hour [kwôrt'ər our] **cuarto de hora** 15 minutes
Example: 4:00 to 4:15 is one quarter hour

quotient [kwō'shənt] **cociente** The number, not including the remainder, that results from dividing
Example: 8 ÷ 4 = 2; 2 is the quotient.

R

ray [rā] **semirrecta** A part of a line; it has one endpoint and continues without end in one direction
Example:

K   L

rectangle [rek'tang•gəl] **rectángulo** A quadrilateral with two pairs of parallel sides, two pairs of sides of equal length, and four right angles
Example:

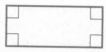

rectangular prism [rek•tang'gyə•lər priz'əm] **prisma rectangular** A three-dimensional shape in which all six faces are rectangles
Example:

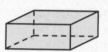

regroup [rē•grōop'] **reagrupar** To exchange amounts of equal value to rename a number
Example: 5 + 8 = 13 ones or 1 ten 3 ones

regular polygon [reg'yə•lər päl'i•gän] **polígono regular** A polygon that has all sides that are equal in length and all angles equal in measure
Examples:

related facts [ri•lāt'id fakts] **operaciones relacionadas** A set of related addition and subtraction, or multiplication and division, number sentences
Examples: 4 × 7 = 28   28 ÷ 4 = 7
7 × 4 = 28   28 ÷ 7 = 4

remainder [ri•mān'dər] **residuo** The amount left over when a number cannot be divided equally

rhombus [räm'bəs] **rombo** A quadrilateral with two pairs of parallel sides and four sides of equal length
Example:

right angle [rīt ang'gəl] **ángulo recto** An angle that forms a square corner
Example:

© Houghton Mifflin Harcourt Publishing Company

right triangle [rīt trī′ang•gəl] **triángulo rectángulo**
A triangle with one right angle
Example:

round [round] **redondear** To replace a number with another number that tells about how many or how much

rule [rool] **regla** A procedure (usually involving arithmetic operations) to determine an output value from an input value

scale [skāl] **escala** A series of numbers placed at fixed distances on a graph to help label the graph

second (sec) [sek′ənd] **segundo (seg)** A small unit of time
1 minute = 60 seconds

simplest form [sim′pləst fôrm] **mínima expresión**
A fraction is in simplest form when the numerator and denominator have only 1 as a common factor

solid shape [sä′lid shāp] **cuerpo geométrico**
See *three-dimensional figure.*

square [skwâr] **cuadrado** A quadrilateral with two pairs of parallel sides, four sides of equal length, and four right angles
Example:

square unit [skwâr yoo′nit] **unidad cuadrada**
A unit of area with dimensions of
1 unit × 1 unit

standard form [stan′dərd fôrm] **forma normal**
A way to write numbers by using the digits 0–9, with each digit having a place value *Example:*
3,540 ← standard form

straight angle [strāt ang′gəl] **ángulo llano** An angle whose measure is 180°
Example:

subtraction [səb•trak′shən] **resta** The process of finding how many are left when a number of items are taken away from a group of items; the process of finding the difference when two groups are compared; the opposite operation of addition

sum [sum] **suma o total** The answer to an addition problem

survey [sûr′vā] **encuesta** A method of gathering information

tally table [tal′ē tā′bəl] **tabla de conteo** A table that uses tally marks to record data

Word History

Some people keep score in card games by making marks on paper (IIII). These marks are known as tally marks. The word *tally* is related to *tailor*, from the Latin *talea*, meaning "twig." In early times, a method of keeping count was by cutting marks into a piece of wood or bone.

temperature [tem′pər•ə•chər] **temperatura** The degree of hotness or coldness usually measured in degrees Fahrenheit or degrees Celsius

tenth [tenth] **décimo** One of ten equal parts
Example:

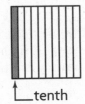
tenth

term [tûrm] **término** A number or object in a pattern

thousands [thou′zəndz] **miles** The period after the ones period in the base-ten number system

three-dimensional [thrē də•men′shə•nəl]
tridimensional Measured in three directions,
such as length, width, and height
Example:

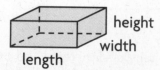

three-dimensional figure [thrē də•men′shə•nəl
fig′yər] **figura tridimensional** A figure having
length, width, and height

ton (T) [tun] **tonelada (t)** A customary unit used to
measure weight
1 ton = 2,000 pounds

trapezoid [trap′i•zoid] **trapecio** A quadrilateral
with at least one pair of parallel sides
Examples:

triangle [trī′ang•gəl] **triángulo** A polygon with
three sides and three angles
Examples:

two-dimensional [tōō də•men′shə•nəl]
bidimensional Measured in two directions,
such as length and width
Example:

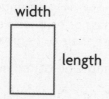

two-dimensional figure [tōō də•men′shə•nəl fig′yər]
figura bidimensional A figure that lies in a
plane; a shape having length and width

unit fraction [yōō′nit frak′shən] **fracción unitaria**
A fraction that has a numerator of one

variable [vâr′ē•ə•bəl] **variable** A letter or symbol
that stands for a number or numbers

Venn diagram [ven dī′ə•gram] **diagrama de Venn**
A diagram that shows relationships among
sets of things
Example:

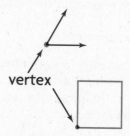

vertex [vûr′teks] **vértice** The point at which two
rays of an angle meet or two (or more) line
segments meet in a two-dimensional shape
Examples:

vertical [vûr′ti•kəl] **vertical** In the direction from
top to bottom

weight [wāt] **peso** How heavy an object is

whole [hōl] **entero** All of the parts of a shape or
group

word form [wûrd fôrm] **en palabras** A way to
write numbers by using words
Example: Four hundred
fifty-three thousand, two
hundred twelve

yard (yd) [yärd] **yarda (yd)** A customary unit for
measuring length or distance
1 yard = 3 feet

Z

Zero Property of Multiplication [zēʹrō präpʹər•tē əv mul•tə•pli•kāʹshən] **propiedad del cero de la multiplicación** The property that states that the product of 0 and any number is 0
Example: $0 \times 8 = 0$

Index

Clocks
analog, 602, 685–688
elapsed time, 691–694

Clockwise, 601–604

Combined rectangles, 729–732

Common denominators, 345–348, 365–368, 409–412, 527–530

Common factors, 291–294
fractions in simplest form using, 340

Common multiples, 299–302, 345–348

Common numerators, 365–368

Communicate Math Ideas
Math Talk, In every Student Edition lesson. Some examples are: 5, 12, 64, 82, 114, 132, 177, 209, 228, 279, 299, 328, 359, 386, 429, 455, 495, 520, 556, 602, 642, 723
Read Math, 555, 685
Write Math, In every Student Edition lesson. Some examples are: 8, 40, 96, 116, 224, 288, 348, 420, 510, 530, 682

Commutative Property
of Addition, 39, 435–438
of Multiplication, 63–66, 107–110, 171

Comparing
decimals, 533–536
fractions, 359–362, 365–368, 371–374
measurement units, 647–650, 653–656, 659–662, 673–676, 679–682, 685–688
whole numbers, 17–20

Comparison problems, 49–52, 69–72, 481–484

Compatible numbers, 152, 221–223

Composite numbers, 305–307

Connect, 99, 163, 260, 435, 607, 703

Connect to Art, 400, 424

Connect to Reading, 84, 224

Connect to Science, 26, 218, 510, 616, 688, 740

Connect to Social Studies, 308

Counterclockwise, 601–604

Counters, 203–206, 235, 236

Counting numbers, 197, 455–458, 461–464

Cross-Curricular Activities and Connections
Connect to Art, 400, 570
Connect to Reading, 84, 224

Connect to Science, 26, 218, 510, 616, 688, 740
Connect to Social Studies, 308

Cup, 659

Customary units
benchmarks, 641-644
converting, 647–650, 653–656, 659–662
of distance, 641
of length, 641, 647–650
of liquid volume, 641, 659–662
of weight, 641, 653–656

D

Data
gathering, 26
using
bar graphs, 116
line plots, 665–668
tables. See Tables
tally tables, 665–668, 671
Venn diagrams, 196, 556, 558, 568, 716

Days, 686

Decimal point, 495

Decimals
comparing
using models, 533–536
using place value, 533–536
defined, 495
equivalent decimals
defined, 508
modeling, 507–510
hundredths, 501–504, 507–510
place value and, 495–498, 501–504, 534–536
relating
to fractions, 495–498, 501–504, 507–510, 513–516, 527–530
to mixed numbers, 495–497, 501–503, 509, 514–515
to money, 513–516
tenths, 495–498, 507–510

Decimeters, 673

Degrees
angle measures and, 607–610

Denominators, 365–368

2. Abstract and Quantitative Reasoning. In many lessons. Some examples are: 11, 17, 23, 31, 63, 69, 75, 113, 119, 131, 145, 151, 157, 163, 221, 241, 247, 279, 297, 311, 333, 359, 365, 385, 391, 397, 403, 409, 417, 423, 435, 441, 461, 495, 501, 507, 513, 519, 527, 533, 567, 575, 601, 607, 641, 647, 653, 665, 723, 737

3. Use and Evaluate Logical Reasoning. In many lessons. Some examples are: 43, 87, 119, 125, 131, 209, 221, 253, 285, 365, 391, 397, 441, 575, 581, 601, 641, 647, 659, 665, 679, 697, 703

4. Mathematical Modeling. In many lessons. Some examples are: 11, 23, 49, 87, 99, 113, 145, 157, 183, 227, 247, 265, 279, 285, 327, 333, 345, 351, 385, 403, 429, 441, 455, 469, 513, 549, 561, 621, 627, 647, 659, 665, 673, 685, 691, 743

5. Use Mathematical Tools. In many lessons. Some examples are: 5, 31, 75, 197, 215, 235, 259, 265, 311, 327, 333, 365, 495, 587, 613, 685, 691

6. Use Precise Mathematical Language. In many lessons. Some examples are: 5, 23, 37, 63, 87, 99, 125, 151, 157, 177, 215, 221, 235, 241, 299, 339, 345, 351, 359, 403, 409, 417, 455, 495, 507, 513, 519, 533, 555, 561, 587, 607, 613, 653, 659, 703, 723, 729

7. See Structure. In many lessons. Some examples are: 11, 31, 75, 81, 119, 145, 171, 177, 197, 209, 215, 227, 253, 285, 299, 311, 327, 339, 345, 359, 409, 417, 429, 455, 461, 481, 501, 507, 527, 555, 561, 587, 607, 641, 659, 673, 685, 703, 717, 737

8. Generalize. In many lessons. Some examples are: 37, 43, 49, 163, 171, 177, 209, 241, 259, 299, 391, 417, 423, 435, 461, 475, 527, 673, 697, 717

© Houghton Mifflin Harcourt Publishing Company

read and write, 11–14
renaming, 31–34
rounding, 23–26
standard form, whole numbers, 11–14
word form, whole numbers, 11–14

Numbers and Operations
adding, 37–40. *See also* Addition
comparing, 17–20
  decimals, 533–536
  division. *See also* Division
    and Distributive Property, 227–230
    estimating quotients using compatible numbers, 221–224
    estimating quotients using multiples, 197–200
    placing first digit, 253–256
    with regrouping, 247–250, 253–256, 259–262
    remainders, 203–206, 209–212
    tens, hundreds, and thousands, 215–218
    using bar models to solve multistep problems, 265–268
    using partial quotients, 241–244
    using repeated subtraction, 235–238
  fractions. *See also* Fractions
    adding fractional parts of 10 and 100, 527–530
    common denominators, 345–348
    comparing, 359–362, 365–368, 371–374
      using benchmarks, 359–362
    comparison problems with, 481–484
    equivalent, 327–330, 333–336, 351–354
      and decimals, 507–510
    multiples of, 461–464
      unit fractions, 455–458
    multiplying by whole number, 469–472, 475–478
      using models, 469–472
    ordering, 371–374
    relating decimals, money and, 513–516
    relating hundredths and decimals, 501–504
    relating tenths and decimals, 495–498
    simplest form, 339–342
  multiplication. *See also* Multiplication
    area models and partial products, 157–160
    choosing method for, 177–180
    estimating products, strategies for, 151–154

by tens, strategies for, 145–148
using Distributive Property, 87–90
using expanded form, 93–96
using mental math, 107–110
using partial products, 99–102, 163–166
using regrouping, 119–128, 171–174
ordering, 17–20
place value, 5–26, 31–52, 75–78. *See also* Place value
renaming, 31–34
rounding, 23–26, 81–84
subtracting, 43–46. *See also* Subtraction

Obtuse angles, 550–552, 555–558
Obtuse triangles, 555–558
Odd numbers, 312
One-digit numbers
multiplication
  four-digit by one-digit, 94–96, 125–128
  three-digit by one-digit, 93–96, 99–101, 125–128
  two-digit by one-digit, 87–90, 119–122
Ones
addition, 37–40
place value, 5–8
subtraction, 43–46
On Your Own, In every Student Edition lesson. Some examples are: 7, 44, 83, 121, 153, 222, 281, 335, 431, 457, 497, 551, 609, 667, 719, 746
Operations and Algebraic Thinking, 63–66, 69–72, 113–116, 131–134
division
  interpreting remainders, 209–212
  multistep problems, 265–268
factors
  common, solving problems with, 291–294
  and divisibility, 285–288
  modeling, 279–282
  and multiples, 299–302
multiplication
  comparison problems, 63–66, 69–72
  multistep problems, 113–116
  two-digit numbers, 183–186
number patterns, 311–314
prime and composite numbers, 305–308

259–260, 265–266, 279, 282, 285,
291–292, 299, 305, 311, 333–334,
339–340, 345, 351–352, 359–360, 365,
368, 371, 374, 391–392, 394, 397–398,
403–404, 406, 409, 417–418, 423–424,
429–430, 435–436, 455–456, 461–462,
464, 469, 472, 475–476, 481–482,
495–496, 501–502, 507–508, 513,
519–520, 527–528, 533, 536, 549–550,
555–556, 561–562, 567–568, 575–576,
578, 581–582, 587–588, 607–608, 610,
613, 626, 627, 641–642, 647–648,
653–654, 659–660, 665–666, 668, 679,
682, 685–686, 691–692, 697–698, 700,
703, 717–718, 720, 723–724, 726,
729–730, 732, 737–738, 743–744
Reason Abstractly, 387
Sense or Nonsense?, 160, 250, 388, 411,
412, 458, 476, 604, 699
Think Smarter Problems, In every Student
Edition lesson. Some examples are: 8,
25, 63, 88, 122, 154, 211, 228, 262,
281, 328, 386, 426, 457, 498, 552, 610,
644, 720
Try This!, 11, 24, 44, 64, 107, 120, 146,
152, 178, 209, 210, 286, 312, 366,
372, 436, 476, 496, 514, 527, 528,
534, 555, 561, 568, 608, 654, 698,
704, 718, 724, 738
What's the Error?, 13, 46, 96, 134, 330,
409, 706
What's the Question?, 20, 342, 362, 478
Problem-solving strategies
Act It Out, 441–444, 519–522, 587–590
Draw a Diagram, 49–52, 113–116,
183–186, 265–268, 481–484, 627–630,
691–694
Make a List, 291–294
Make a Table, 351–354
Solve a Simpler Problem, 743–746
Products. *See also* Multiplication
estimating, 81–83, 99–102, 151–154
partial, 88, 99–101, 157–160, 163–166
Project, 2, 324, 546
Properties
Associative Property
of Addition, 39, 435–438
of Multiplication, 107–110, 145–148
Commutative Property
of Addition, 39, 435–438
of Multiplication, 63, 107–110, 171

Distributive Property, 87–90, 99–101,
108–109, 227–230, 718
Identity Property of Multiplication, 476

Quadrilaterals, 567–570
defined, 567
parallelogram, 567–570
rectangle, 567–570
rhombus, 567–570
square, 567–570
trapezoid, 567–570
Quart, 641, 659–662
Quarters, 513–516, 519–520
Quick pictures
to model division, 203–206, 248–250
to model multiplication, 75–78
Quotients, 210, 235–238. *See also* Division
estimating, 197–200, 221–224
partial, 241–244
placing the first digit, 253–256

Rays, 549–552
Reading
Connect to Reading, 84, 224
Read Math, 555, 685
Read/Solve the Problem, 49–50, 113–114,
183–184, 265–266, 291–292, 351–352,
441–442, 481–482, 519–520, 587–588,
627–628, 691–692, 743–744
Visualize It, 4, 62, 144, 196, 278, 326, 384,
454, 494, 548, 600, 640, 716
Real World
Problem Solving, In every Student Edition
lesson. Some examples are: 8, 45, 96,
148, 200, 237, 302, 348, 411, 437, 457,
498, 552, 603, 649, 699
Unlock the Problem, In every Student
Edition lesson. Some examples are: 11,
49–50, 93–94, 151–152, 209–210, 279,
345, 394, 429–430, 435–436, 441–442,
455–456, 495–496, 533, 549–550, 578,
647–648, 717–718
Reasonableness of an answer, 23, 43, 82, 93,
99, 119, 151–154, 163, 171, 221, 641

Table of Measures

METRIC

CUSTOMARY

Length

1 centimeter (cm) = 10 millimeters (mm)

1 meter (m) = 1,000 millimeters

1 meter = 100 centimeters

1 meter = 10 decimeters (dm)

1 kilometer (km) = 1,000 meters

1 foot (ft) = 12 inches (in.)

1 yard (yd) = 3 feet, or 36 inches

1 mile (mi) = 1,760 yards, or 5,280 feet

Capacity and Liquid Volume

1 liter (L) = 1,000 milliliters (mL)

1 cup (c) = 8 fluid ounces (fl oz)

1 pint (pt) = 2 cups

1 quart (qt) = 2 pints, or 4 cups

1 half gallon = 2 quarts

1 gallon (gal) = 2 half gallons, or 4 quarts

Mass/Weight

1 kilogram (kg) = 1,000 grams (g)

1 pound (lb) = 16 ounces (oz)

1 ton (T) = 2,000 pounds

TIME

1 minute (min) = 60 seconds (sec)

1 half hour = 30 minutes

1 hour (hr) = 60 minutes

1 day (d) = 24 hours

1 week (wk) = 7 days

1 year (yr) = 12 months (mo), or about 52 weeks

1 year = 365 days

1 leap year = 366 days

1 decade = 10 years

1 century = 100 years

MONEY

1 penny = 1¢, or $0.01

1 nickel = 5¢, or $0.05

1 dime = 10¢, or $0.10

1 quarter = 25¢, or $0.25

1 half dollar = 50¢, or $0.50

1 dollar = 100¢, or $1.00

SYMBOLS

$<$	is less than	$\perp$	is perpendicular to
$>$	is greater than	$\parallel$	is parallel to
$=$	is equal to	$\overleftrightarrow{AB}$	line AB
$\neq$	is not equal to	$\overrightarrow{AB}$	ray AB
¢	cent or cents	$\overline{AB}$	line segment AB
$	dollar or dollars	$\angle ABC$	angle ABC or angle B
°	degree or degrees	$\triangle ABC$	triangle ABC

FORMULAS

	Perimeter		Area
Polygon	$P =$ sum of the lengths of sides	Rectangle	$A = b \times h$
			$A = l \times w$
Rectangle	$P = (2 \times l) + (2 \times w)$ or $P = 2 \times (l + w)$		
Square	$P = 4 \times s$